The Future of
Public Broadcasting

Douglass Cater   Editor, Aspen Series on
Communications and Society

Michael J. Nyhan   Project Editor,
Public Broadcasting

Published with the
Aspen Institute Program on
Communications and Society

**The Praeger Special Studies program—utiliz-
ing the most modern and efficient book production techniques and a selective worldwide
distribution network—makes available to the
academic, government, and business communities significant, timely research in U.S. and
international economic, social, and political
development.**

The Future of
Public Broadcasting

Praeger Publishers New York Washington London

Library of Congress Cataloging in Publication Data

The Future of public broadcasting.

(Praeger special studies in U.S. economic, social and
political issues)
"Published with the Aspen Institute Program on
Communications and Society."
    1. Television broadcasting—United States—Addresses,
essays, lectures. 2. Television programs, Public service—
United States—Addresses, essays, lectures.
I. Cater, Douglass, 1923-
II. Nyhan, Michael J.
HE8700.8.F87   384.54'53   76-8889
ISBN 0-275-56990-X
ISBN 0-275-64590-8 student ed.

PRAEGER PUBLISHERS
111 Fourth Avenue, New York, N.Y. 10003, U.S.A.

Published in the United States of America in 1976
by Praeger Publishers, Inc.

Acknowledgment

We gratefully acknowledge the comments and criticism provided by Bruce McKay, Christopher Sterling, Ken Wirt, Charles Clift, and Norman Felsenthal. We also wish to thank James Arntz for his editorial assistance and Diane Willis, Marty Wosser, and Pat Singer of the Aspen Program staff for their help in collecting and preparing the manuscript for publication. Finally, we acknowledge the contribution to public broadcasting of the *Public Telecommunications Review*, in which four of the essays — by Friedlander, Millard, Rowland, and Warnock — appeared in earlier versions.

Preface

Since its inception in 1971, the Aspen Institute Program on Communications and Society has focused on the fate of public broadcasting in America as one of its top priorities. In addition to convening conferences, we have commissioned studies and published articles assessing key policy issues relating to the growth of this enterprise. We have attempted to chart a clear if difficult role in sponsoring reasoned inquiry in a non-adversary atmosphere by those who are committed to public broadcasting's future. Communications in America grows increasingly complex. If public broadcasting is to flourish, it must stake out its claim and make its plans for more than a year at a time.

We believe there is a need in public broadcasting to develop middle range visionaries who are neither blue-sky dreamers nor day-to-day tacticians. Throughout the Aspen Program's activities, we have encouraged participants to put emphasis on "yesable" propositions — that is, concrete proposals for dealing with specific problems.

Over a twelve-month period we asked a number of expert thinkers to examine the many serious policy questions facing public broadcasting over the next decade. While we gave writers wide latitude within their topics, we placed strong emphasis on identifying problems, exploring possible solutions, and proposing future directions.

We hope this volume will contribute to the evolution of public broadcasting in America. The Bicentennial Year is a fitting time to raise our sights and begin to plan for a new level of achievement for our non-commercial communication system.

Douglass Cater
Executive Editor
Aspen Series on Communications

Michael J. Nyhan
Project Editor
Public Broadcasting

Contents

Introduction:
The Haphazard Business
of Institution Building

DOUGLASS CATER

It is not easy to trace a coherent plan for the development of public broadcasting in America. In 1952, Commissioner Frieda Hennock and her colleagues on the FCC set aside a number of TV channels and radio frequencies to serve vaguely specified "educational needs of the community." A few universities, school systems and community associations, supported by a few private philanthropies, responded to this opportunity; but more than a decade later, educational radio and television had still made little impact.

The Kennedy Administration decided to provide facility funds and set loose a station building boom throughout the country. But, then, in just a few more years, educational broadcasting found itself teetering on bankruptcy, and the Carnegie Corporation responded to the urgent appeals of the system by setting up a study commission under the chairmanship of James Killian. At last, early in 1967, the Carnegie Report came forth with an ambitious design for noncommercial broadcasting (henceforth to be designated "public") and President Johnson and the Congress pushed through legislation which created a nongovernmental corporation to help chart the future. There was fresh cause for hope among those who were keenly concerned about a communication enterprise which, carelessly

Mr. Cater founded the Aspen Institute Program on Communications and Society.

1

launched, had evolved so haphazardly.

Much of public broadcasting's more recent history, too, reads like the adventures of Hairbreadth Harry, always one jump ahead of disaster. Luck, both good and bad, has dogged it every step of the way. It was good luck which prompted President Johnson to respond swiftly to the Carnegie Report of 1967 by sending the act to Congress the same year. With only a very few members of Congress showing much enthusiasm for the legislation, the House of Representatives came close to postponing action. Then, in the final days, a vital quorum was lacking and a posse had to be dispatched in search of a Ways and Means Committee member trysting in a local hotel. One can only speculate what would have happened if the vote had been delayed until the next year, when the President, mired down in war and taxes, was getting ready to retire and Congress was preparing for elections. There can be little doubt about the bill's fate if it had been turned over to the tender care of the Nixon Administration.

It was bad luck, however, when Johnson put off a decision on long-range funding for the system. It has taken eight nerve-wracking years to remedy this neglect. (The Carnegie proposal for an earmarked tax on TV sets was likely doomed even if LBJ had been willing to fight for it.) Bad luck also lumped the federal revenues for public broadcasting into the HEW appropriation bill, where they get caught annually in the bigger budget battles between the President and Congress.

On the other hand, it was probably a perverse form of good luck which exposed the early Nixon attempts to play politics with public broadcasting. This threat took on more ominous meaning during the later Watergate revelations, and it has undoubtedly stiffened public broadcasting's will to maintain independence. Ironically, the Watergate hearings also gave public broadcasting a rare opportunity to demonstrate its value to the nation by providing fuller coverage than the commercial networks.

This seems to be the way with institution building. Not everything can be spelled out in advance. Justice Holmes once wrote, "Some things have to be stated obscurely before they can be stated clearly." Such a maxim has certainly applied when attempting to define the principles governing the development of public broadcasting.

Consider, for example, the principle strongly enunciated in the Carnegie Report that public broadcasting must be "insulated" from government. There have been times along the way when this principle seemed to become a mockery. The White House aides under Nixon had few qualms about trying to shape the medium to suit their notions of the President's interest. Some members of Congress have failed to understand why the people's elected representatives should not second-guess decisions of a public corporation whose board is merely appointed. And some citizen groups have not shown much compunction about calling on the politicians to interfere in CPB's business.

The struggle for insulation has focused primarily on the need to obtain multi-year appropriations. But while long-range financing can provide more lead-time for decision-making, it is not likely to reduce the political pressures beating on the system. Indeed, as revenues become larger and more assured, the claims on this public enterprise are likely to become more insistent. Insulation will be achieved only as public broadcast leaders give it meaning by their daily practices and, on occasion, by their courageous defiance of political interference.

A second principle set forth clearly by the Carnegie Commission and affirmed in the legislation is that public broadcasting shall be built on the "bedrock of localism." This emphasis on a diverse system of independent stations and production centers was intended to distinguish the public system from the highly centralized commercial networks. Yet the principle goes directly against the laws of broadcast economics, and it has set public broadcasting at war with itself in trying to budget its scarce resources. How much for local stations? How much for the Station Program Cooperative? How much for ventures in national programming?

An institution with more authority, such as the British Broadcasting Corporation, has felt little need to decentralize its activities. Paradoxically, this has meant that the BBC is able to give greater emphasis to a different kind of pluralism by granting producers the autonomy needed for creativity. Clearly, public broadcasting in the United States must reconcile itself to an unending effort to strike the right balance between centrifugal and centripetal forces.

Still another principle carried forward from the Carnegie Report was that financial support for the system should be diverse. Federal funds, never to be more than a minority of the whole, would be used to encourage funding from other sources. This principle, it was thought, would serve to give the system vigor as well as independence. Yet, with public broadcasting always short of revenues, the principle has also contributed to a chronic and frantic search for dollars. Auctions and membership drives tempt community stations to adopt the hard-sell techniques of their commercial brothers. Corporate sponsorship of high cost programs rouses fears that big business, particularly big oil, may acquire an unnatural claim on broadcast priorities. There is similar danger when government agencies, seeking to promote particular social objectives, offer contract funding for program production.

The harsh reality is that money seldom comes without strings. Public broadcasting's future weal will lie in being alert to undue influence from any source. But this is easier said than accomplished. In addition, the quest for pluralistic funding must somehow resolve the problem of how to finance the types of programming which financial backers are reluctant to underwrite. For example, now that the Ford Foundation is phasing out its generous support, public affairs programming appears unlikely to survive unless some system of tithing can be established within the system.

Even the organizational principles of public broadcasting must be subject to evolutionary change. CPB's structure was set forth in the Carnegie Report, but Congress added what appeared to be a minor caveat: that no more than eight directors of the CPB Board should be of the same political party. This has served to divide the board along partisan lines which are not relevant to such an enterprise. It has also diverted attention from the more important proviso that board members "shall be selected from among citizens . . . who are eminent in such fields as education, cultural and civic affairs, or the arts . . ."

Organizational problems are also arising from the overlap of administrative entities. Nowhere in the Carnegie Report or the congressional legislation was there any mention of the Public Broadcasting Service (though the act did specify that CPB could not "own or operate" interconnection facilities): PBS, set up to manage the schedule on the interconnection, has logically extended its mandate to include operating the Station Program Cooperative by which local stations purchase program offerings. This has given PBS an importance at least commensurate with that of CPB. These countervailing powers undoubtedly add beneficial checks and balances within the system, but they also contribute to red tape, to a certain inertia, and to the temptation for each organization to usurp the other's functions. In recent years, the parallel bureaucracies have moved along in what sometimes resembles a three-legged sack race.

To review the haphazard growth of public broadcasting can

stir feelings of pessimism. So many conflicting pressures are working on this fragile instrument of communication. Organized labor demands that programs imported from abroad, including the popular BBC serials, should be curtailed in favor of native productions. Organized minorities, voicing ethnic and other concerns, protest that the system is controlled by an elite who use public monies and the public airwaves to suit their own rarified fancies. Those who have long fought for public broadcasting's survival respond that rather than strengthening the system, the militant pressure groups may, by their efforts to impose program quotas, destroy it. The battle continually rages over budgets, over the makeup of governing boards, over employment practices and program content. Before public broadcasting has even proved its power to survive, there is already danger of a bitter power struggle to control its future.

The optimistic answer is that this is to be expected of a public institution. To the degree that battles are fought within rational limits, they bring vitality and self-renewal. Better to face a future of struggle than one of moribund calm. But the important question is how much can reason rather than blind chance play a role in shaping public broadcasting's future?

One can draw a degree of comfort from the past. The Carnegie Commission provided a valuable design against which evolving principles could be tested. The Aspen Institute's Communication Program, by its studies and conferences, has helped to take the measure of public broadcasting's progress. The establishment of a second Carnegie-type commission, probably the most significant recommendation contained in this volume, could be of immense help in charting a future for public broadcasting.

Measured in the long sweep of history, public broadcasting can be said to stand somewhere between Runnymede and Philadelphia: It is no longer a baronial fiefdom but its constitutional foundations are not yet fully developed. In terms of citizen involvement, it can barely claim the right to be a public institution at all. The vision and the clout of a dedicated few brought it into being, and its existence still depends in large degree on support that is neither majoritarian nor deeply rooted in popular appeal.

Yet public broadcasting's destiny is important beyond the worth of its present program offerings. We have entered an age when technology ceaselessly invents new ways to process and transmit information. We will soon witness a fissioning of the channels of communication which link our society and our world. Our capacity to employ communication so that it serves both freedom and social order is being severely tested. Indeed, this may be a crucial test for human survival, as well. Amid this relentless technological advance, public broadcasting has a vital role to perform. It is an institution whose building ought never to be finished.

A Crisis of Identity: Reflections on the Future of Public Broadcasting

ANNE W. BRANSCOMB

In late 1975, the staff of the FCC was given the opportunity to comment upon the utility of a panel discussion on the problems of public broadcasting. The panel was being scheduled for the 1976 conference on Telecommunications Policy Research. The response of the FCC was illuminating:

> While this topic does not appear to have any particular relevance to this commission's activities, it is fascinating, and probably merits consideration.

That, in a nutshell, is the primary problem of public broadcasting. If it is not the mandate of the FCC to be concerned about the problems of public broadcasting, whose mandate is it? Some agency, some *one*, must begin the laborious task of resolving the internal conflicts, the inconsistencies, and the inadequacies of today's public broadcasting system. If the public is not to be short-changed and under-served, a locus of energy and responsibility for the system will have to be found — and soon.

The present participants in policy making for the public system

---

Ms. Branscomb is a lawyer specializing in communications law. She also serves as vice-president of Kalba Bowen Associates, Inc., a communications consulting firm.

seem to have too many inhibitions, distractions, and disabilities which divert their attention from this essential task. The FCC, for instance, acts primarily as a regulatory agency. It was also given a statutory mandate to oversee an integrated national telecommunications system, but its office of plans and policy is extremely small and devoted mainly to writing speeches for the chairman's office. The White House OTP, on the other hand, seems to perceive its function as long-range telecommunications planning (as well as an occasional glance at funding for public broadcasting), but the office was originally established to coordinate the uses of the radio spectrum allocated to the federal government. It therefore has an irreconcilable conflict of interest when it considers basic questions of spectrum allocation for the public broadcasting system.

The CPB's statutory mandate is directed toward funding for public broadcasting, while HEW, which was given a planning function for instructional telecommunications by the Public Broadcasting Act of 1967, has not perceived of telecommunications planning as more than a minor appendage to its primary responsibilities. The HEW public broadcasting activities are mainly in widely dispersed categories of programming and include little if any coordination or planning except in the area of satellite interconnections.

In short, much of the present dilemma of public broadcasting is the result of a too "benign neglect" by federal agencies, coupled with a schizophrenia of the public broadcasting entities as to their proper roles, a myopia concerning their potential for development, and a certain lack of self-confidence in their survival quotient. The White House-PBS tensions during the Nixon Administration and the recent struggle to secure a long-range financing act have brought these insecurities and inadequacies in the system to the fore, precipitating much soul-searching among public broadcasters and their regulators concerning the nature of public broadcasting and its development in the future.

This serious crisis of identity has finally raised many rather fundamental questions: What is public broadcasting? What is the justification for reserved channels? What does a noncommercial service really mean? How are noncommercial educational licensees to ascertain and serve public needs, interests, and programming preferences? Who is responsible for what? Do "public stations" have higher or lower standards of responsibility with respect to political and other public affairs programming? How are these various responsibilities and needs to be funded? Who is to decide what? Clearly, until the public broadcasting community itself can sort out its differences, define its purposes, mobilize its resources, and reorganize itself to achieve effective, long-range coordination and planning, the vision of a strong and valuable public telecommunications system will remain less than important on the agenda of public priorities.

What Is Public Broadcasting?

A major problem is that nobody really knows what the words "public broadcasting" should mean. All licensees of broadcasting facilities are deemed to be "public trustees," operating their stations "in the public interest." But the term "public broadcasting" does not appear in the early legislative history of the Communications Act of 1934. Indeed, policy makers have deliberately declined to define public or noncommercial broadcasting functions very explicitly for fear of opening the Pandora's box of programming control — an issue fraught with First Amendment concerns and connotations.

FCC regulations also remain quite ambiguous. For example, Section 73.503, governing the licensing of the reserved FM channels, reads in part as follows:

(a)   A noncommercial educational FM broadcast station will be licensed to a nonprofit educational organization and upon showing that the station will be used for the advancement of an educational program . . .

(d)   Each station shall furnish a nonprofit and noncommercial broadcast service . . .

Similarly, Section 73.621, governing the licensing of television channels, reads:

(a)   . . .noncommercial educational broadcast stations will be licensed only to nonprofit educational organizations upon showing that the proposed stations will be used primarily to serve the educational needs of the community; for the advancement of educational programs; and to furnish a nonprofit and noncommercial television broadcast service . . .

(c) ...noncommercial educational television broadcast stations may transmit educational, cultural and entertainment programs, and programs designed for schools and school systems in connection with regular school courses . . .

It is clear that these channels would never have been reserved had it not been for an overriding concern among commissioners that television be used for "educational purposes." However, it is also apparent that something more than strictly educational and instructional programming was contemplated. Commissioner Hennock, the patron saint of educational broadcasters, spoke of "an unprecedented opportunity for education, both formal and informal" and suggested that educational stations

...supply a beneficial complement to commercial telecasting. Providing for greater diversity in television programming, they will be particularly attractive to the many specialized and minority interests in the community, cultural as well as educational, which tend to be bypassed by commercial broadcasters speaking in terms of mass audiences.[1]

The Carnegie Commission report, from which the Public Broadcasting Act of 1967 was derived, also spoke of the opportunity for "public television" to:

- provide a voice for groups in the community that may otherwise be unheard,

- help us see America whole, in all its diversity,

- increase our understanding of the world,

- open a wide door to greater expression and cultural richness for creative individuals and important audiences,

- seek out able people whose talents might otherwise not be known and shared,

- explore new dimensions of artistic performance not ordinarily available to our nation's audiences,

- carry the best of knowledge and wisdom directly into the home.[2]

Although there can be no doubt that the purpose of the Carnegie report and the Public Broadcasting Act of 1967 was to provide an alternative programming service to what was readily available on commercial channels, the language of the act remained less than helpful in defining the proper content of "public broadcasting." It merely refers to the legal words used by the FCC, "noncommercial educational radio and television broadcasting" and to stations which "under the rules and regulations of the FCC are licensed or eligible to be licensed and which are owned and operated by a public agency or a nonprofit private foundation, corporation or association." Only the term "nonprofit" is truly explicit. (The history of FCC case decisions has also made it abundantly clear that nonprofit agencies may not operate broadcasting facilities on reserved channels for a profit-making purpose.)

The general understanding seems to be that the alternative broadcast service is to be complementary to commercial programming.* It is not clear, however, who is to decide what is complementary. What exists today as public broadcasting has had substantial support in its development from commercial broadcasters, both at a local and at a national level. This assistance, which was fiscal as well as volunteered time and free equipment (many transmitters were given to these educational stations by commercial licensees), was provided for a number of reasons, certainly some of them eleemosynary. However, some broadcasters surely assumed that there would be less pressure upon them because of the existence of the local publicly owned stations.†

To the extent that public broadcasters develop programming which is considered by commercial broadcasters to be competitive to their own programming, there will certainly be animosity from the commercial representatives, as well as monitoring of the noncom

---

*In its membership solicitations, WNET-TV in New York promises to provide programming not available elsewhere.

†Such an assumption would be understandable, even though the FCC's decision to reserve channels for educational purposes explicitly stated that it intended no diminution of responsibility among commercial licensees for educational and public affairs programming.

mercial programming. There is already evidence that public broad-casters are embarked on a collision course with commercial broad-casting. In September 1972, WGBH-TV captured a surprisingly substantial percentage of the audience in the Boston market for coverage of the Canadian-Russian hockey finals. Storer Broadcasting had also bid for coverage of the matches on WSBK-TV, which it has cultivated as the "hockey station" in the market. It is under-standable, then, that Storer sought clarification from the FCC about whether this was the kind of programming intended to be carried on reserved channels.

The basic thrust of Storer's argument was (a) the hockey matches did not provide programming otherwise unavailable in that market; (b) the cost was underwritten by commercial sponsors which were regular purchasers of WSBK-TV air time; (c) extensive newspaper advertising was used to promote WGBH-TV coverage, with substantial credits to the underwriters; (d) the programs carried promotional interruptions and fund-raising solicitations during the intervals, and these "commercials" were considerably in excess of that which would be permitted on commercial stations for adver-tising interruptions. Such programs as "The Way It Was," which is a recap of outstanding sporting events during the last few years, and "A Family At War," which significantly, was produced for a *com-mercial* television network in Great Britain, have also been ques-tioned as infringements upon areas thought by commercial broad-casters to be their natural domain.

As public broadcasters continue to make tentative moves in the direction of attracting a mass audience, they are incurring the wrath not only of the commercial broadcasters but also of another sig-nificant political force in the community — the minority groups whose taste for special-interest programming is not being satisfied by commercial broadcasting. As a result, the FCC finds both groups knocking at its door for the kind of decision-making which the commission has assiduously avoided in the past with its traditional stance of leaving the "educators" alone and regulating by the "raised eyebrow."* Pressure is certain to increase for a clear definition of the concept of alternative programming and for answers to two fun-

---

*A number of petitions to deny the licenses of noncommercial educational stations are currently pending before the FCC or on appeal to the courts. The most notable include: KQED-TV, San Francisco; WETA-TV, Washington, D.C.; KNME-TV, Albuquerque; and KETC-TV, St. Louis.

damental questions: Is the alternative programming requirement enforceable? If so, by whom?

What Is Noncommercial?

The FCC has addressed itself to the definition of "educational" and has determined that licensees on the reserved channels need not necessarily be institutions dedicated to formal educational purposes.* However, very little case law exists on what the term "noncommercial" means, and this is another area fraught with potential difficulties as the "public broadcasters" seek financing from both private industry and the general public. It is clear that overall programming must not operate at a profit and that the programming may not include any explicit advertising messages. However, substantial inroads toward commercialism have been made in the attribution of support from commercial sources, in the solicitation of funds on the air for the support of the station, and in the carriage of nostalgia programming containing commercial announcements.

Credits to commercial sponsors. Some time ago, the best minds in the communications bar gathered to debate whether or not the Mobil Oil Corporation could use its logo in public television underwriting identification. The image in question was the name "Mobil," with gasoline sloshing through the center of the red "o". The group decided that PBS would be unwise to permit this product identification, since it might attract the concern of the FCC.

The rules are explicit concerning commercial credits. Section 73.621 (d) provides that persons or organizations furnishing or producing programs or providing funds for production should be identified by name only — for example, International Business Machines rather than IBM and Chevrolet Division of General Motors rather than Chevrolet.† Companies sharing the same or a similar

---

*At the present time, approximately one-third of the reserved television channels are licensed to state and local educational authorities, one third to colleges or universities, and one-third to nonprofit community organizations. Half the reserved FM channels are licensed to colleges and universities, and about one-fourth each are held by school systems and nonprofit community organizations. (Figures are from the Educational Broadcasting Branch of the FCC.)

†PBS is interpreting this as requiring the full corporate name only on the audio announcement. The logo type (IBM, ARCO or Mobil) is permitted to appear on the television screen.

name may request a waiver of the rule in order to include brief additional descriptive material, and logos have been permitted under such a waiver in order to establish the identity of the company. No mention of the product or service of a company may be made, and credits are permitted only at the beginning and end of a program unless the program lasts longer than an hour.

Since the purposes of commercial interests on public television must necessarily be similar to those on commercial broadcasting — to wit, to obtain the largest audience possible and a positive corporate image — there is a substantial question whether or not it is in the interests of public broadcasting to try to expand funding from this source and to permit greater commercialization. Less than 10 percent of the funding for public broadcasting now comes from commercial sources. However, the programming supported by commercial funding tends to be the most prestigious entertainment programs ("Masterpiece Theatre," for example). It has been virtually impossible for PBS to raise money from corporate commercial sources for public affairs programming, which means that the direction of public programming may be toward more entertainment programming and fewer informational programs of a controversial nature.

Another question concerns the manner in which other media are used to advertise the commercially supported PBS programs. To date, there is no regulation of the corporate advertising in other media. Atlantic Richfield uses the ARCO logo in its newspaper ads promoting PBS programs. The Mobil Oil Corporation, in its full-page ads for "Masterpiece Theatre" and "Mobil Showcase Theatre," actually referred to the program credits as "commercial interruptions." In addition, Mobil used the Mobil logo, but without a commercial plug for oil, in advertising "The Way It Was" and "Upstairs, Downstairs" during the "Today" program on NBC. In 1974, Exxon advertised its offerings on PBS without commercial content, but the ads were invariably in close proximity to the Exxon product commercials on the "NBC Evening News." Aside from a desire to know how and why NBC News decided to carry the announcements, there also arises the interesting question of whether a commercial announcement on a commercial station for programming on a non-commercial station constitutes commercial use of a reserved channel.

Another subsidiary question is whether or not corporations should be encouraged or discouraged from funding programming related to their business. It has always been an unspoken taboo for public stations to accept programming supplied by corporations and related to their business or products. Commercial stations are also leery of carrying such programming. According to case law established by commercial broadcasters, such programs are deemed to be commercial matter in their entirety and are required to be logged as such. On the other hand, what institutions in society have a greater interest in programming related to their business than those in the business?

Actually, it might better serve the public and provide a strong source of alternative programming if large corporations were encouraged to provide funding for informational programs concerning public issues related to their business interests. Since station licensees are subject to the Fairness Doctrine, which requires that both sides of controversial issues be broadcast, the station would have to (1) obtain a program expressing the other sides of the issue, or (2) require the producing corporation to include a discussion of different sides within the given program. Public funds or foundation funds might also be used to produce the "reply" programs to a controversial corporation feature.

Solicitation of contributions. The FCC prohibited PBS announcements of events, such as benefit performances and house tours, which are planned for the solicitation of funds for other nonprofit entities. However, over-the-air solicitation of funds for the public stations themselves is permitted to a limited extent. A popular form of money-raising for the community-owned stations has been annual auctions of consumer products and services which have been donated to the station. This practice obviously contravenes the spirit of the prohibition against commercial uses of the station, since consumer products are being shown and their donors credited over the air. However, the FCC rules have been amended to provide that credit announcements during "auction" broadcasts may identify a particular product or service but "shall not include promotion of such products or services *beyond that necessary for the specific auction purpose*" (note 4, Section 73.621).

The rules have never addressed the question of whether programming time on reserved channels should be used to solicit funds for the support of the station itself, but such solicitations also appear to be generally permitted. In 1974, the Ford Foundation made a $1.5 million grant specifically to promote an increase in viewer support of public television from its current level of 20 million dollars, or approximately 10 percent of the viewing population, to 60 million dollars annually. Certainly, this is a laudable attempt to obtain independent funding for public television stations. However, one wonders whether this effort may create a system of audience-supported stations with goals that will vary from the purposes for which the reserved channels and public funding were originally intended by Congress.

These appeals for listener contributions militate in two directions: (1) They dictate programming content with the most general appeal in order to increase audience response, and (2) they create an audience and subscriber group to which station managements are beholden for their financial support. The question is whether a public station should be catering to the noncontributing rather than the contributing public. One also wonders whether a station can do both without jeopardizing one or another of its obligations. Perhaps there is a genuine need for both public and subscriber-supported stations. If so, the legal constraints might well be quite different. That is, the subscriber-supported stations might seek to provide alternative entertainment programming, whereas public stations could appropriately offer a "common carrier"-type broadcast service.

Nostalgia programming containing commercial matter. Packaged "nostalgia programs," such as "Fibber McGee and Molly," "Amos and Andy," and several other favorite radio series of the 1930s, have become a popular form of entertainment on noncommercial educational FM stations. Because these programs frequently include the original commercial breaks, there has been concern that carrying these shows on reserved channels could make a mockery of the noncommercial prohibition. This would be a problem if the original commercial advertisers would begin to provide this nostalgia programming free of cost to the noncommercial stations. However, the FCC staff has made a number of informal rulings permitting the use of old commercials whenever the program concerns radio history or whenever the "old commercials are an integral part of the nostalgia appeal of the program."[3] The commercials are also acceptable if they are for products or services which are no longer available to the public. Cigarette ads may not be broadcast, regardless of age, because the FCC has no authority to waive the requirements of the Public Health Act of 1969.[4]

All of these questions concerning the definition of noncommercial programming on reserved channels bring us back to the original questions concerning the nature of "public broadcasting." Should public broadcasting be seeking a mass audience? Should it seek financial support from the same sources as commercial broadcasting? Should it be permitted to rebroadcast programs previously carried on commercial channels? May educational institutions charge viewing or listening students for broadcast-related materials? May these institutions charge tuition for the classroom credits received from educational programs?

Since governmental intrusion upon programming choices is prohibited under a strict interpretation of the First Amendment, the easiest definition of "noncommercial" is either "nonprofit," which is easily defined, or "without advertising content," which is not so easily defined, or both. Any effort to define appropriate public broadcasting programming content more precisely would likely lead to much frustration and litigation.

How Should Public Broadcasters Ascertain Community Needs and Interests?

The basic philosophy of the Communications Act of 1934, under which both public and commercial broadcasters are licensed, is that each broadcaster is a "public trustee," serving the specific needs and interests of the community to which each is licensed. Since 1969, under the "Primer for the Ascertainment of Community Needs," commercial broadcasters have come to follow a very elaborate procedure when applying for an initial license and a renewal. There are four aspects to this "ascertainment process": (1) interviewing of community leaders by station management; (2) a general survey of the public in the geographical area served by the station; (3) a statement of needs ascertained by the two surveys; and (4) a statement of programming designed to serve those needs.

For some reason — perhaps because the "educators" have been given special treatment due to their alleged poverty — the noncommercial educational licensees have never been required to engage in the ascertainment process. More recently, however, two independent petitioners filed rule-making petitions asking the FCC to require the noncommercial educational licensees to ascertain community needs and interests. Consequently, a rule-making docket was set up[5] in which all of the concerned parties — CPB, PBS, numerous

The Future of Public Broadcasting

licensees of noncommercial educational facilities, and several public interest groups — filed comments in the FCC proceedings stating their reasons for or against ascertainment of community needs and interests by public licensees.*

Most of the noncommercial licensees have not favored the pending ascertainment requirement. They argue: (1) lack of funds to obtain professional assistance in surveying citizens; (2) money for such ascertainment procedures would have to come from the already limited resources available for programming; (3) programming decisions are substantially influenced by state and local funding sources. PBS, although admitting that some form of ascertainment by public stations would be desirable, also generally opposes the requirement and recommends that noncommercial educational licensees be left to their own discretion to determine how they should ascertain local needs.

In contrast, CPB proposes an amendment to Section 73.503 to require noncommercial educational stations to demonstrate that they would serve "demonstrated community needs within the station's primary service area which are of an educational, informational and cultural nature." Moreover, CPB concedes that the "special treatment afforded noncommercial educational broadcasting through reservation of channels and frequencies clearly warrants higher expectations of applicants seeking to achieve or maintain this special status."

The National Citizens Committee for Broadcasting (NCCB), which has served as a lobby for citizens' groups all over the country, also favors a more general survey of community needs. The NCCB representatives point out that the viewing public most in need of special-interest programming is least often assessed as to its needs and preferences. The reasons for this neglect, according to the NCCB, are obvious: (1) the viewing public "most in need" can seldom afford to become supporting members of a public broadcasting station and therefore do not receive the preference polls used by many of the stations; (2) very few minority-group employees are involved in the decision-making process on public stations; (3) the composition of station boards and directors tends to exclude the

---

*In early 1976, the FCC adopted ascertainment requirements for noncommercial stations. Noncommercial television licensees will follow procedures similar to those of the commercial stations. Public radio licensees are asked only for a narrative report on their ascertainment activities.

least affluent members of the community.

One major problem which has not been addressed by any of the interested parties is the relationship of the concept of alternative programming to the ascertainment requirements. As outlined by the FCC, the ascertainment procedure is not directed specifically to "programming needs" but, rather, to the problems and needs and interests of the particular community to which the station is licensed. The point is to assist the planning of station managements as to their roles in the resolution of existing community problems. Consequently, most ascertainment proceedings are directed toward public affairs programming. However, if one accepts the idea that a major responsibility of the public licensees is to supply *alternative* programming to that offered by commercial licensees, then ascertainment activities by the noncommercial licensees should include an appraisal of the *programming* offered within the entire market and a demonstration that the programs offered by the noncommercial broadcasters are fulfilling unmet programming needs. Yet, only the NCCB has proposed that noncommercial broadcasters be encouraged to deal with programming preferences in the community.*

Clearly, this ascertainment issue has created a focal point for questioning the basic thrust and philosophy of public broadcasting, and a number of very basic issues must now be resolved:

- Should noncommercial broadcasters be treated differently from commercial broadcasters?

- Should noncommercial broadcasters strive to ascertain the programming of commercial licensees and then demonstrate that their own offerings serve well as alternatives to the existing programs available in the market?

- Should ascertainment be related only to the "public programming" portion of the broadcast day (that

---

*Actually, the entire concept of alternative programming is in conflict with the basic requirement that all licensees operate as public trustees. Indeed, if the commercial licensees were meeting all of the needs of the community, then there would be no need for alternative programming. Furthermore, if a noncommercial educational licensee is "a public trustee," then these licensees should be required to ascertain the problems, needs and interests of *all* of the citizens in the community and to design this programming service to serve *all* of those ascertained needs.

directed to general audiences), or should it also include instructional programming?

- Are noncommercial licensees to be held to higher or lower or different standards than commercial broadcasters?

- How shall noncommercial broadcasters meet the requirement of Section 396 (a) (4) of the Communications Act as amended, "to encourage noncommercial educational radio and television broadcast programming which will be responsive to the interests of the people both in the particular localities and throughout the United States"?

- Are noncommercial broadcasters "public trustees"? Or are they pinch hitters for the inadequacies of the "public trustees"?

- Can any of these questions be answered without an integrated look at each of the specific markets?

- Can the FCC or any other publicly funded entity render a judgment which involves evaluating programming choices?

What Are the Responsibilities of Public Stations for Political Broadcasting?

Traditionally, the noncommercial educational broadcasters have not aired a substantial amount of political broadcasting during campaigns. This is mainly due to a combination of circumstances: Political candidates, seeking larger audiences, are more inclined to put pressure on commercial stations to make time available. In addition, noncommercial broadcasters, being largely dependent upon state or local tax sources, are not anxious to bite the hands that feed them. Also, Section 315 of the Communications Act did not positively require that time be made available for political campaign purposes, but only that "equal time" be afforded where time had already been granted by a broadcaster. Therefore, no one had cause to hassle public broadcasters about whether their neglect of campaign politics was in the public interest. Of course, some public stations were also providing a meritorious service in covering local elections.

With the passage of the Campaign Communications Reform Act of 1971, Section 312 (a) of the Communications Act was amended to authorize the commission to revoke licenses "for willful or repeated failure to allow reasonable access to or to permit purchase of reasonable amounts of time for the use of a broadcasting station by a legally qualified candidate for federal elective office on behalf of his candidacy." The act also required that commercial licensees make time available at their lowest unit rate. Since noncommercial licensees had no rate card for advertising, the FCC interpreted the act as permitting a charge by public stations for production services but not for time. Commercial licensees, by contrast, were under no obligation to make free time available.*

Although there is nothing in the legislative history of the act that would indicate that noncommercial educational stations were intended to be exempted from this political-access requirement, neither is there any evidence that there was much consideration by Congress of the consequence of this amendment on public broadcasting. Are public licensees justifiably required to meet a "higher standard" (that is, free time) for political programming? And, if so, on what basis? Certainly, there is room for interpretation of what constitutes "reasonable access," for the carriage of political programming represents a very considerable financial drain on the public stations, as well as a diversion of resources from other programming.

Virtually no use was made of the public broadcasting system by major candidates for the Presidency in 1972.† Since the major net-

---

*Interestingly enough, the amount of *free* programming time given by the national networks to the presidential campaign in 1972 was greatly decreased from previous years. Only one hour of sustaining time was provided to candidates and their supporters on television in 1972, compared with 39 hours, 22 minutes during the famous 1960 debates, and 29 hours, 38 minutes in 1956. The comparable figures for radio are 19 hours in 1972, compared with 43 hours, 14 minutes in 1960, and 32 hours, 23 minutes in 1956. (See FCC Survey 1968, Table 4; Survey 1972, Tables 22 and 23.)

†The PBS program "Election '72," which was conceived by its originators as an in-depth analysis of the Presidential and Congressional campaigns, bit the dust when it stepped on the toes of politically powerful incumbents and also was perceived by commercial broadcasters as competition. Indeed, the public broadcasting community is still feeling the repercussions of this sortie into an area preempted by commercial networks. The Public Broadcasting Financing Act of 1975 wrote into law a system whereby local licensee control of programming content would be perpetuated, thereby effectively foreclosing the advent of a fourth news network which might challenge the preeminence of CBS, NBC, and ABC in presidential coverage.

works and commercial licensees have, by contrast, provided a substantial amount of time — albeit paid political broadcasting — for candidates for federal office, there remains the pressing question of whether it makes any sense to require that public stations provide substantial amounts of free time for candidates for federal office (the Campaign Communications Reform Act applies only to candidates for federal office). However, public broadcasters can provide a valuable alternative service in airing the arguments of local candidates, who are less able to pay for commercial broadcast time and therefore more likely to respond to the invitation of public stations to appear. In 1972 there was also significant use of public broadcast time by third-party candidates, such as Dr. Benjamin Spock. This, too, is consistent with the concept of an "alternative" television service.

If one accepts the current concept of public broadcasting as the source of "alternative programming," it would seem logical to modify the Campaign Communications Reform Act in order to encourage carriage of local rather than federal elections. Certainly, neither state nor local entities have the authority to either prohibit or require specific subject matter on the federally licensed media. The Maine legislature attempted to prohibit educational television systems supported by state funds from being used for the purpose of promoting political candidacies or specific governmental actions, but this law was struck down on the basis of the supremacy clause of the Constitution.*

---

*Oddly enough, a related federal prohibition of editorializing by public television stations or of supporting political candidates (in Section 399 of the Public Broadcasting Act) has not been challenged by any of the noncommercial licensees, although there seems to be general agreement that the restriction is unconstitutional. Section 399 is unlikely ever to be challenged by any of the noncommercial educational licensees themselves because they are very content with a nonpartisan status. For one thing, a positive requirement to editorialize or to support political candidates would be fraught with hazards to public television's funding. Furthermore, Section 399 constituted a concession on the part of the educators engaged in lobbying for the Public Broadcasting Act. They accepted the restriction in order to subdue the fears of congressmen that the federal funds made available to CPB would be used to defeat incumbents. Finally, there is the problem of the IRS restrictions on activities of nonprofit organizations with respect to lobbying for legislation and advocacy of political candidacies. Anyone undertaking to litigate the constitutionality of Sction 399 would probably also have to tackle Section 4945 of the IRS regulations on nonprofit licensees of broadcast facilities.

Anne W. Branscomb

What Are the Parameters of
Controversial-Issue Programming?

Under discretionary authority in the Communications Act of 1934, and now under the written law, the FCC has over the years developed the Fairness Doctrine to serve as a guideline to licensees in the planning of programming on "controversial issues of public importance." The doctrine has always been greatly criticized by broadcasters, and the authority of the FCC in this area was questioned but not resolved by the recent *NBC Pensions* case. The responsibility of deciding what is a controversial issue of public importance, and how much time a station or network must devote to opposing views, has been left substantially within the discretion of the licensee. The present guidelines of the Fairness Doctrine include:

(1) the responsibility for administration and interpretation of the doctrine remains with the FCC;

(2) the responsibility for its application rests upon the licensee;

(3) the Fairness Doctrine applies to the entire programming service, not to individual programs;

(4) the responsibility to evaluate controversiality is upon the licensee rather than the program supplier.

It would appear that Section 396 (g) (1) (A) was intended to insure that CPB, which is not a broadcast licensee and therefore not subject to FCC jurisdiction, would use public funds to promote programming that is consistent with the philosophy of the Fairness Doctrine. However, Section 396 (g) (1) (A) was drafted hastily as an eleventh-hour amendment, and the only thing certain about the terms "objectivity and balance" is that they apply only to programs funded by CPB. Both CPB and PBS have argued strenuously that Section 396 (g) (1) (A) means nothing more or less than the Fairness Doctrine, but it is difficult to rationalize the discrepancies in the language of the two bills. Certainly, consistency could have been easily achieved for the Public Broadcasting Act by referring back to the Communications Act Section 315 terminology.

The Communications Act, Section 315 (a) (4) clearly requires licensees to afford reasonable opportunities for the discussion of conflicting views on issues of public importance. The requirements of Sections 396 (g) (1) (A) of the Public Broadcasting Act would appear to be far more stringent in terms of balancing views to cover far more subject matter. "Programs of a controversial nature" (the Communications Act) is far more inclusive than "conflicting views on issues of public importance" (the Public Broadcasting Act). Similarly, the phrase "programs or series of programs" in the Public Broadcasting amendment is ambiguous but incontrovertibly wide-ranging. It could be interpreted as demanding "objectivity and balance" within a single program, in a single-title series, in all programs involving the same issue, in all controversial programming, or in an entire program package for a season. There is substantial legislative history that something more than a single program was intended, but what that "something more" should be remains obscure.[6]

Most communications lawyers representing public entities agree that Section (g) (1) (A) is unconstitutional. The Court of Appeals has avoided the constitutional question in looking at "objectivity and balance" by reducing its impact to a horatory phrase unenforceable in any court of law.[7] However, the decision is not likely to have much impact on present practice for the very simple reason that public broadcasting is unlikely to obtain funding from public sources unless it strives to maintain an overall "fairness," "objectivity," and "balance" and to air the various views of the politically influential officials who control whatever public funds are being made available at both the national and local level. A more fundamental constitutional question is whether or not a publicly funded broadcasting entity could be challenged for more representative access under the First Amendment, or even under the Fourteenth Amendment requiring nondiscriminatory behavior by public entities.

The *CBS v. DNC* case upheld the right of commercial broadcasters to decline to carry political advertising of a controversial nature, but the minority opinion did not address the question of the obligations of a noncommercial educational licensee receiving more than 50 percent of its funds from governmental agencies (which is the financial situation of most of the noncommercial educational licensees). Justice Douglas did note, however, that such governmentally funded licensees should not be permitted to refuse the programs offered, and he specifically raised the question with respect to programming funded by CPB.[8] Although the Section

396 (g) (1) (A) question is a nonissue in the sense that it is unlikely to generate a substantial amount of litigation in the near future, it nevertheless dramatizes that dilemma of public broadcasting in sorting out the ambiguities of its status and responsibilities.

Which Institutions Have Regulatory Jurisdiction over Public Broadcasting?

When the Accuracy in Media organization petitioned the FCC for an interpretation of Section 396 (g) (1) (A), the CPB filed a brief which argued that Section 398 of the Public Broadcasting Act eliminated any FCC claims of jurisdiction to interpret the Public Broadcasting Act. Section 398 provides:

> Nothing contained in this part shall be deemed (1) to amend any other provision of, or requirement under this Act; or (2) to authorize any department agency, officer, or employee of the United States to exercise any direction, supervision, or control over educational television or radio broadcasting, or over the Corporation or any of its grantees of contractors, or over the charter or bylaws of the Corporation, or over the curriculum, program of instruction or personnel of any educational institution, school system, or educational broadcasting station or system.

Section 398 can indeed be read to exempt noncommercial educational licensees from any control by the FCC. The law is ambiguous since it disavows any intention to amend other provisions or requirements under the act, and the act clearly establishes an intent to honor all previously established responsibilities of licensees under the original Communications Act of 1934. Nevertheless, CPB argued successfully that the FCC had had no jurisdiction over the interpretation of Section 396 (g) (1) (A), which was directed to the programming funded by the CPB itself. The FCC therefore declined to exercise any jurisdiction or to define the meaning of the "objectivity and balance" phrase.

The Accuracy in Media opinion by the FCC dramatizes the current confusion concerning the regulatory authority and institutional responsibility of the various agencies associated with public broadcasting. The question of who has the power to interpret the "strict adherence to objectivity and balance" clause in the CPB enabling act represents merely the tip of the iceberg. There is a much deeper jurisdictional dispute brewing between the CPB and PBS, which CPB spawned under authority granted in the 1967 act. This dispute, which erupted into public view during the debate on the long-range funding bill in Congress, concerns the amount of federal funding that will be directly available to the stations. Currently, the share of the licensees ranges between 30 and 50 percent, with 50 percent proposed under the pending bill. The stations are lobbying for an increase to 70 or 75 percent.

The stations' request for the greater portion of federal funds is a result of their decision to take full responsibility for funding the Station Program Cooperative (SPC). The cooperative is currently financed by grants from the CPB and the Ford Foundation as well as by station contributions. However, if the bulk of federal funds are to be transferred directly to the stations, the authority of the CPB would be greatly diminished. Naturally, this possibility disturbs the delicate balance of power achieved between the CPB and PBS by the "partnership" agreement reached in 1972.

Other than Congress and the President, there are five major entities that retain substantial fiscal and policy control in decisions concerning public broadcasting:

(1) *The broadcast licensees.* There are approximately 246 stations licensed to 155 entities.* The various entities represent diverse forms of ownership including about 14 percent licensed to public school systems; 32 percent licensed to colleges and universities, 20 percent licensed to state organizations (including substantial educational television networks in Alabama, Georgia, Kentucky, Maine, Nebraska, New Hampshire, North Carolina, South Carolina, and Vermont); 1 percent licensed to municipalities (where no local educational authority exists); and 33 percent licensed to independent community nonprofit corporations.

(2) *The Federal Communications Commission.* All broadcasting entities receive their licenses directly from the FCC under its specific authority to license such facilities and its general authority to pro-

---

*Multiple ownership rules, which restrict the number of licenses a commercial licensee may acquire, do not apply to noncommercial educational channels.

vide for an integrated communications system for the nation. The FCC has full administrative and rule-making authority spelled out in the Communications Act of 1934, and no other federal agency has been given any specific regulatory authority over noncommercial licensees. The latter are entirely the creatures of the FCC's rule-making authority, not a specific congressional mandate.

(3) *The Corporation for Public Broadcasting.* The CPB is a funding agency set up under the Public Broadcasting Act of 1967 to receive funds from Congress and to dispense them to other entities to promote and develop programming sources for the noncommercial licensees.

(4) *The Public Broadcasting Service.* The PBS was originally set up by CPB as a program distribution and interconnection service for licensees under authority granted in Section 396 (g) (1) (B). However, the Public Broadcasting Service was organized as a membership organization and, once established, became much more than a distribution or interconnection system. In effect, PBS is now equally a trade association of public television licensees, representing their collective interests and acting as their spokesman. Consequently, PBS has established a separate and distinct existence from the CPB and has developed a considerable amount of political clout. This has left the CPB with little operational or administrative function other than to serve as a "pass-through" for some portion of federal funds allocated by Congress.

(5) *National Public Radio.* The NPR is a program production, distribution, and interconnection system for about 179 noncommercial educational radio stations qualified (as "full service" stations) to receive programs funded by CPB for radio broadcast. Unlike PBS, the NPR does not serve as a trade association for the radio licensees. Instead, they have organized a separate membership organization called the Association of Public Radio Stations. There has been considerable dissatisfaction with this separation of functions since it leaves the radio licensees in a disadvantaged position *vis-a-vis* PBS in dealing with CPB. However, some disinterested observers think the NPR-APRS model may be the better choice.

The Carnegie Commission Report contemplated only a single agency to promote and develop public television. That agency was to be independent of control by Congress and other government bodies. The problem, however, is that in its efforts to insure independence of programming choice unfettered by governmental intrusion, the public broadcasting legislation set up an agency with very little operating authority.

The lawmakers feared that an independent federal agency using federal funds might become a fourth national network outside the jurisdiction of the FCC. Thus, the CPB was prohibited from owning or operating "any television or radio broadcast station, system, or network, community antenna television system, or interconnection or program facility." There was also substantial concern that the non-commercial educational stations should maintain local autonomy and provide a local programming service. If the licensees are to receive 75 percent of federal funds, as they propose, CPB will lose most of its remaining responsibility for fiscal matters. Ironically, the CPB, by spawning PBS, may have served as a dummy corporation to give birth to that which the legislation specifically prohibits the corporation from becoming itself — a fourth network.

Having fulfilled this historic function, perhaps there are those who would wish a timely demise for CPB. However, there is nothing in the legislation to prevent the CPB from spawning other program production facilities, systems of interconnection for the distribution of programs, or even networks for specific purposes. The major purpose of CPB appears to be as a "facilitator" and developer of diverse programming without operational responsibility. Consequently, it may be that the proper role of the CPB is to seek out and develop new forms of program production and distribution facilities.

For example, what would be wrong with promoting production facilities and networks for the distribution of ethnically oriented programming, or developing satellite distribution to cable television systems, or even purchasing time on commercial networks for informational programs which seek a national or mass audience?* A broad range of opportunities are still available to the CPB for the development of diverse programming to serve the needs and interests of the heterogeneous population of this country.

Meanwhile, programming control remains in the hands of those who control the funds — the executive branch and the Congress. Even though the act purported to set up an independent funding agency, the board of directors of that agency is appointed by the President and the funds for the agency come from the Congress.

---

*This would require an amendment to the Public Broadcasting Act for distribution to cable systems and for distribution over commercial stations. It would require larger amounts of funding as well.

Furthermore, both the executive and legislative branches have explicitly stated an intent to exert programming control through the power of the purse strings. In explaining the presidential veto of the public broadcasting funding bill in 1972, Patrick Buchanan, a member of the White House staff, stated publicly that the bill was vetoed because persons in programs appearing on public television (that is, Sander Vanocur, Robert McNeil, and Bill Moyers) were regarded as anti-Administration.[9] Similarly, Senator Cotton, in the debate on the Public Broadcasting Act, stated that Congress could instantly correct any injustice evidenced by public broadcasting:

> First, we can make very uncomfortable, and give a very unhappy experience to the directors of the corporation. Second, we can shut down some of their activities in the Appropriations Committee and in the appropriating process of Congress with respect to this particular network.[10]

In addition, the bill itself provides for the General Accounting Office to audit the books and records of the CPB, and for the Office of Management and Budget to review the budgetary request of the agency annually, even though the CPB submits its budget with a proviso that this is done by courtesy only and not because of any legal requirement that they do so. All of these conditions collectively demonstrate the difficulty of trying to set up an independent agency which must depend upon appropriations either annually or even at five-year intervals from Congressional sources. No less an authority than a Supreme Court justice has stated that "it is difficult to see why it [CPB] is not a federal agency engaged in operating a 'press' as that word is used in the First Amendment."[11]

A completely independent system of public broadcasting will remain a dim and distant hope unless and until some form of insulated funding is available, such as that proposed by the Carnegie Commission. Use of "earmarked" funds set aside in trust could guarantee independence for a CPB, a PBS, individual licensees, or some other new entity.

Who Is To Decide?

Assuming that we will be able to find some resolution for the funding question and for the institutional responsibilities of the various agencies engaged in public broadcasting, there is a subsidiary question of what the composition of governing boards of public broadcasting agencies should be. Section 396 (c) (2) of the Public Broadcasting Act requires that members of the CPB board be selected on a representative basis but from a group of citizens with "various kinds of talent and experience appropriate to the functions and responsibilities of the corporation." This could be interpreted variously as requiring a broadly representative group or one with particular talents related to the corporation functions and to the knowledgable selection of what is truly "alternative programming."

The current board has a substantial number of members from related media — program producers, cable television systems, and the movie industry. Although these members would seem to comply with the provision of 396 (c) (2), such a composition also presents a fairly substantial question of conflict of interest in the management of funds for public broadcasting. The composition of the board has also been challenged by the National Black Media Coalition, the Citizens Communications Center, and the CPB Advisory Committee of National Organizations as seriously deficient in providing representation to "women, youth, and minorities" as well as broad consumer interests.

The present method of selecting the board, by Presidential appointment, also deserves serious reconsideration if insulation from political influence is to be achieved. A system of selection from nominees submitted by the governing boards of participating licensees would be preferable, if such boards were themselves representative of general community interests. However, the National Citizens Committee for Broadcasting has also challenged the makeup of these "blue-ribbon" elitist boards, which are more representative of the contributing audience than of the general community. Public broadcasters are being asked by local citizens' media groups to defend their choices not only of board members but also of their management-level employees.

Reflections Upon the Future of Public Broadcasting

Public broadcasting is asking too much of itself and too little of the public. It is a whole new concept which embodies all the residual and unfulfilled hopes and promise of advertiser-supported, mass-audience broadcasting. With too much public scrutiny, it may die aborning. Without public support, it may also come to naught. Consequently, public broadcast licensees are going through a crisis of identity the resolution of which will be both painful and protracted. The "educators" may long for the peace and quiet of anonymity, but having decided to "go public," they must now live with the consequences: much more public scrutiny, much more public clamor, much more public criticism, and, conceivably, much more public influence.

Some of the more pressing problems might be resolved as follows:

- The concept of "alternative programming" is unlikely to be defined for the reason that no public agency, certainly not the FCC, will want to specify programming content. It is easier to classify types of licensees, and, once they qualify, let them make their own program decisions.

- There should be reconsideration of the concept of reserved channels. The courts are at the brink of a legal breakthrough in recent cases directing the FCC to scrutinize the need for both minority ownership and specialized programming services. Perhaps there are purposes other than educational and noncommercial for which channels should be reserved. Overall communications capability needs to be assessed on a marketwide and nationwide basis, not on the capability of each licensee.

- There should be a thorough reappraisal of the effects of the Public Broadcasting Act of 1967. Is the Public Broadcasting Service — laudable as it may be — the be-all and end-all of the legislative purpose? Clarification of the relationship between the CPB, PBS, NPR, FCC, and licensees is necessary — the possibility of a completely independent system of public broadcasters, or community stations, exempt from supervisory control by the FCC, should be considered.

- CPB should carefully assess its role as a facilitator

of noncommercial public programming and look to alternative methods it can use to increase diverse programming — as the long-range funding bill proposes — by means other than broadcast facilities. For example, nothing is happening out there with all those channels allocated to public use by cable systems.

- There is nothing in the Public Broadcasting Act that says that only one radio and one television system should be developed. Although the PBS might cry foul play, the act could not (and does not), under the antitrust laws, prohibit licensees from obtaining programming from alternative sources. Perhaps the greatest need is to stimulate and develop new production and interconnection facilities in order to provide a wider choice of programming to the public.

- The responsibilities of public broadcasters to make free time available to candidates should be clarified. It makes good sense to exempt licensees from the requirement to carry candidates for federal elective office where candidates for local elections are given time. Moreover, the meaning of "reasonable access" for candidates, whether federal or local, should be defined. Although it is not now a problem, since there is no great clamor from candidates for time, the increasing success of public broadcasters in capturing larger audiences may result in requests from national candidates to preempt the most popular programming ("Upstairs, Downstairs," for example). Such preemption would, of course, seriously disrupt program schedules and could disrupt their funding as well.

- Public broadcasters must ascertain community needs. However, the overall purpose of such ascertainment should be to assess the programming of all stations in the market and to show how the public broadcasters are meeting the unsatisfied programming needs of that particular market. This is vastly dif-

ferent from what is expected of commercial broadcasters. It would provide a useful yardstick by which
the public might assess the performance of all stations
in a market.

- Some soul-searching must necessarily be generated by
  concern about the desirability of increasing the portion of broadcast time paid for by commercial
  sources. Indeed, there is much room for thought on
  the whole definition of a noncommercial service.
  At a minimum, there should be some funding available for the production and purchase of quality
  entertainment programming which is not governed
  by commercial interests nor directed to mass
  audiences.

- The boards of all licensees, as well as of the CPB,
  should be opened to a broader spectrum of appointees. This may require an amendment to the
  Public Broadcasting Act of 1967. Furthermore,
  more careful scrutiny of what constitutes a conflict
  of interest should be written into the law.

This compendium of problems (and possible solutions) is by
no means exhaustive. A number of other problems have been
brought to my attention by public broadcasters, and these lesser but
by no means insignificant issues will also have to be addressed in
the next few years.

- Direct funding of programming by government
  agencies.

- Copyright practices and residual rights which inhibit
  the reuse of material.

- Internal Revenue Service regulations and rulings
  which inhibit the activities of station employees and
  interfere with the free flow of information.

- The overlapping jurisdiction between state-organized
  networks and the national public system.

- The exception to multiple-ownership rules for stations licensed to public entities.

- Legal impediments to branching out into use and development of new technologies.

- Justification of spectrum allocations for public licensees with overlapping signals and duplicative programming.

If a multitude of problems in public broadcasting have been overlooked too long, and a multiplicity of opportunities left undeveloped, the reason is not difficult to ascertain. The noncommercial stations have always been considered the poor cousins of the commercial broadcasting system and have been left to fend for themselves in a highly competitive world. It is different for a system which attracts on a good evening less than 3 percent of the audience to command a position of great public importance.

Why then is the development of the public sector in telecommunications important? For one thing, because this nation, the wealthiest in the world, spends less and produces less in this area than most of our less well-endowed neighbors. We are, in effect, a culturally deprived people. The Japanese spend almost four times as much per capita on their public broadcasting system as the United States (which borrows the best of its programming from the BBC). There are five public channels in Japan — two television (one general entertainment and one instructional) and three audio channels, one FM and two AM. In combination, these channels offer an average of 91.5 hours of public broadcasting a day. This public expenditure on broadcasting might be dismissed as irrelevant if the public system were the only system; but the Japanese also have three national commercial television networks, with a fourth in progress and a fifth independent station in Tokyo.

In addition, there is an English-language cable channel in Tokyo, and the government is actively engaged in advanced experiments with new telecommunications services in the Tama New Town in the suburbs of Tokyo. Here, early in 1976, a working interactive cable system initiated operation with a number of experimental programs, including a facsimile newspaper; a tour guide of sites which can be seen by bicycling near the Tama New Town; an English-language lesson; public safety messages in hard copy; a two-way multiple-choice citizen response for televised public meetings; and library-like retrieval programs which can be viewed on the video display terminal, much like reading a book.

While watching the demonstration of all of these wonders I had a daydream that the American public would be willing to support such a wide range of options to the individual consumer. A new kind of institution would be established in our communities — a public telecommunications information center where children could make use of computer-assisted instruction; where the latest news would always be available; where messages from community groups to their members could be processed and delivered electronically; where the latest technology could be made available on video discs or computer tapes to improve the quality of life for all Americans. The center's pooled resources, both financial and physical, would make this dream possible.

Does the public broadcasting community have the breadth of vision or the personal resources or the will to become this new kind of institution? The answer, hopefully, is "yes." But this means that the major task of the public broadcasters is a quick resolution of the institutional problems which prevent long-range future planning, so that the local public broadcasting entities can begin to evolve naturally into community public-telecommunications facilities.

One of the most urgent goals for the future planning of the public system should be to provide for a separation of the facilities and institutions which have substantially different missions. "Public" is really a misnomer for the interconnection systems currently operated by PBS and NPR. "Public" can mean a system funded out of public funds or a system funded by public subscription. What currently passes for public broadcasting is a hybridization of these two different ideas.

Certainly, a strong network of subscriber-supported stations to deliver good quality general programming without commercial interruptions is of high priority. This network should be spun off from the publicly supported system and operated independently. Within the remaining public system, several separate programming services should be developed: a public affairs channel, a cultural affairs channel (for music and drama), a science service, and a children's channel. These services should be available not only to non-commercial stations but also to cable systems and independent commercial stations. The public would be greatly enriched by fulltime programming in all of these areas.

The Future of Public Broadcasting

There is also a need for discrete state and regional networks devoted primarily to the production, storage, and exchange of educational and instructional materials. On the government-funded information networks, there should be a variety of attractive and effective packages at times and places in which the consuming public chooses to make use of them. Opportunities for such a public service abound not only with television but with video discs, computer-assisted instruction, dial-up information-retrieval systems, imaginative and innovative new uses of cable systems, and the development of data banks and data networks.

The most demanding problem for which no solution has yet been found is in the area of local video programming for local communities. So far, the result of the complex efforts to decentralize the public television system has been to "democratize" the decision-making on nationally distributed programming for local stations without substantially altering the capability of these stations to provide local services. Expanded local service, was, of course, the primary purpose of the FCC's rather generous spectrum-allocation policies. Therefore, the chief mandate for the Corporation for Public Broadcasting for the next 10 years should be to determine how and whether the neglected telecommunications needs of the American people can be met with existing facilities and software. Thanks mainly to federal funds, the public broadcasting system has hardware which in many cases at the local level is superior to that of the commercial stations. The next priority is to develop the software to diversify the available offerings to the viewing public.

Existing statutes (tax laws, labor laws, copyright laws, as well as the communications act itself) must be modified in order to stimulate private industry and encourage innovative practices in the telecommunications industry. And what cannot be achieved by the private sector can and must be achieved by the public sector. The vision of a community telecommunications center which will provide access for all citizens to the latest machines and materials is deserving of high aspiration from all sectors of the society. How public information-delivery systems are designed and developed in the next quarter of a centruy will have much influence on the quality of life in this country. How public broadcasters perceive their role in these changes may determine whether they become leaders or followers in the communications revolution. As a member of the public aware of the new technological opportunities, I trust that their role will be one of leadership.

References

1. *FCC 148* at 591 (1952).

2. Carnegie Commission on Educational Television. *Public Television: A Program for Action* (New York: Harper and Row, 1967), pp. 52-53.

3. WBJC-FM, 40 FCC.2d 936 (1973).

4. 15 USC Section 1331 to 1338.

5. Docket No. 19816.

6. 113 *Cong. Rec.* 29386 (1967).

7. 521 Fed. 2d 298 (U.S. Court of Appeals, D.C. Circuit, 1975); 43 FCC. 2d 851 (1973).

8. 412 U.S. 94 (1973).

9. *New York Times*, May 28, 1973, p. 31.

10. 113 *Cong. Rec.* 13003.

11. *CBS v DNC*, 412 U.S. 94 (1973) J. Douglas dissent.

Heart of the System: The Stations

FREDERICK BREITENFELD, JR.

Power grows where money flows. That's about the shortest possible history of American noncommercial television. It's the only system of broadcasting in the world established with no visible means of support. As a result, it has known almost continual poverty, controversy, internal squabbling, and both tyranny and revolution. It has yet to become a universally accepted, healthy American service. The strongest thing going for public broadcasting remains the purity of the idea and the energy and dedication of the individual stations that make up the system.

There has always been a "national level" in our business as well. Until quite recently, all of the seven-figure money was focused on specific agencies or efforts, so over the years we've developed a strong "centrist" tradition. However, public broadcasting in America — central powers and forces notwithstanding — is a local phenomenon. It doesn't really happen in foundation offices and Congressional hallways; it happens back home. Behind the national shish-kebab of money, status, power, lobbying, statistics and speeches lies the real excitement of public broadcasting: the stations.

Dr. Breitenfeld is executive director, the Maryland Center for Public Broadcasting.

The Future of Public Broadcasting

There are fundamentally only four types of public television (PTV) licensees among the more than 250 stations on the air: *university* stations, operated by institutions of higher learning; *community* stations, which are privately owned; *state* stations, whose licenses are held by state authorities or commissions; and *school* stations, owned by local boards of education.

This handy division of all stations into four categories leads to two unfortunate conclusions. The first is that all stations of similar ownership are the same in every way — which, of course, they are not. They vary significantly in ownership, procedures, budget, operation, style and mission. Most important are the profound differences in their local, internal politics of administration. The *genus* of public television includes several *species*.

The second misconception is that every station must be in one of the four categories in order to have the world spin as it should. It doesn't work that way, since the FCC never put a limit to the types of nonprofit, educational agencies that might own noncommerical stations. Therefore, there are some notable exceptions to these generalized descriptions.

Excuse me, but . . .

. . . The station's best tape editor has just quit.

. . . A $1,000 gift will be given to the station at a dinner on Thursday night. A few words of acceptance would be nice.

. . . Two members of the board have to see you right away. They're upset about that program last night — the one about gun legislation.

One, for instance, is a noncommercial station owned and operated by the City of New York. WNYC is a "city station," the only one in the country, and it has been on the air since 1962. Researchers generally fume as they try to label it as one of the four ownership types.

Another exception is the station that at one time was operated by the board of trustees of a public library. The early operation of yet another station was shared between school and community: A private corporation ran the evening schedule and the local school system took the days. The school officials used the station for classroom television, and the private group raised the funds for out-of-school hours. It was a "school station" in the strict sense, since the license belonged to the school system. But it was also a "community station" (the arrangement was changed a few years ago, and now the station is strictly a "community" licensee).

There are other quirks that make the differences among stations more prominent than the similarities. These differences are the small pieces of circumstance that help to put one station in the basement of an old school, another in a community center, and a third in a garage. These are the local realities that prompt one station to arrange a successful television auction and another to shun such "undignified" activity.

Yet, in the final analysis, there is always the one fundamental sameness about the noncommercial stations: All of them are trying to bring effective educational and informational services to as many citizens as possible. This is the bond that ties the many different stations into a *system* of noncommercial broadcasting in America.

University stations. The university explosion took place while television was becoming an important industry, so it was natural that colleges should develop an early interest in the educational broadcasting idea. The persuasive argument was that an educational television station would be ideally located at a center of teaching and research, and it would allow a university to extend its influence and to reach new audiences. The educational planners have been correct on both counts. Universities have used their stations to train, to educate and to enlighten thousands of people who would not ordinarily be affected by the resources of higher education.

How a university station is set up and operated depends in each case on why the university really wants it and at what administrative level the interest in broadcasting is particularly strong. At one university, the vice president for academic affairs might take an active part in the station, in which case, the broadcast manager reports directly to him. In another case, the station's chief executive reports to a department chairman or a dean. Or perhaps the faculty senate will be given a "program advisory" capacity and will have the power to veto program schedules. Occasionally, a whole new division or special service will be established beyond the usual academic structure.

Station policies remain basically *university* policies, so the life of a university station is quite different from that of other stations. The requirements and procedures established by the university, including purchasing procedures, building specifications and travel allowances, will always apply. Staff members are university employees, and if the station manager is also a faculty member, academic "credentials" can be important. Possession of a master's degree may be regarded as a minimum requirement for a responsible position at the station.

Excuse me, but . . .

. . . An editorial in last night's paper supports a sociology professor who said in a speech that the university's PTV station is "unresponsive to public need." The Chancellor wants to see you.

. . . A heavy light dropped from the grid to the studio floor. Luckily, nobody was hurt, but a meeting on "safety procedures" is in order. The Dean wants to see you.

. . . The Comptroller can't believe that PBS dues will be up to $36,000 next year, and he doesn't think we should join. At least that's what he'll recommend to the state Board of Regents tomorrow. He doesn't want to see you.

The station's annual budget is usually included in the total budget of the University. This means casual lobbying by management at the campus level and then perhaps a presentation to the board of trustees. It could also mean a session at the state capital, since all but a few university stations are at state institutions.

Most university presidents, and their trustees, are only vaguely aware of things like "CPB" and "PBS." The broadcast television responsibility at a university is usually a *line item*, and as such it takes its place at budget time with the school of nursing, the extension division, the alumni office, and the scores of other standard efforts. Therefore, the station manager has to translate PBS/CPB matters into university language. Nor is this merely a semantic exercise; the station's life can depend on it.

Community stations. When the Fund for Adult Education promoted the activation of noncommercial television in the 1950s, it was particularly interested in *privately* owned stations. The idea was that communities would organize existing agencies and services around a new and cooperative "ETV" venture, and that television would help in "liberal adult education." This was a daring dream, and it caught on in many cities. The dozens of private, noncommercial stations on the air today are the most publicized, the most glamorous and the most miraculous of all the licensees.

In almost every case, the story of how a community station got started is a lesson in determination, vision and hard-earned dollars. Usually, a local business leader, educator or political figure learned that an educational channel was available and became impressed by the educational and special services that could be rendered by an "ETV station," an informal council was formed and leading citizens were attracted. At one point or another, a lawyer probably donated services for incorporation and FCC license application.

The community station lives by its own wits, building everything from scratch — hospital insurance for the employees, retirement plans, purchasing procedures, personnel practices and all the operational details of a self-sufficient organization. Cash remains the key to survival, and the stations are engaged in a constant search for new schemes and techniques to bring in money.

Excuse me, but . . .

. . . The chief engineer is worried about how much longer the remote truck can operate without maintenance.

. . . The state superintendent of schools is dropping by in one hour for a tour of the station. He'll have two state legislators with him.

. . . The minutes of the last meeting of the Instructional Television Advisory Council have been lost.

While the boards of many nonprofit agencies can loaf, simply taking credit at public functions for the year's activities, a community station's board of directors must be continually strong, interested and active.

Community stations range from tiny operations, with remarkably small budgets, to huge enterprises with annual budgets in eight figures. Among all the noncommercial licensees, it's likely that the greatest diversity is found in this group. On the other hand, the dozens of private noncommercial stations in the country share the one common characteristic of fierce independence. When the slightest pressure is applied, even from potential sources of money, most community stations rebel. "This station is not for sale" is a favorite statement of one manager. The people involved with these stations generally believe that only their type of operation can be called "pure" public broadcasting.

State stations. States generally measure a commitment in dollar signs. When a bridge must be built or a state hospital expanded, the issue is brought before the legislature and either money is appropriated or the proposal is rejected. The question for state legislators and governors is always one of priorities and costs, so political overtones are as real as in Washington.

Excuse me, but . . .

. . . We have reviewed your request to receive a grant. Try not to accept money from outside sources. If such acceptance is essential, you must get the approval of the Board of Public Services. A letter to the Director of Budget is required, in which you ask that the item be considered. Approval to receive the money will probably be received via the Funds Approval form, which must be signed by four of the seven Board members. With your signature added in the box labeled, "Do not write in this space," you are ready to send the check to the office of the Fiscal Executive. Spending that money will be the same as spending regularly appropriated money, and it must be spent by June 30 or it will revert to the Public Fund. All budgets will be cut by amounts equal to amounts taken in from outside sources, unless a Special Holding Account is established. This is done through the submission of a Fiscal Service Request form . . .

If PTV is to develop as a state service, it must have the backing of the governor, the legislature and perhaps some of the other agencies. Then, to thrive and grow, it must continue to hold that support through the inevitable shifts in elected representatives and executives. This requirement alone makes state-owned PTV stations particularly alert to the political scenery.

Sometimes, state officials learn quickly that television can help in solving educational problems. In a growing number of states, the importance of educational communications has therefore drawn the attention of those who make big decisions. Nevertheless, PTV is not a politically "conservative" idea. It involves expenditures, changes and a gamble. The idea itself, then, is potentially a political issue, and the same questions are asked by careful legislators across the country as they consider statewide PTV proposals: Why does it cost so much? What can it really do to help? Is it like commercial television? Would it present partisan viewpoints? Would it become a political tool for those in power? Who would control it?

That sticky question of *control* often becomes the leading legislative issue. In one state, the university president could be a particularly powerful figure, and it might have been the university itself that started the whole PTV idea. The president could have both friends and enemies in the legislature, and they would surely consider the PTV bill largely in terms of how it might affect the university's power. In another state, the department of education might be considered unproductive and overstaffed. Thus, if the PTV bill calls for that department to become the licensee of the state's PTV stations, then legislative cogitation might center not on the new PTV idea but on an old battle with the department of education. A board of regents, a coordinating group for higher education, a state college board, or a special advisory council on education might also be possible agencies to take over the television enterprise. There is usually some argument about each one, and it's the familiar issue: How can the new service be absorbed most smoothly into the existing administrative structure?

Excuse me, but. . .

. . . The bids for a new film island came in $10,000 above budget. The RCA man called to talk about it.

. . . The Governor just put a freeze on out-of-state travel, due to the budget deficit. What about your report to the PBS Board next month in Washington?

. . . The state auditors are here. They want an office and two desks. They'll be here for eleven weeks.

. . . One of the producers finally blew up at that temperamental teacher for the music series. The teacher demands a meeting with you because, as he put it, "nobody talks to me that way."

Political bodies have a marvelous way of compromising, and in many states the PTV effort becomes a "cooperative" effort. The stations will be built on the state college campuses, but they will be under the administrative control of the state department of education. Or perhaps the state department of public instruction will be responsible for school television production, but another agency will be the official licensee. Several states have even created new agencies to take charge of the noncommercial television systems. The legislators apparently feel in those cases that the responsibility of building a network is heavy and that a special board, authority, commission, or council should be established.

School stations. If a school system is big enough geographically, and if there is a shortage of specialized teachers, then the idea of a public television station is especially appealing. Usually, the superintendent gets a proposal from the supervisor of audio-visual education, or from a group of parents or principals. The next step is the same as with university and state stations: The system's money-granting power must be convinced. The board of education must be persuaded that the education in its district could be improved in one way or another if the school system owned and operated a noncommercial television station.

In just about every case of school-owned PTV across the country, the emphasis is on classroom television. In the early years, school stations usually went off the air after school each day. Then when libraries of available tapes were established, and when other programming services began to appear, they lengthened the programming days. School stations seldom achieve much self-assurance, however; for no matter how professional and extensive the school station's service, when the board of education begins to consider next year's budget (and, then, as the county or city budget agency approves it), the local school PTV station manager has every right to quiver. After all, the signal could be abruptly put off the air if local school tax dollars prove insufficient and the broadcast service becomes an "extra." On the other hand, the station could get a new building, complete with more and better equipment, if the local tax situation is bright and the service is regarded as vital.

The negotiable difference, as with all public efforts, is at least partly political. But in the case of school stations, the ultimate concern is probably educational. If a board of education is forced to re-evaluate its station's activities, it's most likely to do so in terms of the station's effectiveness in *classroom instruction*. Board members can logically complain that school tax dollars should not be used to provide general public television services to the entire community.

Still, many people believe that a board of education should be concerned with the education of all citizens, not just the youngsters. Since everyone pays taxes for the schools, whether he has children attending or not, then shouldn't everyone be able to get some benefits? The answer in many American communities is a hearty yes, and the school-owned television stations are the proof. Television provides the perfect way of reaching a broad new audience among working adults, dropouts, and those who wouldn't ordinarily make use of classroom opportunities.

Civil Service: The Hidden Boss

The majority of public television stations in the country are owned and operated by public institutions — by state authorities, local school boards and state universities. Nationally, we've experimented with a new kind of quasi-public operation; but at most of the local levels, we've gone plainly public. This means that certain freedoms at the station level have been relinquished over the years.

Excuse me, but . . .

. . . That artist you hired away from the commercial station just called to say he's changed his mind.

. . . The incompetent you fired last week after three months of warnings now has a lawyer. She's suing the Board of Education

for "sex discrimination." It'll hit the evening papers.

. . . Somebody called the station to make an anonymous threat about blowing the place up if another program about Nazis is aired. One of the secretaries is nervous about it and wants to see you.

For instance, managers must often conform to hiring practices not of their own making. If a public broadcasting station is told whom it may hire and whom it may not, can programming censorship be far behind? Another serious restriction is that some stations have only limited control over the income realized through contracts, membership subscriptions and grants. They have managed to live with this partial paralysis, but can their situation be tenable in the long run? Here and there around the country, a local licensee is even prohibited by "enabling legislation" from certain kinds of programming. The purpose of such legislation is to protect existing educational territorial rights, but isn't such action a serious warping of federal regulation? If so, what will the FCC do about it?

Is public control healthy? The question is only rhetorical, because that's the way it is. Today, just about two-thirds of the non-commercial stations on the air are supported *totally* with tax dollars. Public bureaucracies are controlling them, no matter how indirect that control may appear. We can ignore it or pretend it isn't so, but the fact is that most public broadcasting stations in America are actually "government-owned."

Excuse me, but . . .

. . . Social Action, Inc. has announced to the press that it is going to study the public television station in town in connection with discriminatory practices in hiring.

. . . One of the board members has written

to ask if a position might be available for his daughter. "She's not sure what she wants to do with her life," he writes, "and I felt confident that you could help."

. . . The telephone company urges us to reconsider setting up our own statewide microwave system since they can provide the TV interconnection. The phone company has three resident lobbyists at the state capital.

This means that state-owned station managers must lobby for funds at the state capital; school station executives must convince boards of education; and university managers must grease the academic gears. Bureaucracies exist to control expenditures of tax dollars and to assume efficient administration. If a public television station is to be owned by a municipality, a school system, a state or a university, then, certainly, the station must be expected to conform to the established manner of doing public things.

A lot of public broadcasters are comfortable with this arrangement. They feel that privately run community stations have to worry far too much about money. They also believe that dependence on shifting financial sources can endanger effective planning and good programming. With public tax dollars, they suggest, a budget procedure is already established and a steady commitment is virtually guaranteed.

Excuse me, but . . .

. . . One of the directors just broke his wrist.

. . . The mobile van is 30 miles away with a radiator leak. How do we cover the school board meeting tonight?

Frederick Breitenfeld, Jr.

> *. . . The Corporation for Public Broad-
> casting has rejected the opera proposal,
> but it wants to see a rewrite next month.*

Community station operators don't often see it that way. They feel, generally, that freedom of decision and administration is more important than financial security. Some of them go so far as to suggest that *public* ownership of noncommercial broadcasting stations is wrong and not in the best interests of the citizens: "You can't run a public television station the way you run a state office building."

Who is right? Everyone. This peculiar tree *does* grow both apples and oranges. After all, the FCC hasn't said which kind of license is best. Noncommercial broadcasting was established with a very general mission and with no way to support itself. The institutions have grown as a result of local political, economic and social factors. There is no "pure" public broadcasting; there is only public broadcasting that *works*. If a licensee can define an appropriate mission for itself — one that its community or public parent can support — and if it can attract dollars, then it will thrive.

Moreover, as this fascinating medium has evolved, the lines between "public" and "private" have become blurred, just as they are growing fuzzy in other parts of our culture. A state-owned public broadcasting facility on one side of the country vigorously conducts fund-raising campaigns and looks to corporations for underwriting. At the other border, a community station negotiates for an unrestricted grant from the county council or the state legislature.

Yes, even the wholly private *community* stations are now enjoying tax support, and such support is increasing every year. Some of this public income is from school contracts, unrestricted public grants, and the usual federal arrangements. Also it's not uncommon for a private station to be subsidized through its housing at a school or public college. Some state public broadcasting networks, including those in Ohio, Pennsylvania and New York, are made up of independent community licensees with state-wide interconnections supported by legislative appropriations.

How can a public broadcasting station operate as one tentacle of a public octopus and also be free and courageous? Can politics

51

be removed from programming judgments when the very same politics dictate part or all of the budget? There is no question that political ramifications must be kept largely separate from public television operations. This is the great challenge facing PTV today, locally and nationally. Public dollars must help support public broadcasting, but it must operate in freedom.

Station Decisions: When the Chips are Down

Most stations, and their boards of directors, make decisions on the basis of current, pressing factors: available dollars, the strength of the staff, available facilities, consonance with the objectives of the parent institution, the underwriting potential, the popularity of some programs over others, and, of course, the FCC requirements. More philosophic considerations are also important, but they undoubtedly have yet to play the prime role in station management. As with other organisms and industries, survival comes first. The aim in most cases is simply to stay on the air and meet the payroll, and some stations still aren't able to do much else.

Fortunately, there is no universal standard regarding the services a PTV station is supposed to offer. The relevant phrases from the FCC regulations are "meet educational needs" and operate "in the public interest, convenience or necessity." The licensees can interpret them in accordance with their own realities, political and economic.

Excuse me, but . . .

. . . If you want to buy a short length of coaxial cable, please fill out a requisition sheet, university budget form 16-j. (Use the orange form if the money is to come from operating funds, and blue if the money is to come from capital funds.) Never indent on any line more than five spaces or the form will be returned. Submit in triplicate to the Office of Budget Approval, Administration Building, Room

1619, attention Mrs. Bagley. After Mrs. Bagley initials the form signifying that you have the $38 in your budget, the form is sent to the Technical Buyer, located in Room 1823. There Mr. Ted Rosler puts out a request for bids. If there is only one coaxial cable distributor in the region, it presents difficulties, but they can be surmounted with a special Sole Source form, which should be approved by the Comptroller's Council of Purchases and Services. The Council meets bimonthly. To get on their agenda, you must submit, in duplicate . . .

Should a station concentrate on what are called "instructional services"? Should it consider itself primarily a medium for "public affairs"? Is a station an agent of education? Is it a social activist? Should it consider "experimental drama" of higher priority than Shakespeare? The answers depend on the cities in which the questions are asked. Thanks to the wisdom of the FCC guidelines, these judgments are left to each individual local licensee. In all likelihood, there is rarely a single national opinion.

Nationally, most of the arguing, voting and petitioning have been on matters that relate to method rather than to content. The placement of power has been the obsession of public broadcasters for years, and only recently have practitioners begun to talk about what public broadcasting might do for America. Particularly since 1973 and the reorganization of PBS, new procedures and new organizational patterns have been given the highest priorities on the national scene.

Meanwhile, the licensees continue to band together in regional and local arrangements, sharing videotapes and establishing program-purchase plans. As always, the stations and their state and regional associations remain, for the most part, quietly effective. As always, it seems, the national machine is still noisily settling in. Certainly, public broadcasting must continue to refine its structure and procedures, but it is also clearly time to start pulling the whole thing together.

The Future of Public Broadcasting

Part of the problem is that the system hasn't been able to get a national feel for services that need rendering. We hold conferences on the lofty subject of "public television potential," and the proceedings are always filled with poetic phrases about the impressive possibilities:

It can be an agent of change.

It can hold a stethoscope to the American heart.

It can provide a showcase for new talent.

It can be a catalyst for social reform.

It can search for excellence.

It can be a mirror for our civilization.

It can serve as society's conscience.

It can be all of the above.

Most local program directors would probably respond to all of that by asking, "OK, wise guy, what do you suggest for Monday evenings at 7:00 p.m., starting the week after next, at no more than $12.95 a show?"

As in American education, we're loaded with philosophers but we're a little short on ideas and money. We need less semantic purr and more action in public television programming. We've got to start matching services to needs.

Excuse me, but . . .

. . . The local association of mathematics teachers has asked to review every math program at least a week before it is aired. A meeting has been set.

. . . The PBS membership meeting in Chicago has been scheduled for the seventh of next month. That's the quarterly meeting of your own PTV board.

An Agenda for the Future

What now? Can we keep the promises made 20 years ago? Can public broadcasting continue to make important contributions

— locally and nationally — without the tugs-of-war and eternal poverty that have been our history? Individual stations have to grow. They need interested, active, influential board members — and that means the university trustees, boards of education and gubernatorial appointees who accept those public broadcasting responsibilities. The stations also need the financial backing that only powerful, enthusiastic and energetic board members can get. And they need the talent that only reliable financial backing can buy.

During the next decade, we might have to look at those hidden political and bureaucratic shackles — the restrictions on income, hiring procedures, travel, purchasing and programming — that tend to keep some stations weak. Somehow, we'll have to develop both national and local systems that allow for heavy public funding along with healthier doses of independence. The precedent has been set with state colleges and universities. The only hurdles are political and emotional.

One way to do it might be to move toward more representative boards of directors, thereby creating "quasi-public" institutions. Some local PTV trustees might be appointed by the board itself or by the governor, mayor or legislative body; but a specific number should be *elected*, either by the supporting "members" of the station or by the public at large. This could provide the variety of political influences that should be guiding and supporting each station. Also, of course, it would help in anticipating the day when some of the stations expand to become "telecommunications centers," serving entirely new functions.

Nationally, we'll have to face a real but embarrassing question — and soon. Do we really want two separate organizations, each with a large staff, both in Washington, and both presumably "leading" the industry? Is there a reason, other than history itself, for these two organizations to function at the same time? It may mean another national spasm on the order of 1973, this time involving the Congress; but we'll have to decide soon whether the stations — and the nation — are best served by both a PBS and a CPB.

Furthermore, regardless of where the national power finally rests, the leaders of the chosen agency must be conscious of its purpose: to serve Americans through the public broadcasting *stations*. That means paying careful attention to the licensees, one by one. It means that the board of directors of the national PTV agency will want to hold its meetings at the *stations*. It means that the newsletter of the national PTV agency will highlight not itself but the *stations*. It means recognizing the system for what it really is — a collection of individual institutions.

At long last, we're determined to settle our power-and-procedure problems. It's none too soon, because the social and educational revolution is raging. We have an opportunity — and a responsibility — to play an important role in restoring national optimism.

Excuse me, but . . .

. . . It's five o'clock, and it's been a fascinating day. It was filled with small reassurances that you are part of something good.

Public Radio:
The Next Ten Years

THOMAS WARNOCK*

Virtually all homes in the United States (98.6 percent) are radio-equipped.[†] In fact, the average home has 5.5 working receivers. There are over 350 million radios in use in the United States today, and 55 million new receivers are sold each year. Virtually all U. S. automobiles (95 percent) are also radio-equipped. The average American adult listens to radio more than 3 hours and 45 minutes each day, and nearly everyone (96 percent) listens at least once each week. In a recent suvey by Roper Reports, a national sample of men and women were presented with a list of 26 possible activities and asked which of the 26 they had personally engaged in during the previous 24 hours. Radio ranked in the second and fourth spots on the list. Reading a newspaper ranked first, and watching an entertainment program on television ranked sixth. Roughly three out of four people said they had turned to radio for news in the last 24 hours.

Radio obviously plays a vital role in nearly everyone's life in

Mr. Warnock is director of Radio Activities at the Corporation for Public Broadcasting.

*The author wishes to state that the views expressed in this article do not necessarily reflect those of the CPB.

[†]These figures come from surveys conducted by Statistical Research, Inc., and the National Association of Broadcasters.

this country today. I wish I could also say that public radio shares a significant part of this role. Unfortunately, the public radio system barely enters into the picture. Although public radio (and educational radio before it) has been with us for over 50 years, until recent years its growth rate has been almost imperceptible. There are two obvious reasons: Of the more then 70,000 radio stations in the United States today, fewer than 200 (less than 3 percent) are public radio stations. Furthermore, public radio is almost entirely FM, while only 39 percent of our 350 million radio sets can receive FM.

Based on these statistics, one might readily conclude that no one wants or needs public radio. I believe, however, that such a conclusion is not justified by a more careful examination of the evidence. There have been, and continue to be, some isolated but encouraging examples of public radio's great potential for service.

The Hidden Medium

The 1967 Carnegie Commission report on public broadcasting provided a kind of blueprint for the Corporation's initial activities in public television, but it neglected to make a comparable report for radio. In fact, the 1967 legislation which created the CPB was originally introduced as the Public *Television* Act of 1967. Public radio was included only in response to testimony offered by National Educational Radio (NER), the now-defunct radio division of the National Association of Educational Broadcasters, during the congressional hearings on the act. As support for its testimony, NER published *The Hidden Medium: Educational Radio*, which listed the past accomplishments of noncommercial radio and hinted at its potential.

Although *The Hidden Medium* succeeded in persuading Congress to include radio in the 1967 legislation, the study lacked recommendations for the appropriate use of federal funds to nourish public radio. One of CPB's first challenges, therefore, was to determine how to go about fulfilling its charge with respect to radio. Thus, in 1969, CPB commissioned a study of public radio designed to identify the major strengths and weaknesses of the existing stations and to suggest the most effective means of encouraging their growth through the newly available federal dollars.

The results of the study not only confirmed public radio's generally slow rate of progress during its first 50 years, but also identified for the first time a major cause for the stagnation. The report revealed that one of public radio's greatest advantages, the economy of radio program production, was also its greatest weakness. Public radio was such a bargain that no one took it seriously!

The 1969 Public Radio Study concluded that with the exception of a handful of stations, public radio had virtually no staff, no facilities, and no funds for programming. Most stations operated on less than $10,000 per year, and most licensees were educational institutions which used the frequencies assigned to them by the FCC to train students as commercial broadcasters or to provide an extracurricular campus activity financed and operated in a manner comparable to the student newspaper. Nearly half of the stations had a transmitter power of 10 watts (a power which could barely reach beyond the borders of the campus). With these deficiencies, it's no wonder that these stations were virtually unheard. Most people didn't even know they existed.

The implications of the 1969 study were quite clear: While CPB's initial activities in the area of public television could build upon an existing base, the base for public radio had yet to be established. Of the more than 450 noncommercial educational stations licensed by the FCC in 1969, only about 25 had a permanent professional staff of more than one or two people. Even fewer stations were operating on a consistent 18 hour-per-day schedule, which is the norm for most commercial services.

A Five-Year Plan for System-Building

Facing an enormous system-building task with extremely limited financial resources, the CPB Board adopted in 1970 the "Policy for Public Radio Station Assistance," which established criteria for the support of individual radio stations and outlined a five-year plan for development of the system as a whole. The plan used a "carrot and stick approach" in which the stations were provided with specific measures enabling them to compute the level of CPB funds they could receive by improving their services and increasing local financial support. The strategy of the CPB was to concentrate the available funds in areas demonstrating the greatest growth potential.

Thus, the first radio-support grants were limited to the 80

stations able to meet the initial minimum criteria of one full-time staff member and a broadcast schedule of 8 hours per day, 6 days per week, 48 weeks per year. Other criteria pertained to minimum transmission power, equipment, etc. Stations which met all of the requirements of the policy, and were therefore eligible for support grants, became known as CPB-qualified stations. Six years later, there are 168 stations meeting the *current* minimum standards: five full-time staff members and a broadcast schedule of 18 hours per day, 365 days per year. These more stringent criteria for staff and operating schedules of "qualified stations" were the heart of CPB's five-year plan and are largely responsible for public radio's recent vitality.

While building the local station base was public radio's greatest need, the 1969 Public Radio Study revealed that the need for a live *national* program service was a close second. Here, again, the differences between public radio and public television are significant: Public television began funding the production and distribution of specifically national programs nearly a decade before CPB was established. Public radio had no comparable activity. Thus, the second major effort of the CPB (in concert with station representatives) was the creation of National Public Radio, a licensee-controlled program production and distribution service. NPR's initial programming has concentrated on those services which stations are generally unable to provide for themselves, such as a daily news and information magazine, "All Things Considered . . .," and live coverage of national events and concert performances.

The other significant development since 1969 has been the formation of APRS, the Association of Public Radio Stations. Incorporated in 1973, APRS is an entirely member-supported organization, representing CPB-qualified radio licensees. APRS currently receives no funds from CPB and struggles along with only two full-time staff members. However, the fact that APRS has a rather narrow and well-defined mission has enabled it to function remarkably effectively.

Now that the original five-year plan has run its course, CPB has begun to reexamine public radio's further development. This time, the CPB analysis has the advantage of a much larger and more precise data base as well as the specific standards and goals by which station performance can be measured in relation to CPB investment. My own evaluation of the evidence leads me to the conclusion that the original objectives of the five-year plan have been reasonably satisfied, although the goal of 90 percent coverage of the nation by 1976 has been drastically revised because less funds have been available than were originally projected. The CPB investment has also been considerably less than was originally anticipated in those areas where stations were already operating. Even so, the fundamental objective (establishment of base level services) has been achieved by an overwhelming majority of those stations which entered the radio Community Service Grant program.

In examining the record of the past five years, I have also come upon three findings which have greatly influenced my recommendations regarding the appropriate role of CPB in public radio's future: The first is that *public radio, given adequate facilities and adequate initial support, can provide a genuine service.* It can develop a substantial and dedicated audience and, as a result, a solid base of continuing financial support. The Minnesota Public Radio (MPR) experiment is the best proof of this premise. In the largest of three demonstration projects, CPB is providing from $100,000 to $200,000 annually for six years to Minnesota Public Radio to provide comprehensive public radio services while the system gradually substitutes local support for its CPB funding (85 percent of the audience and 85 percent of the private support is in the Twin-City area). No parent institution or public television station is associated with Minnesota Public Radio, and although MPR is a state-wide service, there has been no state funding.

CPB has been watching the MPR experiment carefully, and thus far, the results have exceeded all original expectations. Listeners doubled in the first year of the CPB-supported services and nearly doubled again in the second. Local financial support of all kinds increased dramatically, and support from individual listeners has grown and continues to grow at a significant rate. CPB's total investment, when the six-year MPR project is complete, will be well under $1 million, but Minnesota Public Radio's increased support from local sources will exceed that amount on an *annual* basis. In contrast, most CPB-qualified stations today, including many in cities larger than Minneapolis/St. Paul, operate on an income well below the $175,000 which was Minnesota Radio's budget in 1971, the year before the experiment began.

The program fare that MPR offers is not unique. In fact, there is very little that MPR offers its audiences which isn't offered by other public radio stations in many areas of the country. The fundamental differences which account for MPR's increased audiences

61

and increased listener support are a consistent level of program quality and a predictable type of program service. In contrast, the quality of service on many public radio stations varies widely from program to program or hour to hour. Furthermore, the "alternative service" idea in public broadcasting — the desire to satisfy the specific needs of an extremely broad range of listeners — often results in a complex and confusing program schedule which frustrates potential listeners. Even those looking for "alternative" programming seldom can find the service without procuring and then carefully consulting the station program guide. In short, once MPR began to reinforce listener expectations by providing predictable and quality programming on a consistent basis, it began to tap a much larger share of its potential audience.

Our second discovery is that, for maximum effectiveness, *public radio requires multiple channels in major population centers*. WOSU-AM and FM, in Columbus, Ohio, were another demonstration project with six-year CPB funding. Before the project began, 90 percent of the WOSU schedule was identical on both AM and FM. In 1971, the combination of new facilities and CPB's operational support made separate programming possible at WOSU and gave the industry a rare opportunity to measure the impact of two public channels with distinct programming offerings. WOSU-AM concentrated on public affairs and informational programming, while the FM channel began to specialize in music and other cultural offerings.

According to the American Research Bureau, which studied the WOSU audiences before and after the change, the audience for the FM station grew within 18 months to be nearly as large as the combined audience had been when the two stations were offering the same programming. Even more impressive was the rise of the audience figures for the AM channel to more than twice the new FM figure! This three-fold increase in audience occurred because each station was offering discrete (and, of course, better) program services. The cost of the separate programming for WOSU is nearly double the single-service cost, but because the audience tripled, the cost per listener has dropped dramatically.

There is also ample evidence that multiple local radio services can support themselves adequately. For example, the results of on-air membership drives by the three public radio stations in Washington, D. C., during the same 30-day period were as follows: WETA-FM, with a goal of $75,000, raised $96,000 in a continuous, four-day, over-the-air marathon. WAMU-FM exceeded its $50,000 goal during scattered pledge periods over seven consecutive days, and WGTS-FM in Tacoma Park (a suburb of Washington) raised over $20,000 during its six-day pledge week. The local public television station WETA was also soliciting funds over-the-air during this period and managed to collect $75,000 in 10 nights of prime-time pledges.* The point is that the existence of three public radio services (plus a television station) has not jeopardized the support base for any of the three. In fact, WETA-FM leads not only WETA Television in support for the period but also all public radio stations in markets of comparable size, most of which have only one station.

The third discovery of the public radio study is that *local public radio service in small communities is both essential and viable*. The case in point is Buffalo, Missouri, a rural community with but one radio station, the public licensee KBFL. With only 7,000 people in KBFL's primary signal area, it's doubtful a commercial station could survive in Buffalo. Certainly, none has tried. Local commercial or public television stations are financially out of the question, of course.

Thus, KBFL is an essential service, and as proof of this, nearly 70 percent of the people in KBFL's coverage area listen each week. Equally important, over 20 percent of the listeners pledged $21,500 to the station last August during its first, week-long, money-raising marathon. An interesting sidelight to this story is that only three weeks later, KBFL went back to its listeners and raised another $35,000 for the purchase of an X-ray unit to attract a new physician to the community. Only local service could produce such results and only public radio can afford local service in rural areas like Buffalo.

The Future of Public Radio

At the present time, public radio's coverage of the United States looks like this: About 64 percent of the population is within range of a CPB-qualified public radio station signal. That's almost double the coverage five years ago. However, this growth rate can be

---

*It is also interesting to note that the CPB is not supplying special funding to any of the three radio stations and that the radio stations are owned by three separate licensees. As a result, there is less coordination of programming than would be possible under single ownership.

misleading. As the base for the public radio system has been developing, so too has the data base; and one of the most alarming things CPB discovered is that relatively few of the new qualified stations have been established in major population centers. In fact, over one-third of the 100 largest cities in the nation still have no public radio station meeting the current minimum CPB eligibility requirements.*

One major factor here has been the FCC. Like almost everyone else, the FCC has greatly underestimated the cost and support potential of public radio. The commission has been known to grant public radio licenses to applicants proposing to spend only $500 for broadcast equipment and $100 per year to support station operations! Even more unfortunate is the fact that the FCC has never bothered to develop a table of channel assignments for the reserved frequencies in the FM band. As a result, there has been a proliferation of 10-watt stations, especially in larger population centers; and frequently these small stations have, in turn, blocked the growth of significant high-power services.

In 1975, CPB began to address this problem by earmarking $1 million (including a special $400,000 board appropriation from the CPB reserve) under the Coverage Expansion Grant Project. This money is designed to assist the establishment of qualified stations in the major unserved areas. These grants will be followed by significant operational matching grants over the first three years of station operation. Expansion Grant stations will phase into the

---

*In addition to the minimum criteria for staff and on-air schedules, a station must meet the following standards to qualify as capable of performing a sufficient public service to warrant CPB support:

1. Have adequate facilities to transmit an acceptable signal to an appreciable segment of the public.
2. Have access to sufficient funds to cover ordinary operating and program expenses.
3. Have a staff of sufficient size and professional ability to provide a competent service.
4. Maintain an operating schedule of sufficient length and regularity to constitute a reliable and significant service.
5. Assure in its program schedule a substantial amount of programming of consistently good quality, devoted to the educational, informational, and cultural needs of its audience.
6. Be substantially engaged in broadcasting to the public rather than to religious, in-school, or other special classes of listeners, or in serving as a facility for training students in broadcasting or other limited purpose.

regular Community Service Grant program in their fourth year.

Justification for CPB's continued support of the Coverage Expansion Grant Project is dramatized by this example: Buffalo, New York, which is considerably larger (in fact, the 23rd largest U. S. city) than Buffalo, Missouri, has such difficult frequency problems that it has been impossible for public radio to establish a station meeting even the minimum transmission standards of the CPB policy. The only possible solution was the outright purchase of an existing commercial station for noncommercial use, and, finally, WNED, the public television station in Buffalo, was forced to do just that. The purchase price of $2 million (for two stations) points up the enormous cost of adequate facilities once reserved frequencies in major markets disappear. If reserved public radio frequencies had been available in Buffalo, the cost of establishing two noncommercial stations (a full-time 5,000-watt AM and a 125,000-watt FM) would have been well under $400,000, with 75 percent of that amount available through HEW's Educational Broadcasting Facilities Program.

Perhaps even more important than new stations in unserved areas is the development of adequate services in the 30 largest urbanized areas of the country (containing nearly 40 percent of the U. S. population). Of highest priority are the first 10 of these 30, which represent over 25 percent of the population. Three of the 30 and one of the 10 largest cities have no public radio station meeting even the minimum requirements for CPB assistance. Five of the top 10 and 12 of the 30 have stations at or near the minimum standard. These minimum criteria are just that, *absolute minimums*. They are the same in Missoula, Montana, and Bethel, Alaska, as they are in New York or Chicago. Obviously, five staff members and a $75,000 annual operating budget won't go very far in Chicago or New York City.

Four stations in the top 10 cities, and 10 of the 30, require significant improvement (but not the kind of major financial support required to bring the stations at the minimum level up to reasonable service). Stations in this category are those operating on a budget under $250,000 per year, which when adjusted for inflation, is about the starting point for the Minnesota service.

Finally, five of the 30 — *none* of them in the 10 largest cities — have strong public radio stations. Although the strong stations in Minneapolis, Columbus, and Madison, Wisconsin, are certainly needed where they are, services of equal or greater strength are essential in the 10 largest population centers, where they can reach over one-fourth of the nation's population. Without well-developed services in these areas, public radio can never hope to achieve its full potential.

Furthermore, I believe the experience to date in Columbus, Ohio, and Washington, D. C., strongly supports the notion that multiple channels are essential for adequate service in the major population centers. In urbanized areas, audiences have learned to expect generic radio services that can be tuned in and tuned out at the convenience of the listener. Given the wide range of needs and interests that public radio wishes (and often has the obligation) to serve, a single public channel is simply ineffective. I am not suggesting that public radio embrace commercial format program patterns, but I find it equally unrealistic to think that most potential public radio listeners will somehow seek out a half-hour weekly program suited to their individual tastes. The most dedicated listeners will find their special programming, of course, but the vast majority of potential listeners in urbanized areas (people with an interest in the subject) will remain unserved by public radio until specialized channels and stations begin to offer predictable programming suited to their needs.*

The number of specialized channels and stations is in fact increasing, but one deterrent to their progress is a lack of adequate national programming. Original National Public Radio (NPR) programming currently averages about 36 hours per week. Considering the fact that the typical public station broadcasts over 120 hours per week, it's easy to see why public radio is in no danger of becoming a uniform national service. This capacity of the radio medium for local programming is a great strength. On the other hand, stations must have a greater selection of national programs

---

*A possible alternative to multiple channels and stations is sufficient promotion for individual programs. However, since promotion is extremely expensive (the costs are the same for radio as for television), the cost of adequate coverage of individual weekly programs could easily exceed the cost of operating multiple channels. Moreover, the direct service benefits of promotion are likely to be far inferior to the end results of multiple channel programming. Radio has nothing comparable to the TV Guide, and newspaper listings for radio are a "thing of the past" in most areas. Add the fact that most listeners have at least 35 stations to choose from, and the job of matching listeners with programming suited to their needs quickly becomes a complex, expensive, and often futile task. Both local and national public radio need resources to increase listener awareness and to help achieve public radio's service potential; but the trend toward generic program services in multiple station areas is the best way to increase the effectiveness of limited promotion expenditures.

if they are to specialize and build a strong audience/subscriber base.

For example, of the 36 weekly hours currently produced and/or distributed by NPR, much less than half would be useful to a fine arts station. A minority station (and there are a number of these) would find almost nothing suited to its unique program needs. New, national, specialized-audience programs — including major services for the blind, for educators, for the elderly and the poor, for women and minorities — are now in the planning stages at NPR, but none is yet in production.

More general audience programming is also needed from NPR. We know that the early morning, 6 to 9 a.m., is the most active time for radio listening, yet NPR still lacks the resources to mount a significant program service suitable for that time of day. NPR has developed and annually updates a five-year plan based on a comprehensive survey of the future growth and development projected at each of its member stations. The plan documents the need to triple NPR program services over the next five years in order to keep pace with local station requirements.*

NPR'S most immediate need is a satellite interconnection system. The present line interconnection for radio lacks fidelity and stereo, a handicap which is comparable to a television interconnection system capable of distributing only the middle third of a black and white picture. You would recognize Big Bird and Alistair Cooke, but you'd seldom get to see their feet or the top of their heads! Music is an integral part of most public radio services, and stereo-equipped satellite interconnection would allow NPR to make quantum leaps with respect to the quality and range of its cultural services.

Priorities and Challenges— The Next 10 Years

No public radio services exist in 36 major cities and four states. Normally, I wouldn't characterize the activation of stations in these areas as public radio's greatest need, but the fact that a loss of frequencies is currently uncontrollable (and appears likely to remain

---

*Nearly 30 percent of NPR's 1981 revenues are projected from outside sources, whereas virtually the entire current NPR operating budget comes from CPB.

uncontrollable) makes station activation in many of these areas a "now or never" proposition commanding our greatest attention. Two additional considerations tend to support this priority. First, Congress included nation-wide coverage in the list of goals and objectives it set for CPB as part of the 1967 Public Broadcasting Act. Second, private funding sources frequently express concern about public radio's national coverage deficiencies, particularly in relation to the cost effectiveness of national underwriting support.

If frequency availability was not a factor, my second priority would head the list. That priority is the upgrading of public radio services in the 30 largest population centers, and especially in the top 10 urban areas, by strengthening existing stations, by encouraging multiple specialized stations, and by increasing audience awareness of the existence of public radio services and thereby encouraging the development of local support, financial and otherwise. In the past decade, public television proved the importance of strong services in major population centers. My belief is that public radio will find these centers equally essential to its own system development.

The encouragement of multiple channels and services is especially desirable for the major population centers and an absolute necessity for the 10 largest cities, where public radio must compete with literally hundreds of other signals for the listener's attention. Public radio cannot hope to survive in these complex urban environments without specialization; for specialized audiences, while relatively small segments of the total population, are nonetheless significant in absolute numbers. For example, the black audience in Los Angeles exceeds the total population in the coverage of many stations. A service suited to their specific needs could be equated to "first-station" service in smaller communities.

A third major priority for public radio is to strengthen the national program service by establishing a "state of the art" satellite interconnection system; by developing basic specialized-audience programs for such groups as the blind, women, and minorities; by expanding and improving existing general-audience programming to meet the needs of a larger, more diverse system of public radio stations; and by increasing audience awareness of public radio at the national level.

I've set these goals in a 10-year time frame because that is generally the point of reference used throughout this volume. However, several of the priorities, and especially the first, must be achieved in a substantially shorter period of time in order to avoid the extreme financial and technical obstacles which are increasing at an alarming rate. I've also set the 10-year limit because there is still so much more to be accomplished. In round numbers, CPB is projecting the addition of 250 new stations by 1986. But what about 1987 and beyond?

How large is a "full system" of public radio stations? In 1966, the FCC announced its intention to develop a table of allocations for the noncommercial FM band. At that time, the FCC position was that, in general, there should be five Class A, B, or C noncommercial radio stations in each area with a population above 1 million; four stations in areas above 250,000; three stations in areas above 100,000; two stations in areas above 50,000; and single-station coverage in markets below 50,000. If we simplify the calculation by disregarding the "under 50,000" stations, a fully developed system would consist of over 800 stations. CPB's 10-year projection, then, would bring the total to 420 stations by 1986.

In contrast, a similar FCC document issued in 1963 for public television projected a full system of roughly 300 television stations, and there are now over 250 stations in operation. While the next 10 years may well see public television emerge as a mature communication system, public radio will do well if it can rid itself of its amateur, vocational-training-ground image. This problem is not unlike public television's all too frequent association with "chalk talks" in the 1960s. Quality is the key. Program content for public radio can and should vary greatly, according to local needs; but the quality of the presentations must attain new and higher levels. The best of what is available today should be the standard set for tomorrow at both the local and national level.

This is not an unrealistic goal, yet it will not be inexpensive. On the other hand, I believe it will eventually prove to be far more cost effective. If public radio is taken seriously by the FCC and by the public, I am confident it will prove to be the bargain everyone always assumed it was. That is to say, public radio, given significant funding, will render a significant service in return. The key word, of course, is "significant," because in spite of public radio's comparative economy, the value of the service remains directly proportional to the investment. This concept is not new. The only thing we have learned in recent years is how to define "significant" in public radio terms.

Instructional Television
Is Alive and Well

SAUL ROCKMAN

In a series of research notes in CPB's weekly newsletter, Natan Katzman and Karen Farr remarked on the dichotomous nature of the audience for public television's programming.[1] First, there are the households which turn to public television solely for its renowned offerings for young children. A second audience, about equal in size according to Katzman and Farr, consists of mature adults who elect to watch the various public affairs and cultural programs during evening hours. These two audiences rarely overlap, and they each have their own unique characteristics.

A third category of audience was neglected in Katzman and Farr's analysis. Indeed, this large group — the audience that watches programs in formal educational settings — is never considered by the analysts when they tabulate the number of public television's viewers and its program ratings. Despite its scope and importance, instructional television, as this category of programming is commonly entitled, has often been the closeted step-sister of public or educational broadcasting. Among the countless commissions and studies examining educational television during the past decade,[2] many, like the Carnegie Commission research, have studiously avoided consideration of the instructional uses of television. Others, such as

Mr. Rockman is director of research at the Agency for Instructional Television.

The Future of Public Broadcasting

Perkins,[3] have deserted the in-school aspects of broadcast instruction for the academically fashionable fields of post-secondary education, open-university concepts, and the like. Still others have taken a look, not at instructional television, but at the new instructional *technology* of which television is but a part.

The recent ACNO study, *Public Broadcasting and Education*, tried to cover all educational aspects of public television, from cradle to grave; but in doing so, it failed to examine any of the areas in much depth or with much sophistication.[4] The few other studies which have considered the role of public broadcasting in instruction (usually in elementary and secondary education) have almost always taken the perspective of broadcast television and what it could offer to education. Rarely has a study looked at instructional television from the viewpoint of education and its needs.* Perhaps this is one reason for the often heard lament that instructional television is *in* American education, not *of* it; that it does *for* education, not *with* it.

I maintain that instructional television is alive and doing quite well, thank you. The ACNO report's perception of a major chasm between education and television is erroneous. In fact, instructional television has a variety of established functions in *both* education and broadcasting, and more often than not these functions coincide.

Public television stations broadcast programs for the entire spectrum of formal educational activities. In this article, only one educational level — elementary/secondary, or what is frequently called "school television" — will be extensively considered. Three other instructional television categories, pre-school, post-secondary, and adult continuing education, I have left for other writers at other times. That does not mean, however, that lessons to be drawn from this presentation may not be useful for those concerned with the

---

*Until recently, this latter task, if conducted diligently, might have proven disastrous for school television. When pressed about the value of instructional television in the school system, educators would probably have dismissed it completely and placed their limited resources elsewhere. Norman Kurland summarized this position for McMurrin's Commission on Instructional Technology:

> Instructional technology is today largely supplementary to the two primary media of instruction: the textbook and the teacher. Eliminate either of these and the educational system would be transformed. Eliminate all of the technology, and education would go on with hardly a missed lesson.

education of both adults and pre-school children.*

School Television

The size of this nation's educational system is impressive.[5] More than 50 million students are attending elementary and secondary schools, and there are some 2.3 million teachers employed to teach them. During fiscal 1974, more than $62 billion was spent for their education. Expenditures per pupil in 1975 were roughly $1,200, with about $15 of this sum allocated for instructional materials — textbooks, films, computers, and, yes, school television. Although the figures are almost impossible to isolate, a reasonable estimate of education's expenditures for television would be in the range of $50 to $75 million a year for software and operations — only about one-tenth of one percent of the total cost of elementary and secondary education.

The school audience. Within the next few years, long-awaited federal data should provide precise information on the size and scope of the present school-television audience. Until then, we must rely on the best available estimates, which come from the Agency for Instructional Television (AIT). AIT believes that at this time, school television is used regularly (at least once every week) by approximately 15 million different students. This means that between 25 and 30 percent of the elementary/secondary students view television,

---

*In the realm of early childhood education, public television has proven itself particularly effective. Still, as with everything good, people cry for "more and better," and I must join in this cry with the following challenges for the future:

 · One of the first considerations should be that existing pre-school television programs, constructed for 30- and 60-minute broadcast schedules, are often too long to fit comfortably into the limited time allotted to half-day, pre-school settings. Programs of shorter lengths, but which are segmented or modularized, could stimulate additional pre-school and kindergarten utilization.
 · Television producers and stations can work with government agencies and pre-school groups for preparation and promotion of family-structured, at-home television viewing and of community viewing centers.
 · Finally, PBS must eventually deal with the inelastic boundaries of the single-channel broadcast schedule. The children's block can be expanded only to a limited degree before it bumps and strains the rest of the program schedule.

in school, as part of their regular instructional activities.*

The frequency of television use in the classroom depends on the specific television series, of course, as well as on the particular classroom teacher. For example, in a 1972 study of the in-school utilization of "The Electric Company," teachers in grades one through six reported that they generally used between three and four programs per week, with a total audience of 3.7 million students.[7] Contrast these figures with those for the same series in home-viewing environments in 1974: During a four-week survey period, 9.6 million households viewed an average of 4.8 programs, or 1.2 per week.[8] Thus, the home setting provided a much larger audience. However, the in-school viewers use "The Electric Company" on a more regular basis than the at-home audience, and it is this more regular use that produces the greatest instructional impact on the viewer.

The figures on the frequency of in-school uses of "The Electric Company" were generally confirmed by this writer in surveys regarding the showings of several popular AIT school-television series.[9] Teachers who used television in their classrooms reported having their class view an average of between two and three different television programs per week. We can surely conclude that the in-school audience for instructional television is of sufficient magnitude and regularity to suggest that these instructional materials serve a useful function in elementary/secondary education. The available evidence also suggests a large and growing group of teachers who have regularly incorporated school television into their normal classroom activities. Especially if both instructional film and instructional television are accessible, teachers will tend to use increasing amounts of both. However, the concensus of more and more teachers seems to be that the ease and regularity of television presentations make television the desired medium.

The educational function of television. Both by law and by tradition, education at the elementary/secondary level is an activity of state and local governments and the agencies they set up to

---

*These estimates have been used informally by AIT and cited by Cohen (see note 4). They receive partial corroboration from Liebert's study of the in-school audience of "The Electric Company" (see note 6) and from an analysis of NCES data on the availability of television receivers in the schools (see Mielke *et al.*, note 9). More and more ITV agencies are conducting surveys to determine the size of the in-school audience. Where reasonable care has been taken in sampling and data collection, support can be found for the AIT estimate. For example, recent studies of Georgia's school television utilization show about 50 percent of the k-7 students view at least one television series. Dale Rhodes' 1972 study of North Carolina's in-school television, one of the most methodologically rigorous studies available, found 25 percent of the state's pupils received some of their education from television.[6]

accomplish the task for them. School television, by contrast, is a local activity in the extreme. Most of the decisions are made at the individual classroom level. The teacher is the person who decides to use, or not to use, a particular school television program. A television series may be purchased and made available for use by the school district or the state education agency. It may be promoted and broadcast by the local public television station. It may be recommended by the principal or a content specialist working for the school system. But the classroom teacher is the person who turns on the set.

Why would a teacher want to view television in the classroom? What can television do? After Chu and Schramm's 1967 compilation and review of research on instructional television,[10] the question is "no longer whether students learn from it, but rather (1) does the situation call for it? and (2) how, in a given situation, can it be used effectively?" School television is widely used today, with increasing sophistication and effectiveness, to assist the teacher in classroom instruction and in improving the quality and diversity of the educational experience.

In a recent overview of federal policy in funding children's programming, some of the characteristics of the classroom are described from the viewpoint of the producer of children's television.

> In the abstract, the in-school audience is perhaps the most promising of all settings for high-impact use of purposive [children's] television. The audience is grouped more homogeneously than would be the case in almost any other setting. Competing activities can be controlled, and the pupils are in that setting for the purpose of learning in the first place. The viewer can be supervised and controlled, meaning that there can be some previewing preparation, integration of non-broadcast materials, and follow-up activities which can be individualized to needs of particular pupils. ... [T]he in-school program can in principle be more direct, compact, incrementally sequenced, and by implication, more efficient.[11]

Television has brought the specialist into the classroom to present new material or to stimulate class activity. School television now has its stars — John Robbins in literature, Tony Saletan in music, and Louise McNamara in health education, to name a few. These stars may not be the world-renowned experts originally promised in the late 1950s and early 1960s, but they are good communicators and good teachers, which is far more important.

School television materials have been especially emphasized and regularly used to achieve three difficult functions: (1) to assist the classroom teachers in those subjects in which they often have the most difficulty (for example, art, music, "new" mathematics, science and health); (2) to supplement the classroom instruction in subject areas in which limited classroom resources may prevent full examination of historical or international events; and (3) to bring outside stimulation in subject areas, such as literature, where the teachers have difficulty exciting and motivating the students. Generally speaking, school television series in these subject areas do not assume the complete, or even the major, classroom instructional function. The teacher retains control over the presentation of the basic content for each subject area; the television programs merely "supplement" and "enrich" the existing curriculum.

This kind of bread-and-butter television fare has been for years the staple of the national instructional program libraries (NIT, GPN) and of the public broadcasting stations themselves. Production quality has varied; content integrity has often wavered. Most of these school series initially are produced by local PTV stations, though occasionally designed for more than local use or widespread distribution. It is this kind of programming that has caused school television to remain *in* education rather than *of* education.

School television has also served, and continues to serve, by facilitating the rapid dissemination of new curriculum formulations. The relatively new technology was forceably pulled into this role soon after Sputnik was launched in the late 1950s and politicians were demanding overnight improvements in science and language training. Most of these efforts were directed toward higher education,[12] but the methodology was employed also in elementary education for language instruction and the introduction of new math. "Parlons Français" was broadcast as a major part of the FLES movement and contributed to the teaching of foreign languages in schools lacking qualified teachers. New math was introduced to both students and teachers by "Patterns in Arithmetic," a multi-level, heavily researched, and extensive school television series supported by federal funds. The math programs had marginal production qualities, but they were effective in hastening the dissemination of newer approaches to the teaching of elementary mathematics.*

In more recent years, school television has been a major factor in the introduction of affective education into elementary class-rooms. By using series like "Ripples" and "Inside/Out" to provide shared and relatively universal experiences, teachers and students have begun to examine their feelings about themselves and their environment. Other attempts at curricular reform have been less successful. For example, "Ready? Set. . .Go!" is one of school television's few attempts at programming in the psychomotor do-main. It was designed to change physical education from the tradi-tional fun-and-games approach to basic movement education. Wide-spread use of this television program has not been achieved for a variety of reasons.

Similarly disappointing results, for different reasons, are now surfacing for the art series "Images & Things," which was designed to stimulate aesthetic appreciation and critical ability as a com-plement to the traditional how-to-to-it curriculum of making valen-tines and ash trays. In this series, art educators turned to television after noting the existence of numerous television series that did not meet their needs or expectations. The resulting programs were critically successful productions, but in terms of instructional utili-zation, they made no widespread impact.

A more encouraging function of school television has been its effectiveness as a means of equalizing educational opportunity. Un-equal schools and unequal education have been persistent problems in twentieth-century America. From both the fiscal and socio-cul-tural viewpoints, educational inequality remains with us. The broad-cast signal, however, is not limited to wealthy school districts or to poor ones, to new schools or old ones.

Presenting black faces in all-white schools and white faces in all-black schools provides useful role models of all races to facilitate interracial acceptance and understanding. But what school television can do best in equalizing educational opportunities is to provide instructional presentations so universal in nature that they become specific to the viewer and are effective regardless of sex, race, ethnic

---

*As an aside, it's worth noting that television programming is now being developed to re-form the "new" math. EDC's forthright series, "The Infinity Factory," has been in part stimulated by the mathematically confused generation who learned (or did not learn) the new math. It is designed to put mathematics in a reality-based setting rather than a theoret-ical one.

background, or economic conditions.* This aspect of television may not be surprising, but it is often ignored. Children who can view a strong, emotionally-oriented presentation, such as "Inside/Out" or "Self Incorporated" programs, tend to identify and personalize the experience, regardless of the actors' personal or physical characteristics in relation to their own. The highly engaging visual presentations of "The Electric Company," for example, are not race- or sex-related, nor do they depend on these characteristics to teach.

Another educational concern — efficiency and productivity — has focused upon television for answers. Productivity in education means significantly more than merely fewer teachers teaching an increased number of students. It means doing a better job of preparing students to be more effective and more fulfilled members of the community at large. When school television adds to the teacher's choice of approaches to instruction, or when it provides stimulation for improved class interactions, or when it initiates and reinforces cognitive learning, or when it motivates qualitatively different classroom behavior — it is providing better, more efficient education.

The efficiency factor in this increased productivity involves finding the appropriate mix of school television and classroom teaching. By using school television economically — that is, by examining the variety of utilization and programming options available and choosing wisely — improvements in the patterns and effects of instruction can occur with minimal cost increases to the taxpayer. Television is not seeking to replace teachers, only to assist them in reaching education's desired goals.

The programming of school television. The school television broadcast day is essentially that six-hour period during each weekday when schools are in session. Although it can expand its programming hours for in-service teacher programs and post-secondary education, school television can only fill about 30 hours a week. During periods of the year when school is not in session, the average

---

*In that they are designed primarily for a particular ethnic or racial group, the projects developed from ESAA funds may prove counterproductive as instruction. Universal appeal and possibilities for personal identification are effective instructional characteristics; increased salience of social and ethnic characteristics may distort the instructional process for all but a select group within the specific minority. People watch *television*, not black television or Hispanic television.[13] Children tend to see people, not racial or ethnic factors.[14] The value of ESAA projects may be more pronounced in other social and educational areas, such as training minority production personnel and involving various racial and ethnic groups with local public television production agencies and stations.

station's broadcast week drops by about 25 hours. Given these limits, it should not be surprising that school television provides approximately the same amount of television programming this year as it has during each of the past few years. The absolute figures stay relatively static; the proportional figures decrease.

On a normal school day, the average station transmits almost four and one-half hours of in-school programs which surround the PBS-interconnected "Sesame Street" and "The Electric Company." Few if any other school programs occupy the amount of time or appear with such regularity as the CTW programs. The instructional programs are usually 15-, 20-, or 30-minutes long, and the same program is broadcast as many as three or four times during the week to permit repeated opportunities for its use. More than half of all school television hours are repeat transmissions.

Stations obtain programs for transmission to classrooms from a variety of sources. Some of it is produced by the station itself; some is exchanged directly between stations. A large portion is made available through regional networks in which programs produced by one school television agency are made available to all other member agencies. There are also a number of profit-making distributors of school programming, such as Western Instructional Television, Learning Corporation of America, Time-Life, and Encyclopaedia Britannica. Many of their series are widely broadcast; for example, "Sing, Children, Sing," "Alistair Cooke's America," "Western Civilization."

Two of the major sources of school programs are the Agency for Instructional Television (AIT) and Great Plains National Instructional Television Library (GPN). Both agencies began over ten years ago as part of the same federal demonstration project designed to explore the value of exchanging videotaped lessons. Both agencies have prospered, though taking different approaches to school television programming. GPN acquires extant material from state and local television agencies and makes it available, for a fee, to other educational agencies. As a part of the University of Nebraska's educational television communications complex, GPN's course offerings range from pre-school through university and adult education.

AIT has taken an approach which incorporates and goes beyond the acquisition of extant school programs. As its predecessor organization (the National Instructional Television Center — NIT) had done, AIT acquires already produced programs. But it also seeks to help producers upgrade and improve materials in the process of development, and, primarily through the consortium process, it coordinates the development of major school television series. In recent years, AIT's catalog has offered mainly elementary and secondary programming.

During the past two years, two other agencies have made significant amounts of instructional programming available for broadcast use. One, the Ontario Educational Communications Authority (OECA), has entered the United States market with a variety of elementary and secondary programs originally developed for use in Ontario. The other, WETA's ITV Cooperative, has successfully developed consortium arrangements for several television projects. In addition, CTW programs and several projects produced under ESAA funding have attained a place in the school broadcast schedule. The Emergency School Aid Act provided that a certain portion of its monies be devoted to television projects. Although specifically designed for out-of-school viewing, series such as KLRN's "Carrascolendas" and BC/TV's "Villa Alegre" have a significant but undetermined in-school audience.

The materials the public television stations obtain from outside are sometimes electronically distributed via interconnected feeds. More often, the programs are received through a mail distribution system and are available for unlimited broadcast use within a seven-day period. Programs are trans-shipped in sequence from one agency to another, until they return to the distributor. This system of "bicycling" videotapes, which is reminiscent of the early NET, has affected the design of school television series. In the past, series with any promise of more-than-local use were created to be viewed in a lock-step, serial fashion. Now, many series are being designed so that the programs can be used nonsequentially or even individually. Another effect of bicycling has been to limit the timeliness of material included in school television programs.

The production qualities of school television programs are improving in general and, in specific instances, are outstanding. Last year for the first time, a series designed specifically for use in schools won a national Emmy. No longer do talking faces and static chalkboards appear in every program. Katzman's preliminary figures for 1974 show that 21 percent of the in-school programs are, in part or whole, dramatizations; 16 percent are documentaries, 33 percent contain demonstrations, and only 43 percent are lectures, interviews and/or discussions.* It's a pity that this analysis isn't available for the public affairs and other general audience programs broadcast by the public television stations. A comparison might prove enlightening.

Instruction's place in public television. From the viewpoint of contemporary public television, its partnership with education in school television must seem like "a marriage of convenience involving common facilities, capital investments, and talent."[15] Here is public television involved in show business and concerned with audience percentages and "cumes," sharing the same house with the school teacher whose unglamorous interests are in student learning and other classroom effects. How do they treat each other in this marriage of convenience?

Every aspect of public television, save one, has grown in the last few years. That one exception is the instructional and school services of the public television system. Between 1970 and 1975, the number of stations in the system increased by one-third; income went from $100 million in 1970 to $260 million in 1974; the average broadcast week went from 65 hours to about 80 hours per week. In contrast, school television broadcasts still occupy the approximately 25-30 hours per week that they did in 1970. About $25 million was listed by the stations as income for school services in 1970; three years later, in 1973, the figure was nearly the same. School television, it appears, is becoming an ever smaller slice of the growing public broadcasting pie.

Yet the latest complete figures available show that almost 50 percent of public television's income was obtained from agencies which are also responsible for public instruction — state and local governments and boards of education and state colleges.[16] Local and state boards of education, by themselves, provided over $36 million, or 20 percent of public television's income.

That the same agencies fund both education and public television should not be surprising. School television is undeniably the reason that much of the public broadcasting system was built. School television is also the reason that public broadcasting continues to receive a large portion of its operating costs. It is not unusual, for

---

*Programs may not be exclusively one format. Two format choices were permitted, thus totals will exceed 100 percent. See N. Katzman. *Public Television Content: 1974* (Washington, D.C.: National Center for Educational Statistics and Corporation for Public Broadcasting, 1975), p. 59.

example, for physical plants and operating expenses to be justified before legislatures and governing boards on the basis of implications and promises that they will help overcome some of the instructional deficiencies of the school system. Blakely suggested the extent of public television's obligation to its instructional activities when he wrote:

> Television for public purposes needs to serve instruction more effectively because ITV is a major justification for the existence of the public television system and a major part of its broadcasting; because many of the stations receive their basic support from local school districts or state school agencies, and because much of the backing in Congress for the public television system is given with the expectation that it will be increasingly valuable for instruction.[17]

In 1973, this nation's public television stations received as income more than $25 million earmarked for instructional services. Although this accounted for only 14.8 percent of the total system's income (it would have been 26 percent in 1970), the $25 million was, nevertheless, more than subscribers and individuals contributed ($16.6 million), and more than auctions raised ($7.5 million). It was also more income than these two sources provided in 1974, a growth year for both. Moreover, if $25 million in income was directly attributable to the school services of the PTV stations, perhaps five times as much was received indirectly because the school service exists. How much then does the public television system spend on instructional television?

Henry Loomis, president of CPB, was recently quoted as saying that "30 percent to 40 percent of public broadcasting's budget . . . currently is spent on instructional programming." This may overestimate the financial commitment. The Corporation for Public Broadcasting's own figures for 1973 show $8.6 million as "direct operating costs for television operations of instructional and school services." The $8.6 million is only 6.3 percent of the total direct operating costs of the public television system ($137.2 million). If the direct operating costs are assumed to include most of the school service's expenses to public television stations, then the $25 million or so that the stations are receiving as income for these services should result in a healthy surplus (profit) from that part of the station's activities. Actually, instructional income is probably supporting programming for noninstructional audiences.

Even if these figures under-represent the true station costs for instructional services, they accurately reflect the attitude of a large segment of the public broadcasting community toward school television. The station's instructional services are seen as an income-producing activity for those stations that receive money earmarked for school services (and not all stations do). And this income does, at a minimum, permit the stations to recover the costs of programming and air time.* The actual costs are less important than the knowledge that they are probably less than related income and that they have not changed over the past few years while the rest of the system has been growing.

The characteristics of successful school television. In the past, instructional television has been accused of doing insignificant things and doing them poorly. The criticism was harsh but in many cases justified. If school television is to succeed, it must deal with significant educational matters. If school television programs are to be used widely, they must be of high quality, both in terms of production and of proven (or at least demonstrable) effects.

The characteristics of successful projects, discussed below, do not compose an exhaustive list. None of these characteristics is, by itself, sufficient for success; nor can one divine any generic combination of attributes that would be totally sufficient. I should also add that no priority is implied by the order in which they appear.

(1) *The television project is created to deal with a significant educational need.* Success is more likely if the need is identified by

---

*It is not clear from a reading of the report and the questionnaire used in collecting the data whether or not all actual costs were included in these figures. Assuming that the $8.6 million is only for salaries and expenses associated with personnel in the school service — and this assumption may be far from accurate — then other operating costs would have to be added to this figure to arrive at a more accurate estimate of the actual cost of the school service to the station. By figuring the proportion of programming and production hours listed as instructional in nature and then applying the results to various other operational categories, a larger cost figure can be obtained. Adjusting costs by type of licensee (since relative costs and hours of programming vary greatly among them) and applying the percentage of school television hours, I have generated the following figures: The operational costs of technical services attributed to the school service of the television station would be $10.355 million; $5.854 million for the programming costs of the instructional materials, and $5.201 million for local instructional television production. These projections would result in an additional $21.4 million being spent for the school service, assuming that the $8.6 million does not overlap with any of these categories of expense. It would still be difficult, however, for direct instructional costs to approach 30 percent of public television's operating expenses.

education and if the desire for filling the need is explicitly demonstrated within education. The major school television projects are not created merely to teach spelling. Projects should have important curricular implications and the possibility for changing the way children are taught. For example, the desire to extend career development concepts throughout all levels of schooling stimulated an AIT consortium to develop "Bread & Butterflies," a career education series for intermediate students. "Sesame Street" can be seen as a response to the burgeoning early childhood education movement.

Most major instructional television projects dealt with curricular reforms as these new approaches were becoming known throughout education and had the potential for wider adoption. Isolated efforts were successfully producing desirable educational change, and the television series served as the catalyst and focal point for organized dissemination and wider adoption of the new method or curriculum. This process might be called the Panasonic Theory of School Television: The curriculum refinement should be only slightly ahead of its time — not too far ahead, or educational leadership will not be ready to support it; not too far behind, or the improvement may already be part of the existing practice in too many localities.

The local and state education agencies are often in the best position to point to instructional needs that are not being satisfied. Educational goals may be influenced by HEW's Office of Education, but they are ultimately specified and implemented at the local and state levels to satisfy local and state requirements. Thus, the design of a television project must approximate state and local goals or it is not likely to be timely and therefore widely accepted.

The project should also wait upon a commitment by the state and local agency to realize their stated goal through the allocation of funds dedicated to this purpose. Investment of one's own dollars is the verification of commitment. The financial contribution is essential for the extensive production costs of most major television projects, but it is also important in that it places the state and local education agencies in the position of following up on its investment or taking the chance of wasting it. The commitment to work with a significant educational need that they have identified, combined with the contribution of funds, can result in the continued effort to implement the series when it becomes available for classroom use. The investment becomes a permanent record of an agency's responsibility for the most effective use of the project.

(2) *The project adheres to a systematic instructional design or*

development process. For example, the process used at the Children's Television Workshop — needs assessment, instructional design, formative evaluation, production, dissemination, summative evaluation and revision — has been well-documented.[18] Similar but not identical processes are found in AIT's projects and in other national and local school television projects, as well as in Cavert's systematic approach for post-secondary education at the State University of Nebraska/University of Mid-America.[19] If such systematic planning and development is to take place, there must be a high degree of cooperation and integration of activities by representatives from both television and education.

(3) *The project is adequately financed to accomplish its designated tasks.* The precedent-setting costs of the first few years of "Sesame Street" were followed by similar price tags on other major series. Multi-million dollar projects like EDC's math series or BC/TV's "Villa Alegre" have become almost commonplace. AIT's curriculum project budgets have not yet reached the seven-figure category, but they are comparable to the more extensive television projects when analyzed on a cost-per-minute-of-television basis. Projects developed through consortia are now seeing costs in the range of $1,000-$1,500 per minute merely for production. The other necessary parts of a project — writing, designing, evaluating, etc. — consume an equivalent amount per minute of completed television.

Financing these large development and production costs is a considerable problem. Federal ESAA funds assisted many large projects which are just now becoming available for broadcast. (Although these projects were not specifically designed for in-school use, several of the series have been used extensively in the classroom.) CTW involves a variety of funding sources outside the public broadcasting community as well as inside. More and more of the costs for its continuing series are falling within the purview of the public television stations.

The cooperative funding of strictly in-school television programming has come primarily from state education and television agencies rather than from public television stations, because the projects are so closely tied to curriculum planning. In a few cases, the money for these projects was taken from state allocations for public television broadcasting, and the stations in those states received reduced state funding. In others, all of the money came from sources other than the state's media budget, so that the station received, in effect, free television programs.

WETA's ITV Cooperative seeks to fund comparatively less expensive school television projects, many of them "bread-and-butter" projects that, in the past, stations might have funded locally and produced in their own facilities or obtained from an ITV library. The increased costs associated with improved production and design qualities have not placed such projects out of reach of local stations. However, with the reduced cost-per-participant offered by the ITV Cooperative's programs, more of the television stations themselves can again become involved in paying for school programming.

(4) *The project seeks to facilitate use of its materials through extensive promotional activities and an active involvement of the using agency in the project activities.* Involving the using agencies in all phases of a project, from design through evaluation, tends to increase the agencies' willingness to use the material when it becomes available. This does not suggest that committee rule should prevail in school television. However, AIT's experience has been that by informing and involving the potential users of a project, the development agency can create allies and supporters who will carry project information to the appropriate decision makers and will begin to plan for the use of a program even before its completion. That involvement often creates or strengthens commitment is a lesson that has been learned from social psychology.

Another lesson learned by CTW as well as by utilization specialists at state and local television agencies has been that teachers don't turn on television without being motivated to do so. Major promotional activities were the key in CTW's experience in initiating program use. But simple word of mouth and personal contact by utilization and curriculum specialists have proved equally effective.[20] The efforts of utilization personnel are additionally important in generating repeated and sustained classroom use of a series.

Many critics[21] have decried the financial and organizational limitations of the consortium approach in developing the large number of high quality series required for school television's greatest impact. However, they overlook an important advantage of the consortium concept. Its power rests not in the high quality programs that it creates, but rather in eliciting the most effective classroom use of the programs. The impact is not in the station's schedule, but in the classroom. Perhaps public television station schedules must be filled with bread-and-butter school programming and lesser quality materials until the ability to absorb significant television projects have become more widespread in education.

The Future of Instructional Television

The public broadcasting station will probably remain the primary distribution mechanism for school television materials. Over-the-air broadcasting is the more efficient mode, especially since the hardware system is, for the most part, in place. The dilemma of which comes first, quality programming or school television receivers, is moot. Quality programs are increasingly available, although merely broadcasting them is not going to stimulate the acquisition of television sets or their use. If enough quality instructional television series are available and, more important, are desired *by* the schools for use *in* the schools, then instructional television will become another major instructional resource, like textbooks, and will be solidly incorporated into the educational system.

The role of distributor should mean more to the stations than merely transmitting television programs. A recent Battelle study considered the future role of instructional television and its relationship with the public television station. This study suggested some of the distribution problems of school television when it concluded that:

> The role implies a flexible schedule adapted to the individual classroom and teacher. Thus, the distribution system should be designed to provide the material to any classroom, in a manner to suit the style and schedule of the instructor. The variety of materials, schedules, and programs is in sharp conflict with the single-channel nature of broadcasting, and if TV were more popular, broadcast capacity would surely be overtaxed. This limitation is reflected in the current pattern of ITV . . . skewed sharply toward the primary grades, where the classroom can be more easily adapted to the medium.[22]

It is becoming increasingly common for schools to circumvent the restrictions of the broadcast schedule by recording programs off-air for playback in classrooms at times convenient to the teacher. Some schools are refurbishing their ancient one-half inch video-tape recorders; others are investing in video-cassette machines and color monitors. Large numbers of state and local educational agencies are obtaining, recording, and keeping copies of television programs and films. Some are attempting to do it legally (Granite School District in Utah); others are doing it apparently illegally (Salt Lake City Schools).

Since several of the major school television series have been produced on film for television, the film sales of these projects are naturally increasing. Why not? In addition to being shown as films, the films can be transferred to all formats of video-tape for use in that mode, thus increasing the flexibility of their classroom use. This flexibility in the use of materials has proved useful in breaking through the traditional roadblock to the use of television series in secondary schools, where the bell schedule must determine the time and place for television viewing. Several of the school television consortia now provide audio-visual rights to the materials as well as electronic transmission rights. State and local educational agencies also seek the widest use of the programs they purchase. They do not mind and, in fact, support the nonbroadcast use of television materials that would normally be available only through public television stations.

Public television's school services must adapt to these changing patterns of in-school television use. PBS and many stations and distributors recognize the demand for nonbroadcast program use and have increased the efforts to obtain more extensive use rights to programs. For nationally distributed series appropriate for the in-school audience, PBS notifies stations of the available rights for off-air recording and the length of time that the programs may be held before erasure is required. Recent agreements among the major nonprofit distributors of school programming have formalized a seven-day record and reuse policy. Certain programs from PBS, PTL, AIT and GPN can now be used for instructional purposes at times convenient for the teacher. The programs are to be erased within seven days after local broadcast. Many of the state and local school television services now publish the legal-use limitations for all programs listed in their school program guides. In this way, participating schools are made aware of their rights and obligations in re-recording programs.

Public stations must also begin to supplement the traditional broadcasting function with additional services. There is a need for better local program production to serve local needs more effectively. The limits of the school broadcast day mean that changes must come in the quality of programs, not in their number. Series must be updated, replaced, or discarded for improved curricular approaches. A few television stations have the willingness and ability to commit their best production staff and sufficient resources to school television. The same few stations generally appear as the producers of the widely used series in AIT's and GPN's library service. School television has learned the same truth as public television — that by choice and ability there are only a handful of agencies that produce the bulk of high quality materials.

The fact that almost everyone produces instructional television and so few do it well suggests that an ITV-Station Programming Cooperative, as recommended by the ACNO Report, would not result in significant school television projects. Financing major instructional television projects satisfies only one of the criteria for creating a valuable product. The involvement and the commitment of the users are equally as important. If stations receive school television production funds from national sources, there is little reason to believe that they will, in turn, pool their money in a cooperative venture. Since local instructional television production is going to take place and because the money serves as income for the local station, is there any reason for a station to return funds for someone else to use in creating essentially the same material?

Besides distribution and production, an important part of the school television service is *service*. Significant new television projects are useless if they are beyond education's ability to absorb them locally. Stations are now providing teacher and/or student materials to accompany more than one-half of their instructional broadcasting hours. Utilization specialists from state and local education agencies are working alongside station utilization personnel to inform and motivate classroom teachers in the effective uses of television instruction. The price a station pays for state-funded consortia projects may be the price of increased utilization services.

The public television system has relinquished its hold over school television. How programs become available for use, and how they are used, is now answered in the domain of education, not by broadcast television. Although public television stations retain their functions as distributors and producers of broadcast materials for in-school use, their activities must increasingly stress utilization — promoting the most effective use of television to improve the quality of education.

The Future of Public Broadcasting

There is no chasm between education and television. Unbeknownst to public television, education and television have been working together to create and use quality school television. School television is alive and well and has a fine future as a part of education.

References

1. Natan Katzman and Karen Farr. "Focus on Research," parts 2 and 3, *CPB Report* (20 January 1975, and 24 February 1975).

2. For example, the Carnegie Commission on Educational Television. *Public Television: A Program for Action* (New York: Bantam, 1967); the Commission on Instructional Technology. *To Improve Learning, A Report to the President and Congress of the United States* (Washington: U. S. Government Printing Office, March 1970); J. W. Armsey and N. C. Dahl. *An Inquiry into the Uses of Instructional Technology* (New York: A Ford Foundation Report, 1973); Advisory Council of National Organizations. *Public Broadcasting and Education, A Report to the Corporation for Public Broadcasting* (Washington: Corporation for Public Broadcasting, 1975).

3. James Perkins, International Council for Educational Development. *Instructional Broadcasting: A Design for the Future* (Washington: Corporation for Public Broadcasting, 1971).

4. Advisory Council of National Organizations, see note 2.

5. This section is based on materials developed by E. G. Cohen in a speech, "The Education Agency and School Television," presented at the NAEB-CPB 1975 Conference on Instruction, in Philadelphia, May 12, 1975. Also useful to this section were the federal education data from the periodic publications of the National Center for Educational Statistics, U.S. Office of Education.

6. D. M. Rhodes. *The Utilization of the In-School Television Service in North Carolina's Public Schools — A Report of the Audience Services Division of the University of North Carolina Television Network* (Chapel Hill: University of North Carolina Television Network, Audience Services, 1972). Georgia Department of Education. *Summary of Annual Survey Report, 1973-74* (Atlanta: Educational Media Services Division, Instructional Services Unit, 1975).

7. R. J. Liebert. "'The Electric Company' In-School Utilization Study," Vol. 2, in *The 1972-73 School and Teacher Surveys and Trends since Fall 1971, A Report to the Children's Television Workshop* (Florida State University: Center for the Study of Education — Institute for Social Research, in conjunction with Statistics Research Division, Research Triangle Institute, October 1973).

8. J. Lyle. *The People Look at Public Television 1974* (Washington: Corporation for Public Broadcasting, Office of Communication Research, March 1975).

9. See, for example, "Ripples: A Third-Year Survey" (AIT Research Report, 1973); "Inside/Out Teacher's Guide Survey" (AIT Research Report, in prep.); "Bread and Butterflies Teacher's Guide Survey" (AIT Research Report, in prep.).

10. G. C. Chu and W. Schramm. *Learning from Television: What the Research Says* (Stanford, Cal.: Stanford University, Institute for Communication Research, 1967), p. 98.

11. K. W. Mielke, R. C. Johnson, and B. G. Cole. *The Federal Role in Funding Children's Television Programming, Vol. I, Final Report* (Bloomington: Indiana University, Institute for Communication Research, 1975), p. 24.

12. For a fascinating historical review of the uses of television for post-secondary education in both commercial and noncommercial broadcasting during this period, see R. D. B. Carlisle. *College Credit Through TV: Old Idea, New Dimension* (Lincoln, Neb.: Great Plains National Instructional Television Library, 1974).

13. J. Lyle and H. R. Hoffmann. "Children's Use of Television and Other Media," in J. P. Murray, E. A. Rubinstein, and G. A. Comstock, eds. *Television and Social Behavior, Reports and Papers. Vol. II: Television and Social Learning* (Washington: U.S. Government Printing Office, 1972).

14. *A Study of Messages Received by Children Who Viewed an Episode of "The Harlem Globetrotters Popcorn Machine"*

(New York: Child Research Service, Inc., and Office of Social Research, CBS, April 1975).

15. G. W. Tressel, G. A. Janis, J. T. Suchy, D. J. Thielke, J. D. Gammel, and G. C. Johnson. *Final Report on the Use of Instructional Television in Georgia* (Columbus, Ohio: Battelle, 1975), p. 24.

16. These fiscal 1973 data are from Lee and Dunn's *Statistical Report on Public Television Licensees, Fiscal Year 1973*, Advance edition (May 1975). The 1974 data are taken from financial reports in the Corporation for Public Broadcasting's newsletters and news releases.

17. R. J. Blakely. *The People's Instrument. A Philosophy of Programming for Public Television* (Washington, D.C.: Public Affairs Press, a Charles F. Kettering Foundation Report, 1971), p. 69.

18. See H. W. Land. *The Children's Television Workshop: How and Why It Works* (Jericho, N.Y.: Nassau Board of Cooperative Educational Services, 1972); E. L. Palmer. "Formative Research: Educational Television Production: The Experience of the Children's Television Workshop," in W. Schramm, ed. *Quality in Instructional Television* (Honolulu: University Press of Hawaii, 1972); and R. M. Polsky. *Getting to Sesame Street: Origins of the Children's Television Workshop* (New York: Praeger, 1974).

19. C. E. Cavert. *An Approach to the Design of Mediated Instruction* (Washington, D.C.: The Association for Educational Communications and Technology, 1974).

20. See Liebert, note 6.

21. See Mielke *et al.*, note 10.

22. G. W. Tressel, D. P. Buckelew, J. T. Suchy, and P. L. Brown. *The Future of Educational Telecommunication: A Planning Study* (Lexington, Mass.: Heath, 1975), p. 56.

Instructional Television: An Agenda for Self Analysis

BERNARD Z. FRIEDLANDER

Whether or not instructional television in American schools and colleges is in trouble depends a great deal on how one is inclined to see things. If you see the proverbial glass of water as being half full, then you might say ITV is in good shape. If you see it as being half empty, then ITV is in trouble.

What you see depends on where you stand. Saul Rockman, research director at the Agency for Instructional Television, takes the half full viewpoint in his article, "Instructional Television is Alive and Well."[1] Dave Berkman, another competent authority, sees the glass as at least half empty (perhaps *more* than half empty) in his article, "Instructional Television: The Medium Whose Future Has Passed."[2] Both observers — each well informed, each well qualified to interpret data — marshal such compelling and such contrary evidence that their differences are clearly based on selective perception rather than on any single body of facts.

From where I stand, as a psychologist first and a researcher second, I see a very troubled client facing a severe developmental crisis of identity. The crisis is simply stated: ITV has a highly ambivalent self-image — sharply divided between the strength and

Dr. Friedlander is professor of psychology and director of the New England Instructional Television Research Center, University of Hartford.

self-confidence of Charles Atlas, and the anxious insignificance of the 97-pound weakling. In their associations with the world of "big TV," educational broadcasters see themselves as practitioners in an immensely powerful communications medium which dominates society and has transformed politics, entertainment, sports, business, news, and government. In their associations with educators, educational broadcasters know they are fairly visible but nearly impotent. They know in their secret hearts that it would cause more trouble in the schools and colleges if all the pencil sharpeners, blackboards, and wastebaskets suddenly disappeared than if all the TV sets went dead.

It would be hard to find a clearer prescription for a mild, moderate, or severe case of professional neurosis. As it enters its third decade, television in education faces a standoff in its sense of self between the brave new world of its early years and the gray reality of its present troubled status. After a beginning filled with great optimism and self-importance, it is not an easy matter — in fact it is a crisis — to find, as Lloyd Morrisett recently pointed out, that "so far the new communications technology has promise, but the promise has not been fulfilled."[3]

What Comes Next?

If one accepts Morrisett's assessment of unfulfilled promises — and I accept it — then what comes next? As I see it, instructional television can adopt one of three possible strategies for reconciling the identity crisis stemming from this conflict of early hopes and present limitations: *

First, there is the possibility of going on for a while longer, failing to recognize that the bloom is off the rose. That will probably become an increasingly difficult illusion to maintain — if there are any educational broadcasters so comfortable they have been able to maintain until now the feeling of affluence and influence. This strategy is an invitation to a greater identity crisis later on, when the gap between fantasy and reality inevitably becomes even greater than it is today.

---

*Perhaps I should say that individual practitioners and agencies in the profession can adopt various strategies. It is likely that some will cope more successfully than others with the conflict between dreams of glory and constricted opportunity.

Another way to cope would be simply to acknowledge the failure of great expectations and to accept a sharply lowered profile of aspiration and performance with pained but quiet dignity. This strategy offers the advantage of seeming to preserve the collective self-esteem though on a much smaller scale.

Then, of course, there is the strategy of realistic assessment of self and others, the pursuit of greater understanding of what schools really need and want and of what television can do to satisfy these needs and wants in ways no other medium can provide. For those who think as I do that this third strategy makes the most sense, here are some major issues I think professionals in ITV should examine with special care: *

Agenda for Self-Analysis

The fundamental value of television. Whenever spirits flag, it's worthwhile to remind ourselves that television is the most potent medium of communication that has ever been devised. Whatever problems we face in adapting the potentials of television to the actualities of educational practice are simply matters of detail — often crucial details, to be sure, but nevertheless simply detail.

When television is used with the effectiveness inherent in the medium, no other teaching medium can perform as well or as flexibly in making the world of information, imagination, and reality accessible to the thought processes of a learner — or a million learners. No other medium can manipulate action, object, imagery, and speech in virtually any imaginable visual and auditory combination so as to touch its recipients in so many ways. No other medium can as readily combine any visual event with any sound or verbal description; make any conceivable transformation, alteration, or accompaniement; or offer limitless repetitions of these elements in pursuing limitless instructional goals. No other medium can hold these resources endlessly in storage until the exact time they are required, and no other medium can extend its influence over so wide a range of possible receivers — from a single individual in a

---

*I recognize that this is not a complete list. Some very important topics such as costs, delivery systems, and new technologies don't appear on this agenda. What I want to call attention to expecially are the less obvious but perhaps more important topics that other observers tend to neglect.

study carrel, to a city, a region, or a nation.

Though it may seem grandiose to speak in these terms, we need think only of the American-Soviet joint space mission, the moon shots, and the Kennedy assassination to remind ourselves that television can reach and teach the world. Anyone with a sense of confidence that education is worthwhile, and that honest knowledge widely disseminated is one of the great liberating experiences of mankind, *has* to be in love with what television can accomplish as an educational medium. We should start our thinking about the details with these sources of strength as the initial premise for all other considerations.

Formulating ITV learning goals and teaching strategies. Looking back on the early days of instructional television from the vantage point of the present, we can see that television started to lose its way almost from the beginning. The original goals and tactics, which seem never to have been systematically and rigorously re-examined, are dreadfully out of keeping with reality needs and possibilities.

First, the great initial enthusiasm for classroom television was based on a double assumption: Television would be the means (1) for simultaneously coping with the teacher shortage of the post-World War II era, and (2) for multiplying the effectiveness of "master teachers" as examples to ordinary teachers who needed to be inspired to enrich their own performance.

That compound objective committed several fundamental errors. It tied the perception of television's function to solving a short-range problem which now, of course, with the teacher surplus, is completely nonexistent. Even more damaging, it sent an unspoken message to classroom teachers that a television set in the classroom would do the teachers' job better than the teachers could do it themselves. That is hardly a winning strategy for encouraging the adoption of a medium which can never be used in schools without teachers' enthusiasm and trust.

This educational objective also sent a message to program producers — which they are still listening to — to concentrate their efforts on the fundamental curriculum of literacy and numbers. Thus, it loaded the airwaves with programs that simply did, in perhaps a somewhat different fashion, what teachers have traditionally done by themselves.

Second, the initial concept of classroom television as an instructional medium was simply that of a megaphone, an *amplifier* of existing practice. Television was not looked upon as a medium with properties and instrucational advantages of its own. Television's capability as an instrument of educational change simply was not recognized.

This was the era when television in the home was forcefully reshaping America's ideas about human experience in dramas (usually fallacious and deceptive, but nevertheless profoundly affecting to the audience) of the wider world. It was also the era when innovative video admen were amusing and tantalizing families at home with marching cigarettes and dancing beer mugs. Yet when the kids got to school the next day, there were the video "master" teachers ready to paralyze them electronically in the classroom with the same traditional lectures, explanations, and demonstrations they had always used to paralyze their live students face to face.

For the first time in history, teachers had a medium that could bring the vibrancy and vitality of real life and valid human experience into thousands of classrooms at the same time. Yet television educators had a terribly difficult struggle, and generally failed, in pursuing curricular learning objectives free of the scholastic straitjacket of what could be accomplished by a teacher in an isolated classroom.

Even today, television teaching is dominated by the approach of presenting what is often simply a more profusely illustrated textbook. Perhaps the only change from the early days, and I doubt if it represents progress, is that the "master" teacher's talking head is replaced by a hocus-pocus of so-called entertainment and tricky animation — a hocus-pocus that is usually just as remote from the students' real world of personal experience and dynamic interests as the classroom itself.*

At the foundation level of selecting learning goals and teaching strategies, we have to ask seriously whether ITV has done a very good job of utilizing the distinctive characteristics of the television medium. To the extent that it has *not*, we must ask the next question: Does instruction via television deserve any greater potency and status than it has attained?

Gaining acceptance for ITV by teachers and schools. In look-

---

*Incidentally, my laboratory has some very powerful evidence showing that a talking head can generate very high levels of student attention and comprehension *if it is talking about something inherently interesting to the audience.*[4]

ing through the fragmentary written history of the early years of television in the schools, and in talking with people who were on the scene and recollecting my own long-standing involvement with educational matters, there is one important theme I simply cannot trace. I have yet to find, be told about, or remember any strong advocacy for classroom television from classroom teachers, supervisors, or from anyone else who was not already part of the television movement. From the beginning, the process of seeking acceptance for television has been a classic case of "technology push," as opposed to "demand pull."

The teachers who actually do the real work of the educational system were not clamoring for television in the classroom, even though they might have been watching it at home every night. They did not seek it as a solution to the problems *they* perceived and had to cope with every day. The impetus came from the social inventors and technicians, equipment salesmen, administrators, educational top management and statesmen — the leadership people who observe and influence the system from the outside and from above. They are the ones who applied the leverage to get the ball rolling.

People outside the classroom made up their minds that television would be a good thing for teachers to use. Then they tried to make them use it, promising and hoping for a world of benefits. But as it turned out, the results of evaluation research could never report anything better than that television teaching was "just as good." People at the operating level were left to wonder why they should turn themselves upside down for something that was only just as good.

The expensive hardware from which so much had been expected generally came to be little more than an interesting "extra," rather than the central element in what had been envisaged as the new and better way of doing things. Thus, television innovators created another one of the classic confrontations between innovation and existing regularities that recurred repeatedly during the 1950s and 1960s. Instrucational television took its place beside the New Math, the New Physics, the New Biology, and (so it seems now) the New Everything.

The pattern was the same for all of these innovations. One set of people came to the conclusion that it would be a good idea for another set of people to do things differently than they had ever been done before. Then the first set of people, who had influence and authority, tried to get the second set of people to do what was wanted, almost invariably without regard for the true complexities of the intended change. In almost every case, the confrontation between innovation and regularity produced an initial flurry, after which things settled back to a minor modification of prior practice. At best, the results were an equivalent of "just as good." At worst, the results were a dismal failure — that often took years to recognize as such. (In some cases, the damage has never been repaired. Fortunately, ITV is not one of these.)

In evaluating the lukewarm or ice-cold consequence of their efforts, the innovators were usually left with the unenlightened conviction that their project would have really "worked" if it hadn't been for the schools' deeply embedded rigidity and resistance to change. But in the case of television, as in the case of most other innovations, this analysis of the consequences of innovation is just as faulty as the innovation strategy itself. In fact, the schools have a very successful record of innovation in certain *categories of change*. Teachers and schools are not constitutionally rigid and rejecting in the face of change. They are simply very selective in what changes they accept and what changes they reject.

By and large, teachers and schools absorb and thrive upon changes that enhance the operating level of people's sense of themselves and of the importance of what they do. They balk, distort, and eventually reject changes they cannot accept or do not wish to accept as valid contributions to their own sense of importance and job satisfaction. It is easy for a psychologist to see now that the early arguments for classroom television (setting models for "good teaching" by means of the importation, via electronics, of "master teachers") posed a serious threat to the sense of adequacy of the teachers on the local scene. What is hard to understand is how the advocates could have been so clumsy in posing that threat. Recurrently, the advocates stressed the *production goals* of advancing students' learning (without specifying how this was to be accomplished) and paid no attention to the *satisfaction goals* of teachers who were indispensable to the operation of the system.

Rockman points out in his review of recent developments that "education has replaced television as the piper calling the tune for school television."[5] This suggests that instructional television is now evolving in terms of classroom demand, and not of technology supply. If this is really so, it offers the promise that ITV will gain somewhat greater acceptance in the future than it did in the past. It also means that as part of its growing up, educational broadcasting will have to think of itself as a producer obliged by market conditions to attract and please a very demanding consumer. The broadcasters may think they know what's best, but in the end, it's the customer who's always right.

The problem of program quality. My laboratory has special knowledge of this topic, and much of it is dismal.[6] We start off with the basic assumption that students cannot learn from educational materials they cannot understand, and then we test programs systematically to find out which parts of them students at various levels of age and competence do and do not understand. *After* we examine the factor of *comprehension* we pay attention to the factor of learning.

It sounds basic, and it is. Yet as far as I know, mine is the first laboratory ever to have undertaken this kind of work in a systematic way.* The largest share of instructional television programs are completely unevaluated. When we started doing these assessments several years ago as an adjunct to another project, my associates and I were staggered at the thought that millions upon millions of dollars and student hours were invested in an educational communications process in which product testing was not a routine part of the operation, and in which so much of the product was just plain *bad*.

We have made one common finding. About half the students in the age/grade range for which the programs are intended generally cannot understand about half the material in most programs. That's like asking students to study with textbooks in which half the pages are so badly printed the words can't be deciphered. If instrucational television programs were graded the way students are graded, many of them would flunk the course.

Fortunately, just enough of the programs we've assessed have been so very good, they restore our faith in the value of instructional television as a medium that can play a vital role in the educational process. But when one examines the data showing that on program after program the intended students simply can't understand them, it's hard to maintain one's faith in the *system* that produces and

---

*A few of the larger production groups such as Children's Television Workshop and Agency for Instructional Television conduct formative research on their own productions on a routine basis. Yet their productions are only a small percentage of the total daily ITV telecasts all over the country.

disseminates these programs.

What's especially depressing is that the system of developing, producing, disseminating, and attempting to utilize ITV programs *doesn't have any systematic internal checkpoints for quality control.* The system doesn't seem to be concerned with the issue of identifying the difference between good programs that can teach well and bad programs that can't teach at all. When I think hard about this problem of program quality, I have trouble accounting for the widespread lack of concern for it, not to mention the difficulty we have encountered in getting people to see how important it is to the success or failure of the ITV mission.

Perhaps it's no surprise that the schools' response to instructional television has been so lukewarm, especially when the best that television advocates could claim was that television teaching seemed to be "just as good" as personal teaching. But let's spend a moment considering the enormous demonstrated power of broadcast television (often used in a distorted way) to influence children's knowledge, values and behavior. With this power at its disposal perhaps instructional television should have set much higher targets than being simply "just as good." If higher goals had been set and attained (as they could be with good programming), perhaps the demand for ITV would have been very much greater than has been the case.

So we see another reason why teachers have tended to disregard and reject instructional television. Not only is it unconsciously threatening, much of it is of inferior quality. It doesn't do its job because it can't, and it doesn't deserve to be respected. Most teachers are fundamentally conscientious and eager to see their students learn. When classroom television does its job well and has a genuine impact on students, most teachers support it with enthusiasm — even at the cost of being momentarily displaced from the center of the classroom stage. The dynamic success of programs such as AIT's "Inside/Out" series makes that point clear.

It may be part of growing into a more mature identity for educational broadcasting to confront this problem of program quality head-on. People in charge of things must *insist* that programs have a demonstrated record of effective communication to intended audience, and they must stop telecasting programs that don't. When the quality of the product improves, broadcasters can expect schools and teachers to generate a much stronger demand for what they have to offer.

The Future of Public Broadcasting

When we extend these lines of reasoning as far as they go, it's hard to avoid the conclusion that educational television's developmental identity crisis spells real trouble. On one hand, it is overwhelmingly clear that television is a force of enormous power and influence in shaping people's absorption of information, ideas, and values — especially in the most formative student years. On the other hand, it's equally clear that both the educational broadcasting community and the educational establishment have thus far fumbled in their efforts to put video's huge communications potential to work in a truly effective way.

It would be naive to assume that the vast instructional potential of television means that video will necessarily mature successfully and preserve its opportunity to make major impacts upon educational practice. The door of opportunity doesn't stay open forever. Sooner or later, stiffening patterns of organization impose themselves on any process of change. Options become restricted. Growth slows down or stops altogether. Things become settled the way they are.

Future events might very well prove that Dave Berkman is right, after all, in his contention that instructional television is a medium whose future has passed. Film, teaching machines, programmed instruction, computer-assisted instruction — all those innovations shone brightly on the educational horizon just a short time ago. Now they are just a few among many of the now-historic relics of what were supposed to become great energizers of educational reorganization and revitalization. They never really got off the ground.

Will the same thing happen to television? Could the day arrive when it will become apparent that video in the schools will *never* make its way into the educational mainstream? Could it turn out that the educational establishment might be the only great institution of American life to remain substantially unaffected by the video revolution? It certainly would be ironic if the greatest communications medium ever devised were to fail to find a major role in an educational system whose essence is communication, and which ostensibly demands the best communications media available.

New Times, New Prospects

This is a pretty dark view — but it's not the way I really think the mature years of instructional television will evolve. New combinations of circumstances that never before existed now offer television opportunities for a more fully developed and mature role in education than was possible in the earlier years of the television age. I don't have the courage to make detailed predictions of exactly *how* ITV will become more important in the future than it has been in the past, but I think we can see pretty clearly what some of these new circumstances are that could make this happen. Space limitations do not permit extended analysis here, so I will simply list and comment briefly on some of the major societal and professional developments that can combine to give ITV a new lease on life.

Increasing recognition of television's media dominance among youth. One does not have to be a McLuhan disciple to see that the electronic age is rapidly replacing the "Gutenberg Galaxy." Not only do many children prefer television to print as a prime means for receiving information, we now have evidence that children sometimes are more receptive to a television presentation than to a live presentation of *exactly the same material.*[7]

The schools may find ways to resist unwanted changes in institutional structure, but they cannot endlessly resist vast changes in human behavior. Almost all teachers know by now that television influences students more pervasively than they do. When the educational establishment finally understands that students can be reached with educational messages via television that cannot effectively be delivered in any other way, educators will begin to seek out television as a major instructional medium — *if and when television people truly demonstrate that their medium can do the job that needs to be done.*

Improved ITV program quality and elevated instructional goals. New methods of assessment make it possible to determine specific program attributes which do and do not succeed in communicating effectively. These methods of establishing program accountability permit major restructuring of teaching goals in terms of demonstrable results. When ITV documents that it is better than merely "just as good" for certain specifiable types of instruction, educators will have great difficulty rejecting what ITV has to offer.

Open learning and alternate schools. Alternatives to the educational lockstep of traditional curricula have been waiting in the wings for years. Current problems with alternate school models are probably just a temporary setback in the forward progress of a long-term trend. The concept of individualization is gaining force yearly. The accumulation of great libraries of demonstrably effective television teaching sequences, widely available via cable, cassette, or disc, could prove to be the mose important single technical factor precipitating a major educational revolution whose time may well have begun to arrive.

The expanded curriculum. Along with the "de-institutionalizing" and individualization of education, there is a powerful parallel trend toward expansion of the curriculum beyond the cognitive domain to include the affective domain of real life experience. This is a domain where understanding and expanded awareness of self and others cannot be gained by traditional educational methods. Television's great vitality consists of its ability to provide surrogate experience. When properly used, it is the obvious missing link between school and real life, allowing each to illuminate the other.

Knowledge of institutional change. The planning and execution of educational innovation over the past 20 years, including the development of ITV, has been carried out in incredibly naive ways. Behavioral science has begun to identify factors that accelerate and retard social change, especially in the schools.[8] When this knowledge is put into harness with genuine, demonstrable benefits for those affected by change, it will help innovators avoid traps and obstacles that have blocked educational innovation in the past.

Some ITV innovators, notably AIT, have begun to show a far more sophisticated awareness of how to facilitate acceptance of television instruction. Video people who do not take into account a broader view of the multiple interests involved in institutional change than has been customary in the past will have only themselves to blame if they fail to attain their goals.

These five topics touch only the high spots. There are many other factors that can help instructional television develop new roles and new importance in education commensurate with the tremendous vitality inherent in the medium. One factor, however, is more important than any other — as in any developmental process. That is the factor of *time*.

Television is inherently a revolutionary medium. Television in education is *not* simply another New Something, like New Math. It is a whole new way of experiencing the world. Revolutions follow different time perspectives in different contexts. The cultural revolution of commercial network television in our society was greatly accelerated by the profit motive. That motive has operated only marginally or not at all in ITV, so it is logical that the revolution in education should occur more slowly than in aspects of our society where the profit motive operates full force.

But just because a revolution happens slowly does not mean it does not happen at all. In its own way, television is just as revolutionary as printing. In time, its effect on education will be just as great. Our problem now is simply that we can't forecast the details of how the time course of this revolution will operate. But the television revolution in education will come, just as surely as the printing revolution came to education. In fact, it is undoubtedly happening now in ways we only dimly recognize. People involved with television in education must have faith in the truth of that fact if they are to participate in the maturation of a new identity for the medium they serve.

References

1. S. Rockman. "Instructional Television Is Alive and Well," in this volume.

2. D. Berkman. "Instructional Television: The Medium Whose Future Has Passed," unpublished study (Washington, D.C., 1975).

3. L. Morrisett. "Communications Technology in Education," in The John and Mary R. Markle Foundation Annual Report, 1973-74.

4. H. S. Wetstone and B. Z. Friedlander. "The Effect of Live, TV, and Audio Story Narration on Primary Grade Children's Listening Comprehension," *Journal of Educational Research*, 68:1 (1974).

5. Rockman, see note 1.

6. New England Instructional Television Research Center. "Publications and Reports" (West Hartford, Conn.: University of Hartford, 1975).

7. Wetstone and Friedlander, see note 4.

8. S. B. Saranson. *The Culture of the School and the Problem of Change* (Boston: Allyn & Bacon, 1971).

Public Involvement:
The Anatomy of a Myth

WILLARD D. ROWLAND, JR.

Public television in the United States has failed for the
most part because it has never really gained any important relationship with the bulk of the American audience
or even with any really important segment of it. —
Anthony Smith, *The Shadow in the Cave*[1]

Almost unnoticed outside of Washington and New York, one of
Richard Nixon's final decisions as President during the summer of
1974 was to send on to Congress the five-year financing bill for
public broadcasting that had been drafted by the Office of Telecommunications Policy.* For many of those professionals who had
sat stunned and dismayed in Miami in 1971, when Clay Whitehead
launched the White House's two-year assault on public broadcasting,
there must have been some small satisfaction in witnessing the sink-
ing administration being forced finally to honor the terms of the
accomodation it had worked out with the public broadcasting

Mr. Rowland is a Ph.D. candidate in communications, an instructor
in broadcasting, and a fellow at the University of Illinois at Urbana-
Champaign. Previously, he served as Assistant Coordinator of Programming for Research and Evaluation and as Chief Research
Associate for PBS.

*An earlier version of this essay appeared in the *Public Telecommunications Review* (May-
June 1975).

establishment in 1973. But apart from a brief flurry of national and trade press excitement (when, at the last moment, it appeared that Mr. Nixon might renege by holding back the bill), this major step in the long-delayed attempt to build a certain degree of insulation into public broadcasting funding engendered little public attention.[2] Nor, of course, was there much interest in the progress of this measure during the months after its initial introduction. Indeed, with almost no public opposition, the House Appropriations Committee managed to eliminate the combined authorization and appropriation provision of the OTP bill, thereby voiding one of the key elements in its presumed insulation.

Certainly it is not surprising that the unique series of major national events during the period 1974-75 diverted attention from a host of otherwise important domestic issues, including public broadcasting. The Nixon resignation, the Watergate trial, the power struggles inside the Ford administration, the recurring allegations about the CIA and FBI, and the debates over energy and a faltering economy succeeded in all but burying what little public discussion had begun to surface during the previous year or two about federal policy toward noncommercial broadcasting.

Yet one wonders if, under less momentous circumstances, the level of interest in public broadcasting developments would have been any higher. As I have noted, there is good reason to suspect that as late as June 1974, President Nixon had every intention of suppressing the OTP bill. If, unbowed by the Watergate tapes, a still powerful Mr. Nixon had persisted in office, improvement in public broadcasting financing would have remained in jeopardy, and there were even indications that the former President intended to reduce the level of then current appropriations as well.[3]

While extensive debate about the probable policies of now deposed Presidents is somewhat moot, it is important for public broadcasters to realize that the final emergence of an opportunity for Congress to take any affirmative action on the long-range financing bill was due more to an ironic twist of individual political fortune than to any widespread, sustained and adamant public outcry in favor of noncommercial broadcasting. That progress in public broadcasting was still so dependent upon capricious political events suggests that nine years after passage of the Public Broadcasting Act of 1967, there remain a number of serious, unresolved issues in the affairs of this noncommercial enterprise. The current state of public broadcasting also suggests that the remaining problems require more explicit and open attention on the part of public broadcasting leaders than has heretofore been evident.

It is the purpose of this essay to examine two of these problems which appear to be not only among the more crucial, but also among the most readily ignored or even actively suppressed:

- The first of these issues is *the relationship of the public broadcasting institution to its audience(s)* — to the publics it claims to serve and whose names it invokes in the struggle for increased funding.

- The other related issue is *the evolving nature of the structural relationships among the national-level organizations* and the degree to which that structure is capable of promoting, or hindering, an improvement in the relationships between public broadcasters and their audiences.

In attempting to examine both of these problems, it will be necessary as well to review a number of other closely related problems, many of which seem to have been tacitly declared off-limits for public debate. Additionally, in light of my analysis of these several issues, it will be a further purpose of the essay to suggest something of the revised thinking and planning necessary on the part of leaders at all levels if public broadcasting is ever going to begin realizing its assertion that it can play a more important role among the nation's various communications services.

Public Broadcasting and Its Publics

As Anthony Smith suggests in the quotation at the beginning of this article, public broadcasting remains largely estranged from any significant portion of the American audience. Our research, still limited for the most part to head counting, shows relatively thin audience attention to and involvement in public broadcast programming. Clearly the "numbers" are up in comparison to attendance levels during the late-1960s, and there is evidence that the amount of viewing and listening by Americans in low-income, low-education and blue-collar categories is larger than is popularly known.[4] But, generally speaking, public broadcasting audiences continue to come disproportionately from the higher socio-economic brackets, though even within that skew the audience members tend to be widely diffused, and there is little evidence of any widespread collective self-awareness.

Eschewing the goal of amassing large audiences at every given moment, public broadcasters have opted for the alternative of reaching a variety of smaller, special-interest audiences, thereby hoping over time to build up a large cumulative following. The conceptual difficulty here is that the image of those audiences remains cast in the traditional mass society mold. The audience totals may well be thought of in smaller terms, but those terms continue to be expressed as numerical grosses. Most public broadcasters assume that their basic decision to work in noncommercial broadcasting is sufficient evidence of more progressive, less exploitative attitudes about audience characteristics and interests. As a result, there is little willingness to examine the suggestion that at its root, the vision carried around in the heads of many public broadcasters remains one of largely undifferentiated audience collectivities.

For too long, researchers, planners and administrators throughout public broadcasting have allowed their images of audiences to be shaped by the simplistic statistical terminology of American public opinion polling and marketing research. Of course, it must be conceded that much of this influence has been fostered by the low-budget exigencies that dictate that public broadcasting research efforts make do with whatever tools and results are readily and cheaply available. Yet we must be sure that we understand the consequences. For, while the standard survey techniques have their place in certain basic descriptive research efforts, the limited demographics and entirely quantitative methodologies of these ratings and effects research models do nothing to break down the basic mass-audience stereotypes that tempt all broadcasters, commercial and public, in all societies.*

One of the unique and major challenges for public broadcasting is precisely the need to develop, and act upon, a substantially new conceptualization of radio and television audiences. Those intending to provide noncommercial programming services must come to see their audiences, not as passive responders to media stimuli, nor even as less passive seekers of some mysterious "uses and gratifications," but as broadly active, intelligent, individuals whose symbol-hungry minds can, and ought to be encouraged to, participate fully in creative dialogues with broadcasting producers and programmers. In seeking a soul and character for itself, in searching for a viable programming philosophy, public broadcasting is thinking unimaginatively — indeed, it is failing — when it merely ratifies the con-

---

*Public broadcasters and their well-meaning research staffs speak often of the need for more qualitative analytical frameworks. Nevertheless, the results are little more than fancy ratings, and they remain locked in one version or another of the traditional effects paradigms — the legacies of a vapid mass-culture theory that have been passed through the quantitative imperatives of behavioral psychology and functionalist sociology.

ceptual framework of traditional mass politics and commercialism.

Given this perspective, it is not surprising to discover that the target audience or building-block concept and its associated programming tactics have had only limited success. Naturally, it can be shown that scattered individuals will demonstrate an intense interest in this or that program or series. But there appears to be no development of a significant sense of community among such viewers or listeners, no mutual self-recognition as noncommercial publics.

Public television, for example, may be reaching about 31 percent of American television households weekly during the autumn, but viewers in half of those households see nothing other than children's programs.[5] Only about 15 percent of all American television households tune in general-audience, prime-time public television programs each week, and even then there are fewer viewers per household for each program (1.5) than there are for commercial television (1.8). Furthermore, only one or two PTV programs are seen by all household members combined during a week. The total adult audience is thus not only small, but highly infrequent in its viewing habits. It would appear to be an aggregate of many smaller audiences whose members view sporadically and who therefore are probably largely unintegrated with one another.

Given the programming implications of the persistent mass-society images in public broadcasting, I am hardly going to argue that the creation of large audience collectivities is an appropriate response to the problem of weak interrelationships between public broadcasters and their audiences. The answer, as I will argue below, will be more appropriately found through an opening of programming policy-making to broader, more effective public input. But, for the moment, it is important to point out here that beyond the obvious debilitating effects on the public broadcasting imagination, the combination of mass-society perspectives and diffused audience-attendance patterns have important but little understood political ramifications. For, in finding themselves perceived as mere aggregates on the one hand, yet in also lacking any sense of unity as local or nationally participating public broadcast audiences on the other, such publics fail to develop any significant sense of responsibility for the structure and services of the noncommercial broadcasting institution. Scattered as audiences, and ignored as potentially active, creative partners in a public communications endeavor, noncommercial broadcasting publics have been and remain unaware of their rights and potentialities in the formulation of policy for the control and funding of the enterprise.

Not surprisingly, many public broadcasting administrators are not overly anxious to change that relationship. Struggling for funds and some measure of long-term stability, and therefore feeling themselves already harassed by a multitude of real or imagined, direct or indirect political pressures, public broadcasting executives will naturally not actively seek the mobilization of large groups of their audience — unless, of course, that energy can be controlled and directed according to the needs of the institution. In many respects, at both the national and local levels, noncommercial broadcasters have remained less than enthusiastic about following through on the obligations incurred in adopting the "public" terminology. All too frequently one senses that the sole significance of invoking the term "public" has been to provide a rhetorical device that allows the leadership to proceed with the acquisition and expenditure of increasing amounts of state and federal tax dollars, while simultaneously diverting attention from the actual quality and range of the service provided.

Boards of directors. At the local level, among those licensees where direct public participation in governance is possible — for example, in stations licensed to community groups or to state authorities — the memberships of the respective boards of directors continue typically to be drawn from the relatively narrow circle of those high in the ranks of business, commercial broadcasting and politics. For example, a 1973 United Church of Christ study of the boards of directors of the licensees in 25 percent of the communities then served by public television found that among the sample (N= 644) only 7.1 percent of the directors represented minority groups and only 13.7 percent were women.[6]

Since this study was weighted toward the 20 largest cities, the majority of the licensees in the sample were community groups. However, it would seem highly unlikely that a higher proportion of the other licensee types would significantly improve the respresentation profile. Additionally, while the study did not analyze occupations, it is reasonable to assume that the poor figures pertaining to ethnic groups and women are symptomatic of the general lack of representation that would be found if one were to conduct a broader analysis of the demographics, occupations and other activities of licensee board members.*

While at the local level, there is seldom any explicit statutory requirement for this situation to be any different, it should be re-

---

*Narrowly based directorates are also a problem — a particularly more complex problem — among most university and school district licensees, where the lack of representation is usually compounded by remoteness. That is, not only do the boards of many school stations lack breadth, their broadcasting operations are buried so far down in the administrative structure that even in those few cases where the boards are more broadly drawn, direct public input through them is virtually impossible.

called that at the national level, at least in terms of the Corporation for Public Broadcasting board, the situation is somewhat different. The 1967 Act required that the CPB board of directors be selected from among those

> ...who are eminent in such fields as education, cultural and civic affairs, or the arts...[providing] a broad representation of various regions of the country, various professions and occupations and various kinds of talent and experience...[7]

Yet a compilation of the findings of two separate studies in 1971 that included analyses of the early CPB board structure leads to the conclusion that two-thirds of the CPB directors were then representatives of industry and the commercial mass media; that there were serious potential conflicts of interest in many of those relationships; that there was a dearth of representatives from different minority groups, the humanities or the arts; and that a premium seemed to be placed on appointments of those with close ties to political figures and institutions in Washington.[8] This highly selective state of CPB representation was glaring enough to serve as one of the bases for a 1971 suit enjoining CPB and PBS from further operations.* In brief, then, there has been some studied concern that, at least so far, the CPB board's membership has come to be so predominantly reflective of closely circumscribed, elite political and economic interests that it violates certainly the spirit, if not the letter, of the 1967 law.

The representativeness issue does not have the same strictly legal implications for local licensees as it does for CPB (with the exception of certain state authority statutory provisions). It does, however, have important consequences. At the very least, it raises a serious question about how well local stations can be said to be oriented toward broad-ranging, substantive community service. If stations are licensed to boards — be they university trustees, non-profit community groups, local school boards, or independent state commissions — whose memberships continue to resemble those well-heeled and well-connected members of the clubs who meet in private, commercial board rooms, critics will correctly continue to raise doubts about the potential of public broadcasting to proceed with a full range of service, including the controversial and unpopular.

Given the changing organizational structure of the national

---

*The suit, initiated by the Network Project, was originally filed in New York. Its venue was subsequently changed to Washington, D.C., where several motions for dismissal by CPB *et al.* were granted (398 F.Supp. 1332 [1975]).

public television establishment (of which, more below), the problem of representativeness in local station governance is magnified. Since the Public Broadcasting Service corporate body is now dominated by a board of governors that is made up of members elected from among representatives of the local station boards of directors, any distortions in the local governing profile are necessarily ratified and extended at the national level. This situation is even further exacerbated by an uncompetitive election process that permits a nominating committee of the then-existing board of governors to select the slate of nominees and to insure that the number on that slate is no larger than the number of vacancies to be filled.

Obviously, public broadcasting at all levels needs directors with useful political and economic ties. Naivete in this regard would be dangerous. Indeed, as we shall see shortly, such ties and capacity among the PBS governors played a crucial role in the 1973 preservation of a certain degree of PBS independence. But in leaning largely on the generals of industry, politics, military, high culture, and commercial mass entertainment, public broadcasters have allowed the range of policy options throughout the institution to become subtly and severely constrained. We need to ask how long it will be before public broadcasting governance structures begin to open themselves up to substantial inclusion of other Americans: elementary or high school teachers, assembly-line laborers, clerks, students, career enlisted military personnel, Indians, working farmers, nurses, small-businessmen or low-income housewives.

Public feedback. The problem of representativeness can be cast in terms broader than the issue of board structures. For even in the more informal program and policy advisory groups available to national and local public broadcasting agencies, the tendency has been either to ignore such potential sources of feedback or to manipulate them to the self-serving needs of the agency. The experience of the Advisory Council of National Organizations is a case in point. Ostensibly designed in part to help guide CPB policy deliberations by representing the interests of a wide vareity of American organizations, ACNO has found itself appreciated by the CPB board and staff primarily for its lobbying efforts on behalf of funding bills or for its mere symbolic role as a means by which CPB can purport to demonstrate diverse public involvement in its affairs.*

---

*Unfortunately, even at this surface level of significance, it remains doubtful that this Council is adequately constituted to be considered representative of the public at large. While the ACNO membership consists of many diverse groups; those bodies are by definition formal associations whose Washington officials are expected to plead on behalf of their own special interest groups before Congress and the Executive. The pool of potential representatives for this Council is not nearly as broad as it might be if its role was seen more as advisory and less as politically convenient.

Locally, all too few stations can point to any honest, consistent efforts to create panels of citizenry with a substantial role in program and policy decision-making. The criterion for membership in the so-called "Friends" groups is a willingness to provide direct financial support to the stations. As a result, the profiles of public broadcasting "Friends" tend to reflect the interests of wealth, high culture, and commercial power. Even in those few cases where such groups are more broadly representative of the community, they are deemed useful only to the extent that they provide a steady source of income, substantial amounts of free labor for publicity and station clerical work, and additional local political influence.

ACNO and "Friends" groups have been and can continue to be helpful to individual stations and to the system at-large. However, their present constituencies do not provide a reasonable basis to expect that they alone will be useful in the agenda-setting functions which are needed in public broadcasting. It is incumbent upon governors and professionals at all levels to stop just talking about the need for increased public participation. The public broadcasting leadership must create opportunities for the public to move into more active, continuous roles in a wide range of matters.

Feedback cannot be thought of as being adequately or sufficiently provided through increased research and ascertainment efforts. Such work ought instead to be considered as the starting point from which public telecommunications agencies can move on to develop better public ties. Public broadcasters need to ask themselves when the rhetoric of being "on the people's business" will give way not only to the conscientious development of substantial diversity in public broadcasting governance, but also to the active involvement of broad cross-sections of the citizenry in program and policy advisory councils which will have guaranteed, significant functions in local and national schedule building and in general policy determination.

In fairness to the many conscientious public broadcasters, much of their difficulty in defining the role of the American public in its communications systems stems from a long history of public indifference to, and active political avoidance of, efforts to promote conscious, widely debated communications policy. The libertarian and free-enterprise assumptions dominating governmental decision-making about press control and telecommunications development during the nineteenth and early twentieth centuries provided little foundation for erecting much of a noncommercial structure in America during broadcasting's initial decades. It was not until the passage of the 1962 ETV Facilities Act and then, of course, the 1967 act, that federal policy could be said to have made a significant shift in assumptions about the public role in telecommunications.

The Future of Public Broadcasting

Yet even now, it remains questionable whether the changes during the past decade have had much to do with the articulation of general public interests and demand. A close reading of noncommercial broadcasting's history reveals that most of the major strides — the reservation of channels, the securing of federal funds, the establishment of a quasi-independent national agency — all stem from the efforts of a relatively small handful of far-sighted educators, professionals, legislators, and regulators. The motivating force did not come from any strong, broadly based groundswell of general public concern. Whatever the reasons, it would be difficult to argue that public broadcasting has succeeded, through either its expressions of mission or the content of its programming, in establishing itself firmly in the affections and conscious concerns of substantial portions of the American public.

The Fiscal Constraints on
the Development of Public Broadcasting

A criticism of the quality of the vision, drive and breadth of much of the public broadcasting leadership is implicit in this argument about the lack of clear public interest in noncommercial broadcasting and the associated lack of overt efforts to encourage that interest and participation. I will spend the balance of this paper examining certain recent structural changes at the national level which appear to exacerbate what Les Brown sees as the emergence of public broadcasting as "a name without a concept."[9] But, first, I think it is important to outline briefly the handicaps under which the public broadcasting leadership has been working since 1967. One may well tend to agree with Brown, Smith, Paul Duke and others that public broadcast programming policy remains overly cautious.[10] Nonetheless, the critics must be certain that they understand the realities with which the professionals and governors have had to grapple in recent years.

There can be little argument that noncommercial broadcasting today is hardly close to being the modern American Lyceum and Chautauqua envisioned by E. B. White and the Carnegie Commission. Yet, many of the Carnegie recommendations, plus a number of important additional developments, have been successfully initiated in spite of the federal failure to provide the funding levels upon which those recommendations were based. Much criticism too quickly overlooks or dismisses these successes, which are clear testimony to a certain core strength and persistent potential of noncommercial radio and television. Part of this critical pessimism derives from the unwillingness of many observers of public broadcasting, of whatever ideological stripe, to acknowledge the consequences of the final terms that shaped the 1967 act. For in leaving out of the legislation the long-range financing provision proposed by the Carnegie Commission, Congress wrote what was, in fact, only half an act. As a result, the criteria for evaluating the progress of the system in the interim have to be adjusted accordingly.

It has been somewhat disingenuous of recent critics to claim that the public broadcasting experiment has failed when it was not until 1975, during the eighth year after the passage of the act, that federal funds for CPB ($62 million) reached the levels proposed by the Carnegie Commission for the Corporation's second year.* Moreover, in denying insulation for those funds that were made available, Congress and the White House thoroughly invalidated the conditions of the experiment. By reducing CPB to the annual authorization and appropriation treadmill, the lawmakers virtually guaranteed that the kind of political pressure exercised by the Nixon administration would manifest itself. Under such conditions, it is highly likely that Presidential interference in CPB affairs would have developed, regardless of who the White House occupant happened to be.

These defensive remarks aside, there remains a certain lingering veracity to the criticism of public broadcasting's general timidity. No matter how justified the funding complaint of public broadcasters, their lament does not quite parry the thrust of the contention that, during their seemingly endless pursuit of long-range funding, public broadcasting leaders have been carefully avoiding controversy by putting off the boldest productions, particularly in public affairs. Sensitive to this criticism of an apparent *quid pro quo*, many public broadcasters have endeavored to convince themselves that one of the great benefits of the new bill, even as now diluted, is that such extreme caution will no longer be necessary. There has been a general feeling that with at least some degree of insulation, many programming shackles will fall away. (I will argue later that this optimism ignores several crucial points about the bill.)

Even without the bill, however, public broadcasters could be fashioning a new and more productive relationship with the audiences they seek to serve. That they are not, and why they are not, may be understood more clearly by examining the emerging relationships among the major national public broadcasting organizations.

---

*In an important sense, of course, that parity with the recommendations for the second year was still unachieved. For, given the ravages of inflation during the interim, federal appropriations in FY 1975 of $62 million bought far less talent, programming, equipment and operating hours than $60 million would have during FY 1969. Furthermore, the Carnegie recommendations were in reference solely to television. Current CPB appropriations must be divided among both television and radio.

The Future of Public Broadcasting

To initiate discussion of this issue, it is necessary to begin by reviewing a little recent history. Many of the details in the following account are, of course, well-known to members of the public broadcasting community. In fact, many professionals and governors would prefer to forget them. But, because it is upon just that shortness of memory that many of the current myths are being built, it is important for us to reconsider them here, no matter how much the current fashion of national-level "partnership" pretends that they can be ignored.

Developments between 1971 and 1972. The public broadcasting phase of the Nixon Administration attack on most national channels of news and public affairs began with the Whitehead speech at the 1971 NAEB Convention in Miami. Refusing to make any positive proposals for a long-range funding bill of its own, the White House used that speech to begin a period of sniping that culminated in the in the June 1972 decision by the President to veto a two-year authorization bill that Congress had just passed for a total of $165 million.[11]

That administration action was more than a gentle rap on the knuckles. Indeed, it may well be characterized as a determined lunge for the jugular. For the bill in question had been part of a quiet effort by Congress to step up CPB funding to levels more appropriately in line with the original Carnegie recommendations. All planning for the still growing and testing efforts of CPB, PBS and NPR had been based upon the assumption that something close to those new higher levels would be available. Suddenly, as a result of the veto, the national agencies, and therefore the stations as well, had to begin making drastic cuts in their extensive plans for new programming and increased hours of service. Not only that, they now had to scramble frantically to be sure that during fiscal year 1973 they would be permitted to receive the level of funds that had been made available for 1972 ($35 million).

The CPB floundered in the wake of the veto. Frank Pace, the Johnson Administration appointee as first CPB board chairman, resigned his chairmanship, and most of the top staff of the Corporation left rapidly thereafter.[12] To help reach an accord with the White House, the CPB board elected as its new chairman Thomas Curtis, a conservative former Republican Congressman from St. Louis. The restaffing of CPB then commenced with the election to the presidency of a former deputy director of USIA, Henry Loomis, and the subsequent appointment of other men with similar USIA, civil service, or advertising agency backgrounds. Suddenly, in

120

a relatively short period of time, the Nixon Administration had humbled the Corporation board, it had found the pressure points necessary to recast the CPB leadership more in the administration's own image, and it had forced CPB policy to begin turning in directions much more to its liking.

The most immediate effect of the policy change was the Corporation's decision during the latter half of 1972 to take over from PBS the program planning and scheduling process of the national public television interconnection. PBS was to be relegated purely to a technical distribution role.

The White House and OTP attack on CPB had centered on the growth of public affairs programming to roughly one-third of the PBS schedule, most of which was being carried simultaneously by the stations on a regularly scheduled basis. In order to appease these and other objections, CPB opted initially to restructure the national PTV system in a way that would reduce the opportunity for the stations to continue participating in the use of the interconnection in such a standard, and powerful, networking pattern. In calling as well for a lessening of public affairs hours and an increased library-like use of the interconnection, the new CPB policy was rooting itself in the OTP-inspired rhetoric about the need to "return to localism" — a theme which Dr. Whitehead had helped to make the cornerstone of the Nixon assault.

On the other hand, it was becoming clear to many inside the public broadcasting community that despite the CPB claims to be promoting greater decentralization, the Corporation was actually engineering a national system which under its tight, direct control, would be much more centralized and politically vulnerable than the then- existing structure. It also quickly became apparent that both the White House and CPB were gratuitously ignoring the financial shortfall that had been faced by the system and were not accounting for the fact that the operational structure of the interconnection had been shaped by the subsequent economic accommodations that had to be worked out between PBS and the stations.

In other words, the myth of an overly centralized interconnection structure was fostered by the OTP and CPB, despite the knowledge that the stations had not been receiving the amounts of federal funds which the Carnegie Commission had recognized as necessary for the full-blown (and expensive) operation of a program-scheduling process providing nearly complete local self-determination. As a consequence of the fiscal constraints, the stations had authorized PBS to establish a pattern of program distribution, including a large amount of repeat transmission, that was designed to meet the scheduling needs of as many stations as possible. In fact, far from demonstrating the commercial network affiliate pattern of accepting simultaneously well over 90 percent of network-fed hours, PBS member stations were taking simultaneously only about two-thirds of all PBS-distributed programs.*

Another myth was the image of public broadcasters as head-strong liberals determined to saturate the airways with biased public affairs programming. The fact is the vast majority of station managers had read the Carnegie recommendations very carefully and understood that a major part of their mandate as public broadcasters was the provision of a large volume of strong public affairs programming. In making this category of programming a predominant part of the total interconnection schedule, PBS was merely carrying out the clearly expressed goals of the Carnegie Commission, of the 1967 act, and of most the PBS member stations.

Yet another myth — the so-called overly centralized, networking activities of PBS — was fostered by a convenient ignoring of the fact that the PBS board of directors at the time was made up predominantly of local station managers. The rest of that board, variously 25-30 percent, was elected by the station board members from the public at large. Additionally, many of the attacks on the centralized structure chose to omit references to the manner in which the station-directed PBS staff operated the national program service. For, although nearly all PBS funding and most national program underwriting then came directly from or through CPB, the program decision-making process was carried out by PBS in a manner that relied heavily on an elaborate system of station manager and program director feedback and evaluation.†

However, since even this relatively decentralized system left CPB with a powerful veto authority, the stations were already working on plans for a further increase in the amount of control

---

*From 1970 to 1974, PBS kept detailed weekly records of the carriage of its programs by member stations. Review of any of the monthly "Program Carriage Reports" distributed by PBS to the stations during this period will show a fairly consistent overall live carriage pattern of 60-70 percent. When all repeat transmissions of the primary PBS service and the distribution of extra or library programming is included, the amount of station live carriage of all hours of PBS transmission drops to below 50 percent.

†Working with the several elements of this evaluation process — activities that also included audience data and program carriage analyses, station surveys, close consultation with the producers, analyses of press coverage and evaluation by expert outside advisory groups — the stations, through PBS, had been responsible for taking the lead in developing long-range programming profiles. As the chief funder, CPB had, of course, also been consulted and involved at each step along the way. But the initiative had lain largely with the PBS staff, as advised by the stations. The PBS staff recommendations were then forwarded to the PBS board, that is, to a group dominated by elected station managers. After review at this level, the recommendations were passed on to the CPB board for approval.

exercised by the local stations. In authorizing the PBS staff to propose the establishment of a program-marketing procedure — a version of which later came to be known as the Station Program Cooperative — the stations were in part acknowledging the problem of CPB political sensitivity. They were also searching for a process that would guarantee a maximum check on the ability of CPB to influence the content of the national program service.

The cooperative proposal essentially called upon CPB to give up to the stations most of that portion of its budget which was held for national programming.[13] Instead of expending those funds directly, CPB would distribute the programming money to the stations in the form of larger community service grants. The stations in turn would pool those funds through a bidding and contract procedure which they would administer through their own agency, PBS. With these changes, the only centralized fiscal control remaining for the network would be in the amount of money CPB would continue to pay to PBS for the technical operations of the interconnection. In sum, at the very time that the White House was criticizing public television for being overly centralized, this infant system, struggling under severe financial constraints it had never been intended to bear, was in fact developing a unique system that tempered the economically necessary centralization of certain technical-distribution processes with a heavy decentralization for program policy-making. Under the pressures of extremely limited resources, public broadcasters had cooperated in achieving a national-local balance that was far more responsive to the Carnegie recommendations and to the terms of the 1967 act than the White House chose to acknowledge. Although mistakes were made and a measure of hesitancy necessarily crept in, the stations had begun to discover that there need be no irremedial incompatibility between local control and a reasonably strong national service.* Even prior to the initiation of the cooperative in 1973, the amount of station control over the policies and the product of the network was at least as great as that of any national broadcasting system in the world and clearly far greater than that of American commercial television.

In this light, it is now clear that at its core the localism issue raised by the White House was spurious. However, because the

---

*The automatic assumption by many "East Coast" critics of public broadcasting that caution is a function primarily of local control usually ignores the realities of the continuing fiscal uncertainty in the institution. Except when CPB makes a decision that offends the differing ideologies of these critics, they generally fail to comprehend the political vulnerability of the centralized public broadcasting organization. There is among such critics a great deal of silly and over-romantic idealization of the efficacy of centralization in public broadcasting.[14]

Congresses during the 1971-73 period would take no initiative in regard to public broadcasting legislation, choosing instead to defer consistently to the White House, OTP held the cards. Given CPB's control of most of the national service purse, and the influence of OTP on the Congressional attitude toward that purse, the issue came to be defined to suit the joint OTP-CPB interests.* The PBS board attempted to inject itself into CPB deliberations, but after a series of rebuffs by the CPB board, it became all too evident that, under their organizational structure, the PBS directors lacked the political muscle necessary to secure continued hearings before the CPB board. In addition, the stations themselves were still rent by a number of internal disputes — notes of disharmony which added to the directionless image of public broadcasting and played directly into the hands of the OTP and CPB.†

Given this atomization of station opinion and the inability of the managers to secure a hearing before the reorganized CPB board, the stations found that they were going to have to erect a more powerful leadership structure if they hoped to turn aside the effects of CPB-White House collusion. The most effective solution appeared to be in granting legitimacy to the efforts of an ad hoc group of representatives from many station boards of directors around the country. This group, the National Coordinating Committee for Governing Board Chairmen, led by Texas industrialist Ralph Rogers, consisted predominantly of individuals who were chairmen of local community station licensee boards. Operating through the power of their strong ties to local financial, cultural and political institutions, and representing a broader power base than the CPB board, this council of so-called "lay representatives" was able during the winter of 1972-73 to demonstrate to the station managers that it had the political clout necessary to gain that attention from the CPB board.†† The new group soon forced the White House to realize

---

*Beyond all this, there was also the general problem that between 1968 and 1973, many CPB board members — whatever their views in the public broadcasting controversy — nonetheless enjoyed being seen around the White House. They had not yet come to understand the degree of integrity and autonomy required of them as directors of a non-governmental, public communications corporation.

†These disputes included the debate about differences implied in "public" as opposed to "educational" broadcasting, the bitterness associated with the transfer of networking from NET to PBS, and the jealousies involved in attempts to define the proper role and relationship to PBS of the older Educational Television Stations (ETS) division of the NAEB.

††The somewhat euphemistic term, "lay person," was ostensibly designed to serve as a way of differentiating those who, as local station governors, served in a voluntary capacity from those who, as professionals, earned their living from work in public broadcasting. However, the term also served to connote that image of broad public input and representativeness which, while successfully projected in negotiations with CPB and Congress, nonetheless overstated the actual public breadth among the licensee directorates.

that at the higher level of their boards, the local licensees were not without the means of creating a Congressional stir about the OTP-CPB effort to circumvent the stations.

Meanwhile, other political factors had begun to affect White House strategies. For one thing, in spite of the size of Mr. Nixon's majority in the 1972 Presidential election, the Administration was becoming increasingly aware of how heavy a price it was going to have to pay for its failure to work more diligently for the Republican Congressional candidates that year. With the reduced GOP minority in both houses and a bitter sense of betrayal among important elements of that remnant, Executive branch legislative proposals were running into stiffer Congressional opposition. Moreover, with the increasingly dangerous pressures being generated by the Watergate revelations (in part supplied, ironically, by full PBS and NPR coverage of the Senate Select Committee hearings), the Administration hardly needed further criticism from within its own ranks on such an issue as public broadcasting, with all its overtones of governmental control of opinion and suppression of free expression. Aware of the added opprobrium it would generate with further efforts to contain public broadcasting and fearful that the issue might become a partisan one, the White House began to pay more attention to the new voice from within the public broadcasting fraternity, and the word soon passed to CPB to begin negotiations with these local licensee representatives.

An immediate consequence of this shift in attention to the licensee board members was to encourage a corporate restructuring of PBS that subordinated the old board, the managers, to a super board of governors made up of those "lay" representatives. By the spring of 1973, the stations had agreed to this formal change in the PBS governing structure.* No longer an ad hoc group, the new Board of Governors now held the legal authority over PBS operations. In creating this dual board structure in PBS, the stations were able to end the earlier quibbling about whether or not the previous organizational structure had been adequately station-controlled. They were now capable of calling the OTP-CPB bluff. Here, they said, was a sincere station response to the charges of a lack of local community control over the affairs of the network. No longer could the White House and the CPB board pretend that the network was out of the hands of the stations. Nor could they continue to claim

---

*The restructuring also brought ETS into the "new PBS," presumably unifying the station lobbying efforts at the national level. (See *ETV Newsletter*, April 2, 1973 for reorganization details.) The NAEB, divesting itself of control by institutional divisions, now became an association of individual professional members.

they did not know with whom they were dealing.

At least two major results were rapidly achieved either directly or indirectly by this political maneuvering of the stations. One, CPB called a halt, at least temporarily, to its attempt to take over the total national service programming function in PTV. It agreed instead to allow the stations to formulate a compromise — the so-called "partnership" agreement[15] — that would clarify the respective CPB and PBS roles and preserve a certain autonomy in the station organization.*

Two, OTP was forced to begin work on the long-range financing plan. Faced with what now appeared to be a more unified public broadcasting industry, as well as a politically more adept segment of it, OTP found that it could no longer stall by pretending that there was not a clear institutional structure with which it could negotiate.

Whereas in the past CPB had largely contributed to its own undermining by failing to push openly and explicitly for a long-range financing bill, the CPB board under Dr. Killian's leadership now quickly moved to stiffen its posture relative to this issue. Using the machinery of a pre-existing special board committee (the Long Range Financing Task Force) that had been sputtering along without much effect during the preceding period of political uncertainty, the new board leadership re-endorsed the Task Force mandate and energized its effeorts to develop a firm funding proposal. Inviting the new PBS governors to participate in this process, CPB served notice that at least for the present the White House could no longer count on CPB to avoid pressing for a solution to this pivotal problem. Given the other difficulties then facing the Administration, it too found that continued confrontation was likely to prove counterproductive to its own interests, and it therefore authorized OTP to sit down with CPB and the station representatives to begin drafting

*This occurred, however, only after CPB itself went through one more leadership catharsis and faced a final showdown with the stations. The crisis began during the winter of 1973, when chairman Curtis and a committee of the CPB board were engaged in compromise negotiations with the then ad hoc Coordinating Committee of the licensees. Those negotiations were designed to culminate in an agreement that was to be ratified by CPB shortly after the March 30, 1973, reorganization of PBS. However, a band of hardliners within the CPB Board still insisted on absorbing the interconnection programming function, and they put together a majority which on April 13 voted against their chairman to reject the compromise. Within a week, Mr. Curtis, having served as chairman for only eight months, resigned from the board and triggered wide-spread reports that several of his fellow members on the CPB board had actually been operating on direct instructions from the White House.[16] Apparently embarrassed by the allegations about the way it was continuing to be manipulated by the Administration, and unprepared for the subsequently harsh reactions of the newly reorganized station organization, CPB began to reconsider its precipitous actions. In May, the board elected Dr. James Killian, former chairman of the Carnegie Commission, as chairman of the CPB. In elevating Dr. Killian, who had been one of the leaders among the moderates, CPB was signaling both the White House and the stations that it had had enough of the direct confrontation.

the long-range bill. The bill placed before the 93rd Congress during its last session, and the much-changed version which was finally passed by the 94th, were the result of that collaboration.*

1974-76 and the long-range financing bill. It has been the official public broadcasting position to hail the Public Broadcasting Act of 1975 as a significant forward step. Indeed, it has become the fashion to argue that the White House-inspired actions of CPB during 1972-73, the stations' reorganization of PBS, and the two organizations' declaration of partnership in 1973 were all necessary and worthwhile in the effort to achieve passage of this measure. Between 1973 and 1976, serious discussions of the many issues that plagued public broadcasting were frequently superseded by appeals to unify behind the pending long-range financing legislation. Debates during this period seemed to pretend that such problems as that of public involvement were somehow not real — or, in the few instances when they were understood as real, that passage of this legislation was the direct path to their solution. Yet, given the problems raised in this essay, and in light of the actual provisions of the bill, one may legitimately question the validity of these popular rationalizations.

It is not my intention to argue that the financing bill is entirely without value. Perhaps its passage has given public broadcasting some badly needed breathing space in which to tackle other problems. But it must be recognized that both as originally conceived and as finally passed, the bill had and still retains serious limitations and drawbacks that are seldom acknowledged by its supporters.

To begin with, the public broadcasting leadership and its White House and congressional supporters have been unsuccessful in preserving the crucial feature of combined, full-term authorization and appropriation (the cornerstone of the original OTP and CPB versions of the bill). During the bill's progress through Congress, the House Appropriations Committee agreed that the authorizations could be provided as a block for the full five-year period, but the committee insisted that, as in the past, the appropriations must be provided in separate legislation. It finally forced

---

*In its recommendations, the CPB Long Range Task Force asked for a five-year combined authorization and appropriation measure with a ceiling beginning at $100 million the first year (FY 1976), moving up to $200 million in the fifth (FY 1980) — all geared to a formula that would provide $1 in federal funds for every $2 raised by public broadcasting. OTP countered with a recommendation ranging from $70 million in FY 1976 to $100 million in FY 1980, based on a $1:$2.50 matching ratio. The Senate and House each offered additional versions. In the end, the Public Broadcasting Act of 1975 was a House-dominated compromise. It eliminated the simultaneous appropriation feature, and it provided an authorization starting at $88 million and rising to $160 million, though still based on the $1:$2.50 formula.

the bill's sponsors to delete the combined appropriations provision.*

Secondly, the bill includes a stipulation that the CPB board members and officers be available each year to testify before the appropriate congressional committees about any matters determined by those committees. This requirement is ominously similar to the oversight proceedings imposed on governmental agencies. It also adds yet another bureaucratic burden (the CPB is already required to file an annual report with the President). These two points demonstrate that Congress remains reluctant to acknowledge that publicly supported broadcasting must be considered unique among all those social and cultural programs receiving federal aid. In maintaining a separate appropriations process and in establishing an annual CPB testimony requirement, Congress is continuing to undermine a key feature of the Carnegie recommendations and the 1967 act, namely that CPB must neither be, nor be treated as, a governmental body.

Thirdly, even in its original form, the bill was, and remains, hardly long-range. Its five-year provision is, at best, medium-range. No sooner has the bill been passed than it has become incumbent upon public broadcasters to begin a campaign to insure its later renewal. To be successful, of course, that campaign will have to demonstrate evidence of "responsibility" in public broadcast programming, and the implications of that requirement are all too clear.

Fourthly, the bill's mechanism for drawing on federal funds is not thoroughly enough insulated. Admittedly better than the annual or biennial authorization process used heretofore, the five-year matching grant provision of the 1975 act still contemplates using general treasury funds, not a dedicated tax, for the appropriations.

It has been argued that the matching formula reduces the political vulnerability of the funding process by guaranteeing that a predetermined federal subsidy will automatically be made available. Up to a certain maximum, the only restriction on the federal total will be the limitations represented by whatever amounts are raised by the licensees and national organizations from all other sources.[17] The problem here is that both Congress and the White House still retain discretion over the terms of that formula. General

---

*The Committee has indicated a willingness to provide up to three of the five years of appropriations as a block. But even if this provision emerges in the subsequent appropriations legislation, it appears that the remaining two years will have to be sought in separate measures. Additionally, of course, a congressional promise is not always a guarantee, and even the three-year block of appropriations could ultimately be denied CPB or used to extract further concessions. Moreover, as public broadcasters know from painful past experience, the amount of funding authorized is not necessarily the amount finally realized in the appropriations process. CPB might end up with far less than the ceilings contemplated in the 1975 act.

authorizations are the easiest to rescind, and, even though a given ratio of federal-to-other sources will be promised for a multi-year block, the fact remains that a new authorization has to be provided at the end of that period. With no dedicated funding source available, public broadcasting producers and programmers are going to continue to find themselves susceptible to a great deal of internal and external pressure to be circumspect and noncontroversial.

Modeling the matching formula authorization process on aspects of the public assistance and Medicare programs, most proponents of this system are assuming that somehow public broadcasting will remain as sheltered from the day-to-day political winds as those other programs are presumed to be. Without dwelling on the question of the putative invulnerability of the other matching formula arrangements, it is sufficient, and more important, to suggest that the assumption of adequate shelter ignores the unique political visibility of the public broadcasting enterprise.

All in all, the 1975 authorization bill and the economic theories underlying it are probably most notable for their reaffirmation of the general socio-economic and political context in which American telecommunications policy-making has traditionally been set. Given that any broadcasting system in a society requires a certain degree of governmental regulation, and given that politicians have certain basic needs for and fears of broadcasting, it is clear that any form of broadcasting is more vulnerable to political manipulation than almost any other social institution. As the recipient of governmental funds in a society that has traditionally associated free enterprise economics with allegedly maximum guarantees of free speech and press, a public broadcasting system is even more subject to attacks on its autonomy.

There are two other considerations in this regard. One is that serious conflicts of interest persist among public broadcasting directorates *vis-a-vis* the dominant commercial broadcasting, telecommunications, and press systems.* The other is that in the American

---

*Given the particular character of the power structure represented on public broadcasting boards of directors, it ought to be apparent why those boards choose not to push for more thoroughly insulated and long-range financing. For one thing, to the degree that truly insulated funding depends upon the implementation of such proposed taxes as those on receiver sales, on commercial broadcasting licenses, or on common carrier or commercial broadcaster revenues, those on the various public broadcasting boards who have direct or indirect financial interests in such affected industries are hardly likely to support such proposals. For another thing, if greater insulation were achieved, public broadcasting might emerge with sufficient strength to allow aspects of it to become a consistent source of controversy and challenge to various elements of the nation's dominant political, economic and cultural forces. Finally, that same protection and strength might encourage public broadcasters to develop the type of attractive, broad-ranging programming, that, without sacrificing quality and educative value, could well begin to undermine the mass audience structure supporting commercial broadcasting.

environment, issues of accountability and control assume major importance in the strategies of Congressmen and Presidents as they jockey with one another over decisions about how to apportion the public purse. Therefore, with a limited-duration, limited-insulation general treasury authorization as their sole major federal funding source, public broadcasters are going to have to be so careful in their self-control that a restrictive pattern of programming is virtually ensured — a consequence that is not in the best public interest.

Other current problems. Clearly, the financing bill's drawbacks are serious, and they carry the potential of restimulating overt political manipulation of public broadcasting when the bill comes up for renewal or change as well as during the intervening period when appropriations will be sought. But there are additional consequences which may take effect at any time and which in a long-term sense may be more serious. It is to help create an understanding of these consequences that this long discussion of recent PTV history has been necessary.

One of the conditions of establishing the ceasefire with CPB was PBS's agreement to accept the terms of a compromise or "partnership" declaration that was adopted in May 1973. On the surface, the partnership agreement was designed to provide the image of unity necessary to impress Congress that public broadcasting was going to cease continuing to explode into a messy political issue. However it also had the effect of formally ratifying for the first time an open, substantial role for CPB in program policymaking, and it may well be that one of the most serious structural weaknesses of noncommercial broadcasting now lies in this provision. For, while CPB permitted PBS to continue the day-to-day work of scheduling, and while it even allowed the network to initiate the program cooperative, CPB nonetheless reserved for itself what ultimately is the much more important role of long-range program planning.

As we have seen, it had been the CPB goal during the 1972-73 takeover attempt to shift to itself most of the detailed planning and scheduling operations, leaving PBS with primarily technical functions. Although the direct takeover bid faltered, CPB found that the new PBS board of governors was not as clear about is own goals as CPB itself was. While the backgrounds of many of the governors had prepared them for the Byzantine politics of national level public broadcasting, some of these new board members remained uncertain about how broadly they should insist on defining the functions of the interconnection service. Thus, ignoring the recent excesses of their Presidentially appointed counterparts at CPB, the PBS governors apparently decided that under the terms of the 1967 act and the new professions of CPB good will, there was a degree of legitimacy in the CPB claim for a direct role in programming. Still relatively naive about the subtle power patterns at work in program development, the PBS governors were willing to concede to CPB a formal program-planning function if CPB would cease questioning PBS's right to its own programming department and reaffirm the essential role in the national service of public affairs programming.

The stations were also agreeable to the CPB proposal. They had been considering the initiation of the program cooperative any-way, and given their assumptions about how thoroughly the coop-erative mechanism would reserve for them the vast bulk of the details involving the program planning and scheduling process, the stations could not conceive of the partnership terms representing any serious threat to their increased control. To allow CPB to proceed with long-range piloting and planning, particularly when such work was to be coordinated with the PBS program staff, appeared to be a small price to pay for the peace supposedly being established by the part-nership agreement.

However, the stations and the PBS boards have failed to recog-nize at least two important operational implications of this agree-ment. The first problem is that in acceding to the Corporation's de-mand for an increased formal programming role, the stations have al-lowed the Washington-based programming process to become vastly more complex and debilitating. Under the terms of the partnership, CPB has been permitted not only to greatly expand the size of its programming staff, but also to draw the PBS programmers into an inordinately detailed program-planning and review system. That is, aspects of the national programming service now require the kind of complex, inter-institutional bureaucratic negotiation process that can thoroughly sap the vitality, imagination and daring that otherwise might have become the hallmarks of contemporary public television.

The second implication of the agreement is that CPB's control of program pilot and development funds ultimately gives it the upper hand in defining the eventual scope, character and content of the na-tional public television service. For in reserving for itself the right to commit substantial pilot funds in a given year, CPB strongly shapes the range of program options that will be available to the cooperative two or three years later. Operating the cooperative under the terms of a free market model, the stations proceed on the assumption that their bidding and competitive procedures will make available the best and most necessary national program offerings. However, what the stations ignore in relying so heavily on the cooperative concept is that through its long-term development work, the Corporation

131

has the time and freedom to begin, well in advance, a subtle molding of the choices that will be available in upcoming station bidding rounds. No matter how elaborate the provisions for consultation between the staffs of the two organizations, the reality remains that the different masters served by those staffs dictate substantially different programming priorities.

In his farewell address to a joint meeting of the CPB and PBS boards, retiring CPB chairman Killian correctly pointed out part of this continuing fact of life by noting the different immediate responsibilities and constituencies of the two organizations.[18] Under the law, the Corporation is accountable to the Congress and the people for those aspects of public broadcasting which its use of federal funds affects. PBS has no such centralized, federal accountability. Its constituency is the collectivity of the stations, with all their differing organizational structures and community needs.

Where Dr. Killian would appear to err, however, is in his contention that the struggle for power between these organizations can be down-played; for a persistent reality in public broadcasting is that the different terms of accountability *do* imply different and often contradictory priorities for the exercise of power. A review of noncommercial broadcasting history will suggest that what is at stake here (just as it was two decades ago during the early days of NET) is the issue of the distribution of programming power between national and local interests. To pretend that one can, or should, paper over the differences between these powerfully opposing forces in a partnership agreement is to ignore the reality of a fundamental tension in public broadcasting.

Nor is the problem of power limited to the national-local dichotomy. It also includes the needs, rights and responsibilities of such other interests as the regions, radio, regulatory bodies, legislatures, executive branches, producers and, of course, a multitude of publics. Since the initiation of federal funding for noncommercial broadcasting, the tensions among these different power centers have inevitably become even more acute. While at any given moment (e.g., during the recent effort to secure the longer range funding legislation) it may be politically advantageous to de-emphasize the conflicting goals of such organizations as CPB and PBS, it is unduly wishful and finally dangerous to imagine that the substantially different power roles and objectives of the separate organizations and constituencies can be forgotten or suppressed for any length of time.

In terms of the specific issue of program development, no one denies the necessity of program piloting for the national service. This process and the requisite supportive research have too long been delayed in public broadcasting. But the stations must come to realize the implications for them of leaving these activities predominantly in the hands of the Corporation. In spite of all the fine rhetoric about partnership, the stations have given up the most important, pace-setting phase of the complex program development procedures. As a result of the 1973 compromise, CPB has been able to take over from the interconnection service most of the initiative for national program policy-making.

In any case, one may argue that the partnership has failed its first major political test. The stations were coerced into the PBS reorganization and the CPB partnership agreement with the promise that such compromises, by substantiating the claim of unity and consensus at the national level, would guarantee delivery of an acceptable long-range financing bill. But in spite of all this maneuvering and rationalization, it is clear that the image of length and permanence associated with the bill is essentially false. In the cold, hard light of morning, this financing measure is a pale reflection of what the Carnegie Commission had in mind when it called for the establishment of a dedicated tax trust fund.

The licensees and their audiences might well begin to inquire whether all the restructuring and compromises made on behalf of the bill's passage were worth what little has, in fact, been achieved. Many will conclude that, all the station machinations notwithstanding, CPB has been allowed to achieve the essential elements of the goal it had set its sights on after the 1971-72 White House assault and the subsequent CPB board and staff shake-up in 1972. What is more, CPB has been able to accomplish this openly and with station approval. The partnership agreement has allowed the Corporation to give the appearance of graciously disengaging from its initial, all-too-obvious and unattractive battle for outright annexation of PBS staff functions. But while the bloody frontal assault, with all its attendant bad press, has been abandoned, a fierce rear-guard action has been pursued and CPB has used the terms of the partnership to secure for itself effective control of the character of the national service.

While arguing that the issue of control and power is still very much with us, I intend no implicit suggestion here that a certain degree of centralized program decision-making leadership in public broadcasting is unnecessary. Purely democratic and marketing-based selection techniques will not provide for all the courage, zest, and experimentation that is necessary if public broadcasting is ever to stake out a clear series of concepts and actual programming results appropriate to its promise. Yet it is unclear that the best form of that leadership can be provided by a large programming bureaucracy which is (1) centered in an organization dominated by a Presidentially appointed board of directors and (2) still without a truly long-range and insulated funding base. In spite of the emergence of a few CPB board members of high caliber and integrity, there persists the problem that most of these appointees reflect neither a wide representative base nor a high degree of political autonomy. The CPB board has proven susceptible to overt political pressure before; and since the terms of its appointment and operations have not changed, there is no evidence that it will not prove equally manipulable in the future.

Given this view of the Corporation board, and in light of my earlier argument about the system-wide problem of public involvement in public broadcasting policy-making, it should now be apparent that the relatively closed nature of the local and national governing boards contributes directly to the inability of the several elements within the institution to recognize the shortcomings of one another. Look-alike boards at all levels do not question the make-up and representativeness of their sister organizations. Indeed, most of the members of these boards tend to come from the same or closely affiliated "old boy networks." They simply do not have significantly divergent world views; their perceptions of the nature of society and culture are more striking for their similarities than for their differences. Retaining certain common understandings and allegiances, they tend to perceive most public broadcasting problems through similar lenses — a distortion that naturally leads to a large amount of relatively narrowly focused consensus about just what those problems are and what might constitute suitable solutions.

A direct consequence is that battles like those over funding and the shape of the national institutions continue to be fought rather silently, albeit ferociously, well behind the scenes, without any substantial questioning of the assumptions underlying the terms of the dispute. Since they all speak essentially the same language, these power brokers on the different boards find it all too easy to reach decisions (e.g., "partnership" agreements) that are worked out privately, not through any form of open, public debate. This relatively closed process strongly militates against the development of new and broader program and general policy philosophies, and it restricts the subsequent range of service options proposed and then finally adopted. Even national conventions and annual meetings, which ought to provide forums for developing a dialogue among differing professional and public interests, tend to serve as vehicles for rubber stamping compromises previously, and often secretly, arrived at.

Conclusions and Recommendations

At the very least, then, it would appear that the stations, the national agencies, and the publics they all claim to serve must begin a mutual re-evaluation of the terms under which they interact. The public needs to take a more active role in the affairs of its noncommercial broadcasting system, and the several local and national agencies must find ways to open their board structures and advisory procedures to encourage such increased, and substantive, public input. The stations and the national agencies must resist the temptation to conceive of their audiences in traditional mass-society terms. If partnerships are to be spoken of, it would be better to conceive of them as creative, mutually supportive understandings between public broadcasters and the live bodies and minds that make up their audience-publics, not solely as politically efficacious pacts between the closed, narrowly representative agencies that constitute the public broadcasting establishment.

Additionally, the stations and CPB must re-examine the terms of their recent accommodations in a more open forum. Like any centralized, money-dispensing agency, CPB will naturally tend to fill power vacuums wherever it finds them; and as a result, it will probably choose not to question the current arrangements so long as its power continues to grow unchecked. Again, there is no denial here of the need for a certain substantial role for centralized planning and development. The question is whether the public broadcasting community is fully aware of where programming power has recently come to rest and whether that is where they want it to stay. Accordingly, there may well be a growing consensus among the stations, CPB, and the public that the time has come for a thorough re-examination of the entire structure of public broadcasting.

It is of more than passing interest that in his farewell address, Dr. Killian raised just this issue of review. Sensitive to the serious dissensions and exclusions continuing to lurk beneath the surface of the current arrangements, the former CPB leader called for re-evaluation by at least the joint CPB-PBS Partnership Review Committee, and perhaps even by a coordinating committee of representatives of PBS, APRS, and CPB. However, it was Dr. Killian's additional reference to the possibility of reconvening the Carnegie Commission that is perhaps the most sound and important recommendation.

The furious pace of events during recent years has let so much time slip by that it is startling to pause and be reminded that 1975 marked the tenth anniversary of the formation of the first Carnegie Commission. On many different fronts, public broadcasters found it possible to be successful in rapidly implementing certain of the Commission recommendations. Yet in other areas, most notably in the effort to develop an insulated, long-range funding provision, success has been elusive. Indeed, as I have tried to explain in this essay, the problems reflected in public broadcasting's fruitless search for an insulated funding bill, in its restricted governance structure, in its closed policy making, and in its uncertainty about how to envision and interact with its audiences are all becoming chronic.

These symptoms suggest that the cultural and political principles underlying the 1967 act have become severely strained and that the continuing validity of the first Carnegie blueprint is now open to question. Additionally, it is clearly necessary to bring out some other issues which continue either to be ignored or to be handled quietly without much debate. At the most basic and general policy level, such issues include the need to examine (a) the proper definition of "noncommercial," "educational," and "public;" (b) the constitutionality of the anti-editorialization provision of the 1967 act; (c) the fundamental provisions for CPB governance; and (d) the degree of programming and other authority that ought, or ought not, to be invested in the Corporation. At the operational and specific policy level, such issues include an examination of the need for the addition of second national radio and television interconnection services, of the proper interaction of public broadcasting with cable systems, of the optimal use of satellite resources, and of the long-overdue problem of developing stronger, interconnected regional networks.

In this light, it is highly appropriate to heed and advance the call for a new, comprehensive Carnegie-type study effort. While it may not be necessary to develop a proposal for an entirely new structure, there are enough substantial problems and omissions under the current arrangement to warrant a thoroughgoing examination of even that possibility. However the recommendations of a new planning commission might take shape, I want to attach two conditions:

- The first is that this project be mobilized quickly while there still remains at least a semblance of peace within the public broadcasting institution. The study process would have great difficulty being sufficiently broad and careful if it were forced into existence in reaction to another major battle.

- The second condition is that the study be conducted openly. The importance of this proposed re-evaluation is such that, rather than hiding it inside a closed coordinating committee made up of representatives of the public broadcasting establishment, it must be carried on publicly by some such disinterested body as a second Carnegie Commission or, given the fundamental political issues involved, a joint Congressional-Presidential commission.

Since the issues facing the current public broadcasting enterprise remain serious and potentially explosive, delay is dangerous. We cannot afford to be side-tracked any longer by such questionable campaigns and events as the enactment of the financing bill. We have already seen that the image of long-term stability associated with that bill is misleading. More important for the argument here, the five-year authorization of that bill might, ironically, provide too much of a respite. That is, the breathing room it offers also carries with it the danger of encouraging a complacency that might prove fatal in its potential for masking and delaying attention to other continuing and serious policy and organizational problems and disagreements.

We must realize that 1980 will come much more quickly than we expect. Public broadcasting must move immediately to initiate a study process that will lead to a reconceptualization of the optimal structural and policy directions for public broadcasting. Otherwise, the arrival of the new decade will be marked by a reappearance of all those issues that were either ignored after 1967 or so hurriedly swept under the rug in 1973.

References

1. Anthony Smith. *The Shadow in the Cave* (Urbana: University of Illinois Press, 1973), p. 282.

2. "Nixon Kills CPB Funding Bill," *Variety* (June 12, 1974), p. 29; "Whitehead, White House Appear at Loggerheads Over CPB Funds," *Broadcasting* (June 17, 1974), pp. 24-27.

3. See note 2.

4. This interpretation of contemporary viewing patterns was originally offered in a PBS Programming Department, All-Station Memorandum, issued July 31, 1973 by W. Rowland and entitled "Public Television Audience Data, 1972-73." That analysis was based on data supplied by the A. C. Nielsen Company for the fall of 1972, the first national estimates of PBS audience demographics. For examination of more recent data and an extended analysis of this issue, see the CPB monograph by Jack Lyle, "The People Look at Public Television — 1974."

5. *CPB Report* (January 20, 1975), and Lyle, see note 4.

6. R. M. Jennings *et al.*, *Public Television Station Employment Practices and The Composition of Boards of Directors* (New York: Office of Communication, United Church of Christ, 1973), pp. 10-12. Data was compiled from Ownership Reports (Form 323E) filed with the FCC and through personal contacts in the 31 communities represented in the study. The FCC material reflects data available as of June 1, 1972.

7. The Public Broadcasting Act of 1967, PL 90-129, 90th Congress, Sec. 396, (c)(2).

8. W. D. Rowland, Jr. "Public Broadcasting: An Institutional Analysis of the National Level Organizations," (unpublished master's thesis, The Annenberg School of Communications, University of Pennsylvania, 1971), pp. 99-102. See also The Network Project, *The Fourth Network* (New York: Network Project, Columbia University, 1971), pp. 16-27.

9. Les Brown. *Television and The Business Behind the Box* (New York: Harcourt, Brace, Jovanovich, 1971), p. 319.

10. In addition to the books by Smith and Brown already cited, see the articles by Duke, "Public Affairs: The Commitment We Need," and Harry Skornia, "Has Public Broadcasting Lost Its Nerve?" in the *Public Telecommunications Review* (October 1974), pp. 22-29 and pp. 34-38.

11. A good account of this affair is by Ron Dorfman. "Gelding Public TV," *Chicago Journalism Review* (April 1973), pp. 3-5.

12. See note 11, Dorfman, p. 4.

13. For a description of the market plan as it was originally conceived, see H. N. Gunn. "Public Television Program Financing," *Educational Broadcasting Review* (October 1972), pp. 283-308. Then for an analysis of the cooperative as it came into operation, see "Inside the Program Cooperative, An Interview with Hartford Gunn," *PTR* (August, 1974), pp. 16-24.

14. For a more thorough discussion of the central vs. local control issue, and for a good, concise analysis of the public broadcasting structure and the major issues facing the system in the 1968-1972 period, see Steve Millard. "The Story of Public Broadcasting," *Broadcasting* (November 8, 1971), pp. 30-36.

15. "An Agreement for Partnership," CPB and PBS document adopted May 31, 1973.

16. See Alvin Krebs, "Curtis Resignation From CPB draws Mixed Reaction," *New York Times* (April 19, 1973), p. 86; and John Carmody, "Public TV Chairman Resigns," *Washington Post* (April 18, 1973), p. 4.

17. For a strong argument (with which I nonetheless disagree) in favor of the general treasury matching formula mechanism, see Chapter 8, "Public Television," in R. G. Noll *et al.*, *Economic Aspects of Television Regulation* (Washington, D.C.: Brookings Institution, 1973), especially pp. 229-244.

18. *CPB Report* (January 13, 1975).

Financing:
Problem or Symptom?

No one will be surprised with the statement that financial support remains educational television's greatest single problem. Inadequate funding has made it necessary to cut corners in operation, to eliminate everything but the bare essentials and even to compromise with program quality.[1]

This gloomy assessment of the financial health of public broadcasting could be from testimony in support of The Public Broadcasting Act of 1975. But it isn't. The quotation is actually from Lyle Nelson's study, "The Financing of Educational Television," which was completed in 1960. In the intervening 15 years, there have been many rearrangements and reorchestrations, but public broadcasting's theme song has remained the same: If only the "financing problem"

Mr. McKay, a doctoral candidate in the Institute for Communication Research at Stanford University, is completing a study of management decision-making within the Canadian Broadcasting Corporation. His earlier work at Stanford included the 1971 *KQED and its Audience* report and collaboration on the 1972 Aspen Institute study, *The Financing of Public Television*. Mr. McKay's background includes work as a professional engineer and a producer/director in both radio and television, and as research associate to the CBC's managing director.

could be solved, virtually all of public broadcasting's other difficulties would fade away.

The magnitude of public broadcasting's financial troubles has not, in fact, been overstated. Indeed, the financial requirements of the system have been systematically underestimated (or at least understated) over the years, and the consequences of this under-financing are much more alarming than is generally appreciated. Recent estimates indicate that over $100 million is currently needed simply for television equipment upgrading alone,[2] and that annual operating cost funding ought to be doubled if public broadcasting is to meet its responsibilities to the public.[3] There is also the in-tangible problem of the effects of this perennial poverty on the morale of those who continue the struggle to better serve their audiences.

But the real tragedy in the seemingly endless financing debate is that it has almost totally distracted attention from the funda-mental questions about how the public broadcasting system should relate to and serve the public — questions which the system must eventually confront unless it is prepared to abandon the great experi-ment and quietly fade away. The "financing problem" cannot and should not be dealt with in isolation; for financing, and most of the other basic problems of public broadcasting, are all related to the more fundamental issue of public broadcasting's relationship with its audience. If public broadcasting is to succeed — indeed, if it is to survive — there must be a thorough re-examination of public broadcasting's general assumptions and specific objectives, of its shortcomings and achievements, and of its overall "mindset."

"To Educate, Enlighten, and Entertain"

In the chapter on public television in their book *Television Economics*, Bruce Owen, Jack Beebe, and Willard Manning begin with the following set of questions:

1. What ought to be the goals or objectives of public tele-vision in the United States?
2. Given these objectives, what is the best institutional structure for decision-making (program choice) within the public broadcasting system?

3. How should we go about deciding how much money to spend on public television?[4]

Economists have an infuriatingly rational way of looking at the world. The questions, and especially their sequence, are eminently sensible. Yet in the real world of public broadcasting in our society, they have been taken up in precisely the reverse order.

Numerous studies of the financial requirements of public broadcasting have been completed. Widely accepted cost estimates have been developed. New funding legislation has made its way through Congress. There have been evolutionary changes in the institutional structure of public broadcasting, and experiments with program-selection mechanisms continue. But with regard to the primary need for precise "goals or objectives" — for a clear definition of the role of public broadcasting — relatively little progress has been made toward reaching any consensus.* In reflecting on his years as CPB's first president, John Macy observes:

> All too frequently McLuhan's claim that the medium is the message has been valid in public broadcasting. The overpowering concern about structure, relationships, and technical means has preempted the basic purpose of the system: to provide to the citizen-viewer programs which will educate, enlighten, and entertain.[5]

Although many public broadcasting philosophers would argue with the conclusions of at least some of the "consumer-as-king" analyses of public television economics, the agenda put forward by Owen, Beebe, and Manning nevertheless holds the greatest promise for lifting public broadcasting's sights above the operational obsession described by Macy. Without a more precise set of objectives than the often cited "to educate, enlighten, and entertain," public broadcasters cannot begin to identify the institutional structures

---

*Complicating this role definition task is the tendency for legislators in any country, in attempting to relate the power of broadcasting to the public interest, to draw up mandates for programming and services which are global in scope. The problems of interpreting these sweeping charters and defining realistic service objectives are then passed on to the broadcasting institution itself — not because of noble intentions to permit institutional self-determination, but because of the inherent difficulties in being more specific. Thus, public broadcasting in the United States, and most everywhere else, has been handed a global charter and must face the problem of defining its precise role by itself.

best suited to the accomplishment of public broadcasting's mission. And, given the absence of specific service objectives — of a sense of what public broadcasting should actually be doing — any discussion of how much money to spend is really a meaningless exercise.

Evolution as System Design

Of particular significance in explaining the pattern of development of public broadcasting (and the role of financial considerations in shaping the system) is the fact that public broadcasting is the product of a long *evolutionary* process. And like any institution which has evolved, public broadcasting in the United States bears marked characteristics clearly resulting from its attempts to adapt to its environment — an environment dominated by private-enterprise commercial broadcasting and seemingly scarce in resources available for the support of public radio and television.

Throughout public broadcasting's history, there have been two constants: a striking lack of any strong public convictions about the value of this type of broadcasting service, and an equally striking lack of coordination in the planning of the services which have managed to develop. In both radio and television, the FCC's initial allocation of broadcast channels gave no consideration to noncommercial broadcasting. After the FCC finally reserved FM radio channels for educational broadcasting in 1945, the growth in the number of FM stations was impressive. However, the actual growth of public radio *service* was not as dramatic as the number of new stations would suggest. Even as late as 1969, less than 100 of the 420 noncommercial radio statons then operating had a permanent staff of at least three people. And more than half of these stations operated with a power of only 10 watts — a power so low that some college stations could not reach all potential listeners on a single campus.

In the case of television, provision for educational stations came relatively eariler, undoubtedly because educators and public-service supporters of noncommercial broadcasting had learned a lesson with radio and mounted an intense lobbying effort. In 1952, the FCC authorized the reservation of 242 station channels for the exclusive use of noncommercial educational television. However, over two-thirds of these allocations were in the UHF band, and regulations requiring that new television sets be capable of receiving UHF stations did not take effect until 1964, twelve years later. The net result was to shunt much of noncommercial television onto a technological siding, out of reach for a large proportion of its potential audience. Efforts to recover from this early derailment continue in many communities to this day, and the costs of VHF channel acquisition and UHF technical innovation — though certainly justified — continue to drain away dollars and energy that might otherwise be devoted to program services.

Concern for the development of a *system* of educational broadcasting stations arose relatively earlier in the case of television. In 1952, the same year that the educational channels were reserved, the National Educational Television and Radio Center (later NET) was created with funds from public broadcasting's major independent benefactor, the Ford Foundation. Lyle Nelson's 1960 study contemplated a national educational television *system*, and provided estimates of the number of stations required and the associated capital and operating costs of "a national 'live' network, providing instantaneously anywhere in the country the finest in cultural and educational programs."[6] In 1962, Congress finally moved to provide capital assistance to the stations, but the legislators failed to make any provision for the coordinated planning required for an efficient nationwide system. The integration of a station's services with those of other stations or with regional or national systems was not considered.

This absence of what is now referred to as "family planning" led to costly and inefficient duplication of facilities in areas already served by existing educational stations. Thus, as in the case of radio, a simple count of public television stations on the air is a misleading indicator of the growth of television *service* to the public. Because of the 161 grants made under the HEW Educational Television Facilities Program between 1963 and 1967, and because of improvements in the prospects for UHF utilization, the rate of new stations construction doubled during this period. However, coverage remained far from nationwide, an integrated national system did not emerge, and the rate of capital investment far out-stripped increases in station operating budgets.[7]

Throughout the evolutionary development of the public broadcasting system, attempts to integrate services and coordinate development have always had to face the fact that "the stations" are really a collection of understandably but dramatically dissimilar local entities — university licensees, public school systems, state and municipal systems, and the nonprofit "community" stations. Because of the differing nature of their local responsibilities, from the outset these various types of local stations not only provided different levels of local program service but also had (and continue to have) differing preferences for programming to be shared on a national basis.

The Carnegie Commission and Public Television

At the end of 1964, the federal Office of Education underwrote the cost of gathering station managers and board members together to consider the financial future of their system. The conference urged the creation of a national commission to "study ways and means by which educational television can become a permanent instrumentality in the United States." The conference also identified certain specific needs: partial federal support for community service programs, more support and additional production centers for national programming, funding for program libraries, and the necessity for regional and national interconnection.[8]

The subsequent Carnegie Commission investigation and report (released in 1967) stands as a landmark on the road to the development of a national public television system. At the heart of the commission's recommendations was the creation, by Congress, of a central agency — a "federally chartered, nonprofit, nongovernmental" corporation — to receive and disburse governmental and private funds to subsidize local stations and to finance national production centers, independent producers, interconnection of stations, research and development, experimentation, and recruiting and training. The suggested title for the new institution, the Corporation for Public Television, and the change in name from "educational" to "public" television were not intended to be wholly cosmetic:

> Although it provides for immediate assistance to existing stations, this is a proposal not for small adjustments or patchwork changes, but for a comprehensive system that will ultimately bring public television to all the people of the United States: a system that in its totality will become a new and fundamental institution in American culture.[9]

Even so, no guidelines were offered by the commission for the integration of the existing stations into the differentiated system proposed in the study. Nor did any "family planning" advice accompany the recommendation that the Educational Broadcast Facilities Program be expanded. Finally, the commission insisted that it had "no expectation" that programs transmitted over the interconnection would be immediately rebroadcast by local stations, if at all.

The financing mechanism suggested by the commission — a separate trust fund supported by a manufacturer's excise tax on the sale of television sets — is an unmistakable indication that Congress was expected not only to provide federal funds to support the system but also to free the corporation "to the highest degree" from the annual budgeting and appropriations procedures of the government. The commission was attempting to establish an institution of information and ideas for which there was no American precedent — an institution which could be financed by government and responsible to the public but at the same time free from political interference. The move was in the direction of the British and Canadian public broadcasting models: The "federally chartered, nonprofit, nongovernmental" corporation was, in its independent but responsible relationship to government, strikingly similar to British crown corporations; and the separate trust-fund financing recommendation was put forward to ensure that the new corporation would have BBC-style autonomy from its source of funding.

The commission recommendations were translated into federal legislation in near-record time. But, as John Macy has noted, "that speed of passage should never be interpreted as evidence of unrestricted support for the concept of federal involvement in broadcasting."[10] The concept of true institutional independence vanished at about the same time that the ink dried on the Carnegie report.* Perhaps the barrier has been a failure by legislators and the public to comprehend the overriding importance of independence for public

---

*Distrust of a federally supported national broadcasting system manifested itself while the Public Broadcasting Act of 1967 was still in Congress. Amendments prohibited CPB from becoming too central an institution: the Corporation was prohibited from owning or operating any broadcasting facilities and from creating a "network" which would impose a national broadcast schedule. Political activity and editorializing were prohibited, and language was inserted into the bill requiring "strict adherence to objectivity and balance in all programs of a controversial nature." The importance of these amendments lies more in their spirit than in their letter: The BBC conducts its public affairs programming under similar guidelines — though it developed them itself, and it has not been deemed necessary to insert them into its charter.

broadcasting. Perhaps the problem has been fear of the creation of a federally controlled propaganda channel. Perhaps a publicly supported, independent broadcasting institution is an impossible dream in this time and place. Whatever the cause, public broadcasting has been under seige since before its creation. Put bluntly, public broadcasting has never been trusted to act in the public interest.

The solid evidence of the federal government's lack of understanding and/or distrust of the corporation it created was, of course, its failure to provide appropriate funding — both in terms of the amount of money and in terms of the degree of insulation of this financial support from political interference. Ironically, the failure to provide *insulated* funding made the system temptingly vulnerable to precisely the types of political influence that were most feared in Congress. As Willard Rowland has noted, "by reducing CPB to the annual appropriation treadmill, the law-makers virtually guaranteed that the kind of political pressure exercised by the Nixon Administration would manifest itself. Under such conditions, it is highly likely that Presidential interference in CPB affairs would have developed, regardless of who the White House occupant happened to be."[11]

The failure to provide *adequate* funding invalidated the conditions of the public broadcasting experiment at least as seriously as the denial of insulation. It should not be forgotten that, at the time of the passage of the 1967 Act, the development of public broadcasting in the United States faced a series of hurdles unique in world public broadcasting experience. Chief among the obstacles to success was the prior existence of the fully developed private, free-enterprise, commercial broadcasting system. Public broadcasting had not only to shake off the "dull, dry, stuffy, and boring" image that had become associated with educational broadcasting but also to capture the attention and interest of a public which had been conditioned to think of television as that which ABC, CBS, and NBC provided.*

---

*Public broadcasting in Britain never faced such a problem. The relationship between the BBC and its public was developed during a period when public broadcasting was monopoly broadcasting. Competitive commercial broadcasting was not permitted until long after the BBC's responsibility to the public (as opposed to political institutions) was clearly established and the BBC was entrenched in the public consciousness as the cornerstone of any mixed public/private system of broadcasting which might develop. The mixed public/private systems of broadcasting in other countries such as Canada were developed in the same sequence.

The most immediate need of public broadcasting was to develop a strong and vital rapport with the American people — to clearly establish its channel of responsibility to the public, rather than to political institutions, and to generate the public support urgently required for the ultimate survival of the system. The only possible basis for the establishment of this strong relationship between public broadcasting and its public would have been — and *is* — the provision of attractive, high quality program services.

If the public broadcasting experiment was to have succeeded in its first try, it clearly required a massive "start-up" infusion of dollars. Vast sums were required for promotion — to cause viewers to at least sample the fare provided on the educational channels which they had been routinely bypassing for years. But the most crucial financial need was for bold, vigorous, and ambitious program development, encompassing large-scale research, experimentation, piloting, and evaluation efforts. The addition of a few new programs to the old educational television schedules stood no chance of transforming the existing system into a public television system of any consequence for major segments of the American population. Because wholly new segments of the potential audience had to be reached, wholly new programming concepts were necessary.

It is now history that the necessary levels of federal funding were not provided. And since the stations had experienced severe financial problems throughout the 1960s, they were scarcely in a position to embark on ambitious service-expansion programs. As a result, program development, though bold and vigorous in some instances, was severely limited in extent. The overall orientation of program services remained largely the same. Not surprisingly, viewership increased very slowly, and the viewers continued to come disproportionately from the same better-educated, upper-middle-class audience segment which had been reached earlier by educational television.

The relationship between public broadcasting and the bulk of the American people remained basically unchanged. As a result — again not surprisingly — public broadcasting was forced to muster practically all of its defensive forces from within during the Nixon/Whitehead assault of the early 1970s. There was no widespread public indignation, no groundswell of support, no clear public demand that public broadcasting be permitted to play its obvious role in the consideration of national public issues. Public broadcasting survived the Nixon Administration offensive in the same way in which it was created: on the basis of the tireless efforts of a strikingly small number of committed advocates of public-interest broadcasting.*

The Public Broadcasting Financing Act

In 1973, the Nixon Administration, preoccupied with the Watergate revelations, found itself forced to begin work with public broadcasting representatives on a financing bill. The restructuring of PBS into a membership organization indisputedly under local station control, the negotiation of the CPB/PBS partnership agreement, and the completion of a long-range financing plan by an industry-wide Financing Task Force — all in the same watershed year of 1973 — had presented the government with an unprecedented demonstration of the unanimity and singleness of purpose of the public broadcasting community. The Administration was no longer able to argue that the system had ignored the concept of localism or that the elements of the system were in disarray. And it was faced with the determination of the CPB board (by then under the chairmanship of Dr. James Killian, who had headed the Carnegie Commission) the provision for long-range financing must be made.

The various draft versions of the Public Broadcasting Financing Act were substantially transcriptions of the original recommendations by the industry Task Force in 1973. The Administration bill, the Public Broadcasting Financing Act of 1975, included a five-year appropriation on a matching basis of one federal dollar for every $2.50 of nonfederal income. Ceiling levels ranged from $70 million in 1976 to $100 million in 1980, and provision was made for 40 to 50 percent of the federal dollars to go directly to local public radio and television stations.

The general feeling within public broadcasting in early 1975 was

---

*The attacks upon the institutions and emerging traditions were formidable. The White House specifically attacked the presence of national public affairs programming on public television. Public broadcasting was repeatedly the victim of battles over the Health, Education and Welfare appropriations with which it had been lumped. One CPB Chairman resigned with angry accusations that the President's men were engaged in backstage manipulations. For a detailed look at how public broadcasting responded, see Willard Rowland's "Public Involvement: The Anatomy of a Myth," in the May/June 1975 issue of *Public Telecommunications Review*.

optimistic. The political warfare of the Nixon era had passed. All that remained was some work with the Ford Administration and with Congress to convert the recommendations of the Financing Task Force into law. Although the Senate Commerce Committee quickly voted to raise the ceilings to higher levels — to $88 million in fiscal 1976 and $160 million by 1980 — other House and Senate committees and subcommittees proposed further and less favorable changes:

- The matching provisions were to be changed so that, after the first three years, one federal dollar would only be provided for every *three* nonfederal dollars.

- Language was to be inserted into the bill requiring CPB's availability for testimony at any time.

- A "significant" portion of CPB's federally appropriated funds was to be devoted to instructional programming.

- CPB was to be made responsible for compliance by the station licensees with provisions of the Civil Rights Act of 1964.

- And, most significantly, the five-year appropriation was to be removed — with the promise of an interim three-year appropriation and then advance appropriations in separate annual bills.[1][2]

In June 1975, with the bill still in committee, a continuing resolution took care of funding for another year at the subsistence level of $62 million.

One "reaction" from the public broadcasting community came in a joint statement by Henry Loomis, Hartford Gunn, and Matthew Coffey, the presidents of CPB, PBS, and the Association of Public Radio Stations:

> Although we are disappointed that the Appropriations Committee adversely reported five-year appropriations which would mean true insulation and protection for public broadcasting from undue interference and control, we

recognize that some features of the funding mechanism recommended in the report are superior to the present method of annual funding of public broadcasting.[13]

Their restraint was remarkable considering that the general tenor of the proposed Congressional amendments amounted to a complete rejection of the position and proposals developed by public broadcasting over the eight incredibly frustrating years since the passage of the Public Broadcasting Act in 1967.* The Public Broadcasting Financing Act of 1975, even in its original form, was far from a long-range solution to public broadcasting's problems. A five-year appropriation would have been merely *medium-term*, not long-range financing. Furthermore, the financing mechanism of "matching funds" was hardly ideal. Matching had been selected over other more reliable approaches (notably a dedicated tax) not because it was better for the system, but because it was the most politically tenable.

By the time that the bill emerged from conference, resolution of the differences between the House and Senate versions had removed most of the proposed amendments — with one notable exception. The five-year appropriation was gone. *Any semblance of either insulated or long-range funding was gone.* CPB was due to go before the Appropriations Committee *within the year* to begin the annual advance appropriations process for 1979.

The mutilation of the Public Broadcasting Financing Act should stand as sufficient evidence of the fact that the real problem of public broadcasting lies in its relationship with its public. The legislators who considered the financing bill were not under pressure from any groundswell of public support for public broadcasting. Nor have they ever been. Seen in that light, the actions of Congress are more understandable. The apparent indifference of Congressmen to public broadcasting's funding problems and to its need for political independence is merely a reflection of the general attitude of the public.

If public broadcasting is ever going to "make it," it will have to address Owen, Beebe, and Manning's first question: "What ought to be the goals or objectives of public television in the United States?"

---

*But then, what could Loomis, Gunn, and Coffey have said? With the watered-down act still under consideration by Congress, they could hardly take the occasion to observe either that the politicians failed to understand why insulated long-range funding was required or that the politicians understood but apparently didn't care.

It will have to change the way it *programs*, not just the way it draws internal flow diagrams. The fact that public broadcasting's relationship with its public is integrally based on its programming role is embarrassingly well-illustrated by its major success story, "Sesame Street." Survey respondents who identify their local public television station as "The Sesame Channel" are providing an assessment of a program service, not of the management style of the Children's Television Workshop or the institutional arrangements under which the development of "Sesame Street" was carried out.

Planning for the Future

In fairness to those who have charted public broadcasting's survival course in recent years, criticism must be set against a clear recognition of the nature and the power of the pressures which have been applied to the system. It is important to recognize that political frustrations and financial desperation have had a profound effect not only on the development of the institutional structures of public broadcasting but also on any consideration of its role in serving the American people. It is understandable that there has been a preoccupation with structures and with finance. And given the current situation, it would even be understandable (though fatal) if these preoccupations continued to distract attention from consideration of the system's programming role. Richard Moore, a former station manager, has observed:

> Noncommercial television has seldom taken the subject of programming seriously. What *is* taken seriously is the issue of control and participation in the hierarchy that makes the programming decisions. However, even in these disputes, the issue is not really programming and audiences, but rather the distribution of available monies for the purpose of institutional survival. . . .The questions of how to attract the best talent and produce programs in an optimum cost-effective manner become merely a masquerade for the real issue of station survival and system building. . . .The current battle between CPB, PBS, and possibly a third force represented by the larger producing stations is the same old struggle for the control and distribution of monies.[14]

The Future of Public Broadcasting

In recent months, there have been a number of calls for a complete review of the conditions and direction of U. S. public broadcasting. Serious questions have been raised about the distribution of program decision-making power within public broadcasting's institutional structure and about the extent to which public representation on public broadcasting's various governing bodies is representative of the full public and of the public interest. I suspect that behind these specific concerns is a general uneasiness about program services — an uneasiness which stems from the fact that somehow public television's programming hasn't seemed particularly important to a substantial proportion of the public.

In his farewell address as CPB chairman in 1975, Dr. Killian raised the possibility of reconvening the Carnegie Commission. That suggestion is a step in the one direction that holds any real promise for extricating public broadcasting from its present predicament. What is required now is a complete reappraisal of the role of public broadcasting in the United States. Small adjustments or patchwork changes will not set public broadcasting on the road to a more significant relationship with the American people. Nor will minor alterations improve its chances of securing appropriate financial support through the people's representatives. A new commission must be formed to question all of the assumptions which underlie both the current approach to program services and the current institutional structures of public broadcasting.

Such a reassessment will not be easy to conduct properly. When the original Carnegie Commission was at work, the public television "establishment" was much smaller. Also, many problems which the Carnegie Commission then considered only minor have turned out to be significant. A comprehensive review will have to give special attention to the role of the Corporation for Public Broadcasting, the senior national public broadcasting institution which was the centerpiece of the original Carnegie recommendations. Having CPB's record will be a distinct advantage for the new commission, but the commission will also have to be wary of the particular perceptions and preoccupations of CPB as a resource for the examination of public broadcasting as a whole. The commission's review should be independent of all of the public broadcasting institutions, from the smallest station to CPB itself. On the other hand, the task of the new commission must be, in the pure sense of the word, political — for political answers will be required to sort out the pile of assumptions, interpretations, and political considerations upon which

154

U.S. public broadcasting now rests.

Areas of Concern for a New Commission

"Alternative" programming. The first set of issues that must be faced by a new commission concern public broadcasting's program service goals. It is generally agreed that public broadcasting's role is to provide alternative or supplementary services that do not duplicate commercial television offerings. It is also generally accepted that public broadcasting must have a special concern for the public's interests and needs. But beyond these guidelines, there seems to be little consensus on how these broad principles should be translated into program services.

One interpretation is that alternative service means specialized and minority audiences. Others argue that alternative program services need not imply small audiences. Many public broadcasters feel caught in a "double bind" between a responsibility to serve minority audiences and a need to demonstrate the relevance of their services to large segments of the public. The issues are complex and not the kind that get sorted out at board meetings. They are questions not of black and white but of balance — balance between mass-audience and highly specialized programming, balance between local and national services, and balance in the types of audiences served.

Public broadcasting already knows that devising "alternative" programs is not easy. It continues to experience serious problems in reaching substantial segments of the public. A 1975 CPB research report contained the following observations:

> When we look at the types of programs named by "blue-collar" and minority families, we find that the children's programs account for almost all of their public television viewing. The evening programs of public television draw primarily viewers with more education and high-status occupations. . . .
>
> When we look only at the evening audience, public television draws disproportionately more viewers from the older age groups — those over 50 — than from the younger ones. Given the nature of most of the programs presented by public television in the evening, this should not be surprising. Not only are most of them "adult" programs,

but they have a rather eclectic appeal. . . .

Most persons meeting the criterion of "public television viewers" were able to name only one program or program series viewed by someone in the family during the pre-ceeding week.[15]

Clearly, public broadcasting must begin to give serious con-sideration to how it can best complement the commercial system and thereby ensure not only the most effective and equitable use of public funds, but also the optimum level of service to the American people. It must begin to think about programs, about programming schedules, and about how these can best relate to the lives of real people. Useful answers to questions about structure and funding can come only after a careful re-examination of the system's role in serving the public.

Local service. The issue of "localism" will have to be recon-sidered. If locally originated programming really is to be a major element of the public broadcasting service, then everyone is going to have to get serious about the costs. *Quality* programming cannot be produced without financial resources, regardless of whether the pro-gram is intended for a local audience or a national one. Lloyd Morrisett has pointed out that not only is it generally much more efficient and economical to produce high quality national program-ming, but also that viewers almost inevitably prefer national pro-gramming.[16] Schramm and Nelson estimated in 1972 that as a result of the multiplier effect of the number of local stations separately producing similar programs for their own communities, local pro-gramming would require 2.3 times more money than the national programming. The point is that the time has come to make some determination of the optimum balance between the two.

Local control. "Localism" is also the term for another impor-tant issue in public broadcasting: the question of local control of national services. Again, this is not the place to sort out the best balance between centralization and decentralization, between sys-tematic planning and local independence. In fact, it will not be easy to sort out this balance at all.

First of all, the widely varying forms of station ownership and control result in significant differences in programming preoccupa-tions and services. In such a setting it will always be difficult for any national service to meet everyone's needs satisfactorily. Also sig-nificant, at least for the immediate future, is the fact that the system's perspective on the matter of local control was badly distorted by the White House pressures of the Nixon/Whitehead era. As a result, the matter has come to evoke emotional rather than rational responses. Still, I suggest that there are serious implications here both for the quality of program services provided and for the associated costs.

Strenuous efforts to avoid centralization have run throughout the development of public broadcasting. These efforts have certainly not been without cause, but in the scramble to preserve some minimum level of political independence for the system, it may well be that the decentralization impetus has gotten out of hand in certain decision-making areas. It is also possible that the power to make other types of decisions remains overly centralized. Some degree of centralization must be accepted as necessary for a national system, but it would seem unwise to leave the resolution of the balance between central and local control entirely in the hands of competing institutions.

Funding requirements. Although a specialized tradition of public broadcasting finance studies has come into existence, virtually all of the cost estimates which have been constructed are basically projections of the existing system, with minor adjustments for, say, slightly increased levels of local production. Under the circumstances, this has been inevitable, but the resulting estimates are less than an accurate assessment of the real needs of a fully developed public broadcasting system. Any comprehensive new study of funding must take into account both the program objectives and the institutional structures best-suited to the provision of optimum services to the public.

Insulated funding and independence. Given the pattern of events of recent years, securing truly insulated funding will not now be easy. Here again, public broadcasters find themselves in a double bind which is not unique to the American scene. The BBC has commented on its own comparable situation:

> It should be stressed that the policy of impartiality is closely bound up with the independent status of the BBC. Without genuine independence, it is difficult, if not impossible, for broadcasters to maintain the highest standard of truthfulness and impartiality. Conversely, without having established a reputation for just those qualities, it is difficult for any broadcasting organization to be truly

independent and worthy of trust.[17]

The implication for American public broadcasting is clear. Although public broadcasting must ultimately secure insulated funding, in the meantime it must begin to develop a meaningful relationship with its public and, thereby, establish the basis for this independence. The original version of the Public Broadcasting Financing Act would have provided a five-year breathing space in which to begin work on establishing such a basis for independence. Such a breathing space is required now more than ever.

Funding mechanisms. The "matching funds" approach to financing — though attractive in many respects — has the serious drawback of draining off station and system energies badly needed for the improvement of program services. The current costs of fundraising, especially in terms of personnel time, are not known; but it is clear that many public broadcasters have been forced to devote so much of their attention to their financial problems that attention to programming has suffered. The matching approach has a tendency to reinforce this pattern, and it also introduces a temptation for public broadcasters to cater to those segments of their potential audiences most likely to provide subscription dollars and other direct forms of support. Seen in this light, proposals for dedicated tax support seem superior in freeing program planners and program planning from inappropriate financial (as well as political) influences.

The Steps from Here to There

Those who have been closest to the evolutionary changes in public broadcasting over the past few years should not be defensive about a call for a comprehensive reappraisal now. The system has become the prisoner of assumptions and political considerations to such an extent that only a very high level, comprehensive, and independent review of the role, structure, and requirements of public broadcasting can free it from the inevitability of carrying on as at present. To the extent that funding difficulties are an indication of the overall state of the system, there are clearly many basic and serious problems. These problems should not, however, be seen as "financing" issues. And no further attempts should be made to deal with funding problems in isolation. It is time now for some serious thinking about the role that public broadcasting *could* be playing in American society — and about the steps that might lead the system from here to there.

References

1. Lyle M. Nelson. "Financing of Educational Television," in *Educational Television: The Next Ten Years* (Washington: U.S. Government Printing Office, 1965), p. 166.

2. CPB Office of Engineering Research. "A Report on the Minimum Equipment Needs and Costs to Upgrade the Facilities of Public Television Stations" (Washington: Corporation for Public Broadcasting, March 1975), p. 10.

3. See S. Young Lee and Ronald J. Pedone. "Status Report on Public Broadcasting 1973" (CPB/HEW: Advance edition, December 1974), p. 34; and *Report of the Task Force on the Long-Range Financing of Public Broadcasting* (Washington: Corporation for Public Broadcasting, September 1973), pp. 32-3.

4. Bruce M. Owen, Jack H. Beebe, and Willard G. Manning, Jr. *Television Economics* (Lexington, Mass.: Heath, 1974), p. 155.

5. John W. Macy, Jr. *To Irrigate a Wasteland: The Struggle to Shape a Public Television System in the United States* (Berkeley: University of California Press, 1974), p. 40.

6. Nelson, p. 174.

7. Wilbur Schramm and Lyle M. Nelson. *The Financing of Public Television* (Palo Alto: Aspen Program on Communications and Society, 1972), p. 2.

8. Macy, p. 20.

9. Carnegie Commission on Educational Television. *Public Television: A Program for Action* (New York: Harper and Row, 1967), pp. 2-3.

10. Macy, pp. 27-8.

11. Willard D. Rowland, Jr. "Public Involvement: The Anatomy

of a Myth," *Public Telecommunications Review,* 3:3 (May/ June 1975), p. 11.

12. "Long-Range Funding," *CPB Focus on Legislative Affairs* (25 August 1975), p. 1; and "CPB Authorization Approved in House, with Amendment," *CPB Report,* VI:44 (17 November 1975), pp. 3-4.

13. "House Appropriations Committee Acts on Long-Range Funding Bill," *CPB Report,* VI:28 (28 July 1975), p. 10.

14. Richard O. Moore. "Programming: The Illusory Priority," *Public Television: Toward Higher Ground* (Palo Alto: Aspen Program on Communications and Society, 1975), pp. 19-20.

15. Jack Lyle, *The People Look at Public Television 1974* (Washington: Corporation for Public Broadcasting, March 1975), pp. 29, 33-4.

16. Lloyd N. Morrisett. "Rx for Public Television, " in *The John and Mary R. Markle Foundation Annual Report 1972/73,* p. 14.

17. *BBC Handbook 1975* (London: BBC, 1974), p. 285.

R_x for Public Television

LLOYD N. MORRISETT

The potential audience for public television is considerably smaller than the commercial broadcast audience of 68 million homes.* Some of the potential public television viewers are not within range of a public television station. Others are in areas served only by UHF public television stations and own television sets which either are not equipped for UHF reception or receive the UHF signal poorly. As a consequence of these limitations, the true potential audience for public television is estimated to range around 60 percent of American homes, equaling 41 million homes or over 100 million people.

Taking the smaller potential audience of public television into account, the distressing fact remains that few people in the United States who are able to receive a public television station are frequent viewers of that station. Robert Bower, a sociologist who conducted a recent survey of the audience for commercial and public television, was able to say in *Television and the Public*,[1] "ETV has not seriously altered the over-all viewing patterns even of the college educated." If public television had won a large, fanatically loyal audience, then it would be incomparably easier to justify increased financing. The

---

Mr. Morrisett is president of the John & Mary R. Markle Foundation.

*This paper is a revision of the essay "R_x for Public Television," first published in the annual report of the Markle Foundation for 1972-1973.

rather lonely ranks of public television advocates would then be filled by people who were regularly utilizing this public service. So far public television has not won a large, fanatically loyal audience, and few plans have been suggested to show how such an audience might be gained.

Does Public Television Need an Audience?

Although it seems frivolous to ask this question, an argument can, in fact, be made that public television should exist and be adequately financed, regardless of the size of the audience. Indeed, there are times when proponents of public television have seemed to advance this idea.

One side to this argument is that public television should exist primarily in order to provide flexible standby television facilities to be used when needed. There are, for example, instances when events of great public importance are occurring but are not presented by the networks at times of the day convenient for a majority of the population. Public television can provide such coverage, as in its replay of the Senate Watergate hearings in prime time. The standby facilities of public television can also be used for other types of programming that are deemed socially valuable or for events that should be covered but are not or cannot be broadcast commercially.

Looked at in this way, public television is the luxury in the American broadcasting system. However, there is little evidence that society is ready to support such a luxury at this time. The networks and independent stations clear time for events they believe to be of overwhelming national importance, as in the broadcast of the Kennedy funeral, of presidential speeches, and of the Watergate hearings. There are very few instances when such events were not adequately covered in one way or another by the commercial broadcasting system. The coverage might not have been as extensive or at the time of day that the newscaster or public affairs expert would like, but in most cases it did bring the essential character of the events to public attention.

The costs of public television would appear to be exorbitant if both capital and operating costs were to be justified solely by the few times when the system was being used for events of national significance not adequately covered by the commercial system. If unlimited funds for broadcasting were available, it might be reasonable to look at public television as a standby luxury. Today, when many public priorities are underfinanced, this is an untenable view. Nor is financing ever likely to be so plentiful as to make such a luxury view of public television reasonable.

There is another side to the argument that public television does not need to concern itself with the existence of a large audience. Some feel that there should be a noncommercial outlet for talent, as well as a place where people can air unpopular views. These claims have merit. It is apparent, for example, that many people today feel that they cannot reach society with their ideas. Public television could remedy this by enabling people of diverse views to have an access to broadcasting that is apparently not now available.

The national system of commercial broadcasting has also tended to diminish the importance of those outlets for local talent that at one time existed in small clubs, theaters, and other places where people went simply to be entertained by whatever talent was available. Public television could serve as the replacement for such outlets by providing a vehicle for talent to develop away from the tremendous exposure and harsh spotlight of commercial television. This reasoning may make sense, but the public now has such a high national standard of talent that it isn't interested in watching performances of lesser professional quality.

While neither of these proposals depends directly upon a large audience for public television, they both suggest the need for *some* audience. Talent requires recognition; an unfamiliar viewpoint will remain unknown if it is not heard. Regardless of the merits of the argument, there is little evidence that the public will support public television for these purposes alone.

Public Television and Its Audience

After examining alternative arguments and on the basis of simple common sense, it seems that public television can be justified only on the basis of serving an audience. The questions are: Where is the audience for public television? How should public television go about acquiring its audience?

One way for public television to attempt to acquire an audience is to compete with commercial broadcasting and the networks for a share of the mass audience. Although public television was not created to do this, competing for a share of that mass audience is exactly what public television has done and does do much of the time. Unfortunately, it does not do this very successfully.

The viewing audience for television in the United States tends to be divided approximately equally among the three networks. If public television were to attempt to gain a proportionate share of the mass audience, it would need to present much the same fare that is currently on commercial television. There are several lines of evidence which support this conclusion:

A special documentary program or a program of topical interest that deviates from the regular schedule will almost always attract a lower share of audience (as measured by the Nielsen and Arbitron polls) than that normally obtained by the network at that time. In cities in which there are independent television stations as well as network affiliates, the successful independent succeeds by providing programming like that on the networks. Through long experience, the networks seem to have found what the public wants to see during prime time.

A survey conducted by Gary A. Steiner[2] in 1960 showed that viewers who wanted a greater vareity of programs tended to want them in the already popular categories — action programs, sports, comedy and variety programs, the assorted panels, game shows, and melodrama — that make up the typical fare of commercial television. When this survey was repeated in 1970,[3] people were spending more time watching television than in 1960 and reported a more favorable assessment of the programs they saw. Only a small fraction of the additional six hours per week the average family watched television in 1970 can be accounted for by public television. (The tentative experience of pay television also shows that people are most willing to pay for the same kinds of programs they already receive on commercial television.)

There is no evidence whatsoever that public television could gain a proportionate share of the mass audience unless it produced the same kind of programming already available on commercial television. Of course, public television programming would not have commercials, and it would be produced somewhat differently. However, if public television were to take this road, its fare would necessarily consist largely of light entertainment, action, sports, and variety programs. In competing for the mass audience, the cost to public television would be similar to the networks' costs under present conditions.

Some proponents of public television believe, or at least have seemed to believe, that public broadcasting should attempt to obtain a share of the mass television audience and become a standard-setter for commercial television. In Great Britain, the government-funded British Broadcasting Company competes very successfully for a share of the mass audience. It does so by presenting a wide variety of programming, including much in the light entertainment categories. There is evidence to suggest that this would be a viable course for public television in the United States. According to the available surveys and rating systems, the public favors more choice within the present range of program categories. Thus, on the basis of what the public seems to be willing to pay for and what the public says it wants, public television might try to be a "fourth network."

Ranked against these arguments, however, are strong reasons why public broadcasting is unlikely to become a "fourth network." First, direct competition between a publicly oriented broadcasting organization and the commercial broadcasting system is simply not in the tradition of private enterprise in the United States. It would be vigorously resisted by commercial broadcasters as well as many others who would consider such competition plainly wrong. More important, perhaps, is the fact that this is not the role that Congress or the Federal Communications Commission envisaged for public broadcasting. It is not the concept that has been used to justify public television to the American people. According to the FCC rules and regulations covering the licensing of educational television stations:

> Noncommercial educational broadcast stations will be licensed only to nonprofit educational organizations upon showing that the proposed stations will be used primarily to serve the educational needs of the community for the advancement of educational programs and to furnish a nonprofit and noncommercial television broadcast service.

While noncommercial public broadcasting stations may transmit educational, cultural, and entertainment programs, there is nothing

167

in the FCC rules and regulations that would suggest direct competition with commercial broadcasting for a proportionate share of the mass audience. Similarly, the Carnegie Commission on Educational Television stated that public television "includes all that is of human interest and importance, which is not at the moment appropriate or available for support by advertising and which is not arranged for formal instruction."

The Special Interest Audience

If public broadcasting must be justified on the basis of serving an audience, yet it can't compete with commercial television for a share of the mass audience, then public television must attract its primary audience by presenting material aimed at subgroups of the population that share special interests. In fact, this direction for public television has already been proclaimed, even though the record of success is mediocre.

Aside from a very few programs such as "Sesame Street," there has been little attempt to define specific audiences, discover material that satisfies specific interests, and present that material in highly attractive formats. The relatively few shows aimed at special interests — such as in painting or gardening — were produced without any thorough audience assessment and usually on low budgets. Where relative success has come — as with Julia Child's "French Chef" — it is a tribute to the flair of the performer.

Furthermore — again excluding the success of "Sesame Street" — the audiences for public television programs have always been extremely small by normal broadcasting standards, and they do not change substantially from year to year. In the Fall of 1974, the average weekly prime-time audience for the most popular public television programs was approximately 1.2 million television households, or 3 percent of the audience within the reach of public television stations ("Masterpiece Theatre" was the only exception, reaching 2.5 million households). This is a tiny fraction when compared to the audience share of a low-rated commercial network program (one that would not be sustained by the network). Such a program might reach as much as 10 percent of the broadcast public, or 6.8 million television households. In short, although public broadcasting now reaches more American people than ever before, the total audience is still extremely small by any normal standard of commercial broadcasting in the United States.

168

The Philosophy of Localism

Much of the difficulty in finding an audience can be assigned to the fact that public television is still pursuing an uncertain philosophy. This is, perhaps, to be expected. In the early years of any evolving system, its philosophy is likely to undergo changes and be subject to the uncertainties of development.

Historically, the philosophy of public television in the United States has evolved from educational broadcasting and the concept of localism — the idea that a public television station should be a servant of its community and provide programming designed to serve that community. On the surface, the localism concept seems entirely meritorious. It suggests that geographical interests somehow unite and motivate television audiences and that locally produced programming can therefore be the staple of public television. Such a philosophy is stated and restated.

The Carnegie Commission Report says, for example:

> Committed to diversity and to the differentiated audience, public television is deeply reliant upon the vigor of its local stations. Admittedly, like commercial television, it must have central sources of programming, but unlike commercial television, it will depend also upon a strong component of local and regional programming, and it must provide the opportunity and the means for local choice to be exercised upon the programs made available from central programming sources.

Hartford Gunn,[4] president of the Public Broadcasting Service, states in his plan for public television program financing:

> The single most important attribute of the approach suggested is that it would maximize financial and program decision-making at the point closest to the individual communities and their citizens, namely the local public television station.

Presley D. Holmes,[5] of the National Association of Educational Broadcasters, in his presentation of a financial plan for public broadcasting, makes much the same point:

Both the decisions on national programming and the day-to-day mechanics in operational responsibility of program acquisition, production, promotion, publicity, and distribution can and should be in the hands of the stations and an operational agency responsible to the stations.

Finally, Wilbur Schramm and Lyle Nelson[6] of Stanford University, in their report on the financing of public television, reiterate this point:

The primary objective of noncommercial television, in its truest form, is to cater to *all* of the audience . . . *some* of the time . . . This obviously requires special concern for *local* audiences and local programming needs.

The idea of localism, or local control over broadcasting, is rooted deeply in the history of radio and television in the United States. Roger Noll, Merton Peck, and John J. McGowan,[7] economists at the Brookings Institution, studied the economic aspects of television regulation and revealed how the FCC's vision of broadcasting developed and reached maturity on the basis of a special conviction that (1) there would be a local television station in as many communities as possible, and (2) these stations were to be instruments for community development, education, and enlightenment, much like the small town newspaper of the preceding century.

In its Sixth Report and Order, the FCC commented: "In the Commission's view, as many communities as possible should have the opportunity of enjoying the advantages that derive from having local outlets that will be responsive to local needs." Later, FCC Commissioners Kenneth Cox and Nicholas Johnson, in a study of broadcasting in Oklahoma, stated the objectives of the commission as follows:

Congress created the present scheme in order to promote specific policies in specific kinds of programs. The system of locally based stations was deemed necessary to ensure that broadcasting would be attentive to the specific needs and interests of each local community. It was also considered a guarantee to local groups and leaders that they would have adequate opportunity for expression. Ultimately, our broadcasting system is premised on concern that the very identity of local states and cities might be destroyed by a mass communications system with an exclusively national focus.

The Carnegie Commission appears to have based its case for public television on a similar view:

Educational television is to be constructed on the firm foundation of strong and energetic local stations. The heart of the system is to be in the community. Initiative will lie there. The overwhelming proportion of programs will be produced in the stations, scheduling will be performed by the local station and staff, local skills and crafts will be utilized and local talents tapped.

Although the philosphy of localism in public broadcasting has long roots and is reiterated frequently, the practice of public broadcasting has been quite different. Schramm and Nelson show, for example, that between 1962 and 1970, the number of broadcast hours over public television rose steadily. During this same period, however, the hours and proportion of local programming *fell* steadily.

Despite the philosophy of localism, the fact is that for one reason or another during the decade of the 60s, public television stations came to depend more and more on nationally produced programming and less and less on locally produced programming. The models for the financing of public television presented by Hartford Gunn, Presley Holmes, and Wilbur Schramm and Lyle Nelson all take this into account. In the Schramm and Nelson model only six hours out of the total of 28 hours per week of prime time are designated for local and regional programming. Thus, the facts of public television broadcasting differ markedly from the philosophy on which public broadcasting has been based.

Although local programming will continue to be an important part of public television, it is not and cannot be the basis for public television in the United States for two primary and overriding reasons. First, viewer preferences are almost inevitably for national programming. Second, broadcasting costs make it much more efficient to produce high quality national programming than to produce high quality local programming. These two factors hold whether one looks at commercial broadcasting or public broadcasting.

171

The experience of commercial television, for instance, shows that audiences overwhelmingly opt for highly professional talent and highly professional production methods when they have a choice between national programming utilizing those ingredients and local programming that must draw upon smaller pools of talent and smaller budgets. The only major exceptions are local news, weather and sports programs, which can be produced cheaply and are popular for some stations.

The same viewer preferences and cost factors hold true for public broadcasting, although it is not supported by advertising and therefore does not share all of the economic characteristics of commercial broadcasting. Public broadcasters find it much more efficient and economical to produce a high quality show for national production and distribution than to produce a high quality local show. A single station that might be able to afford $1,000 for an hour's production can, when combined with many stations, afford a $50,000 show. That show is almost certain to be preferred by viewers to the $1,000 show that one station could afford. The establishment of the Station Program Cooperative was an attempt by PBS to remedy this dilemma by allowing individual stations to combine resources to purchase programs.

This analysis shows that public television is unlikely to attract a large audience if it depends primarily upon locally produced materials directed at individual communities. This does not mean that localism does not have a place in public broadcasting. It simply means that the philosophy of localism cannot serve as the basis for audience attraction in public television.

Finding an Audience for Public Television

Based on the experiences of both commercial and public television, the primary audience motivation for watching television is the desire to be entertained. The desire to know what is going on in the world and the desire to learn are also motives for viewing, but they are much weaker. The shows that attract the largest audiences in prime-time television are usually light entertainment, including melodramas. Sizable audiences are also attracted by the news and information show or the special documentary that informs about a particular topic. Further down the list are programs that attempt to teach the audience. These are consistently less attractive than the other types of programs unless they include important elements of entertainment and information as well as pedagogy ("The National Driver's Test," for example).

People who watch a specific television show do so with their free time. There are many other things that compete for the use of that time — first of all other television shows, then possibly books, music, movies, exercise, extra work, or household chores. If a television program is to be watched, it must command the viewer's interest more than the competing options.

Thus, the most important questions that public television can ask are (1) What audience interests can be capitalized upon to draw significant numbers of viewers to public television programs? (2) How can these interests be characterized? (3) What determines these interests?

Where a person lives may have some influence on his interests, but this influence is likely to be small. People who live in Chicago are not very different in their viewing interests from those in New York, Miami, or Seattle. More important than geography are the traditional sociological attributes of age, sex, occupation, ethnicity, income level, and education. Countless numbers of sociological studies have shown these and similar characteristics to be determining factors in explaining a person's interests and attitudes. As a result, specific interests influenced by these general characteristics — such as interest in sports, in drama, or in children — are most likely to create an audience for public television.

Since public television ought not to compete with commercial television for the mass audience and cannot do so successfully, and since it cannot attract a sizable audience with locally produced and locally oriented programming, it must find its audience by appealing to special interests and special tastes. To do this successfully, public television must have leadership and inspiration based on a sound understanding of special audience interests and tastes. Also needed are criteria for determining which interests and which tastes are to be satisfied first. Finally, public television needs some sort of measure for judging and rewarding the degree of success in satisfying those interests and tastes. Together, these elements provide a new prescription for public television — a procedure by which public television may be able to find its audience and begin to achieve its potential.

By experience as well as trial and error, commercial broadcasting has developed programs to appeal to the mass audience. The economics of commercial television, dependent upon advertising revenue, dictated a simple criterion for choosing programs — the largest number of people possible should be satisfied. Several rating systems have been devised to indicate how many people watch commercial television and which programs please and interest the most people. Programs that are successful (defined currently as programs attracting approximately 17 percent of the total audience) are retained; those that achieve lower ratings are dropped. To the extent that the rating systems accurately measure public preferences, commercial television is an honest system. It attempts to satisfy the majority of the audience; it has techniques for measuring the degree of success it achieves; and it uses these measures ruthlessly to weed out programs that are not up to the rating par.

Commercial broadcasting's simple methods for defining audience interest, for determining which interest should be initially satisfied, and for measuring the degree of success of a program cannot be directly applied to the problems of public television. Public television faces a more complicated task: how to measure the appeal to *special* audiences and *special* interests. Talented producers and television executives already do this on the basis of experience and intuition. There is, however, a great deal of evidence available that could be used along with experience and intuition to provide a sound basis for the development of public television programs.

Compiling a report on audience interests. What the public television industry needs is a systematic report on the special interests of Americans. This report should be periodically updated so that a body of information is available to the television executive or producer when he begins to determine that portion of the audience to which he wishes to appeal. Program ideas will not spring automatically from the report: television executives will still have to call upon their full creative potential to choose target audiences and to develop program ideas. But with the report at hand, there will be a foundation on which creativity can build.

No one can simply ask people what they are interested in and expect an accurate guide to special interest audiences. Interests are related to what is available. In the absence of experience, a person tends not to know his own interests. Also, there is often a discrepancy between what people *say* they are interested in and what they actually *do* with their time. Thus, while any report on audience interests should utilize direct questioning, it must also utilize other sources of information to try and portray the size, strength, and diversity of special interest audiences.

One basis for the report on audience interests should be the past experience of commercial and public television. This experience is particularly valuable in defining or beginning to define the *size* of some potential special interests. Unfortunately, commercial television experience provides very little information on the *strength* of those audience interests. The audience does not have to pay for commercial programs, hence, there is no way to register effectively the strength of interest in any individual program.

A second source for the report on audience interests should be the mass of surveys conducted by commercial and nonprofit polling organizations. Over the years these surveys have included many questions that can be used to define both the strength and size of special interest audiences. A third source might be studies of voter behavior and the factors that tend to determine voting outcomes in local and national elections. Examination of these studies may show enduring themes that motivate voting decisions — themes that are indicative of compelling interests.*

The initial cost of a periodic report on audience interests would be high — perhaps on the order of half a million dollars. The periodic updating of the report, however, would be considerably less costly, and these updating costs would probably be balanced by the gains from having such a report available. For example, a report on special interests should greatly reduce the number of public television programs that are designed for audiences that actually do not exist or for audiences that are not sufficiently interested in the subject to turn to the public television channel. Thus, overall production costs would be reduced by decreasing the number of expensive programming failures.

Some of the research sponsored by the Corporation for Public Broadcasting is already headed in this direction. In addition, there is at least one major audience study being developed under foundation sponsorship. However, the first step of public broadcasting should be to produce a report on the special interests. If the report proves valuable, then consideration should be given to longer term problems

---

*During the 1960 presidential election, a number of social scientists were brought together to collate the information from past elections and surveys. Their purpose was to put this information into a form that could be used to determine which issues were of paramount interest to particular segments of the voting population. The resulting model of voting behavior was quite accurate. This Kennedy campaign model cannot be transferred directly to the problem of defining special interest audiences for television, but some of the techniques can be utilized.

of administration and funding.

Selecting the audience to be served. Having a systematic report of audience interests will not completely solve the problem of what programs should be produced by public broadcasting. In all probability, there are many special interest audiences of considerable size and strength. The choice of which of these audiences to serve will depend on (1) value judgments as to the social importance of a program, and (2) broadcasting judgments as to which subjects can best be treated by television. Choices must also be made between serving an audience of substantial size but only average interest in a subject, or serving a smaller audience which is highly interested. Again, value judgments as well as broadcasting judgments will enter the picture.

Successful choices in the design and development of programs will depend, as they always have, on the experience, talent, imagination, and intelligence of the people involved in production. A report on special interests would, however, inform that talent, experience, imagination, and intelligence so that choices might be made on a more rational basis than in the past.

In contrast to what one might think, special interest audiences are not necessarily small. Some evidence is available which shows that at least some of the special interest audiences for public television are likely to be on the order of 10 percent of the total broadcast public, or between six and seven million American homes. One example would be the American Broadcasting Company's "Stage 67," a program aimed at those interested in serious drama. On a commercial network, this special interest program attracted about 10 percent of the potential audience.

This example, as well as others, suggests that reaching 10 percent of the people who receive public television stations on a regular basis should be the goal of many programs. By commercial television standards, these audiences would be insufficient to justify the continuation of a prime-time program. By public television standards, however, these audiences are many times the size of those that are currently reached.

Devising a rating system. Under the system suggested here, the production of most public television programs would begin with the definition of a specific audience, plus the definition of a specific job to be attempted for that audience — entertainment, information, or instruction, or some combination of the three. The final element in the system being proposed here is the design and operation of a rating system that can be used to measure how successfully individual programs attract and satisfy their particular audiences. For example, if a program were designed to reach those people seriously interested in tennis, and it were known that about 10 percent of the broadcast public fit this definition, then the rating used for that program should be based on the number of serious tennis lovers who have been attracted to the program. Without a rating system of this type, there is no way for public television to judge the degree of its effectiveness.

In a sense, public television should be just as ruthless as is commercial broadcasting in judging its success. If a program is designed to reach a special interest audience and fails to do so, or if it fails to reach as large a percentage of that audience as the typical public television program, or fails to satisfy the people it does reach to the degree that public television programs normally do, the program should be dropped or revised so that it will meet normal standards of success. Without a way of judging successes or failures, public television cannot improve its programs or weed out the unsuccessful ones. Given an appropriately tailored rating system, public television will have a way to justify its work and thereby the public investment of money.

Until an appropriate rating system is developed, it will be difficult to spell out precise goals for successful public programs. But again, on the basis of commercial experience, coupled with the limited experience of a public program such as "Sesame Street" (which was designed for a special interest audience), it might be argued that a public program should attempt to reach at least 50 percent of its potential audience. Experience may modify this standard, either upward or downward, but this suggests a goal towards which public television might initially strive.

A rating system for public television will be a costly operation. It is difficult to estimate in advance how costly it might be, but something on the order of $500,000 to $1 million per year would not be surprising. The cost would be high not because of frequency of the surveys, but because it will be difficult to develop a survey technique that correctly identifies special interest audiences and polls them reliably. Ratings for public television need not be nearly as frequent as those used for commercial broadcasting. The goal is not to get an overnight rating of a show so another show can replace it, but rather to judge whether or not a public television program is meeting its objectives over the course of a season. This might mean that the ratings could be on a monthly, quarterly, or even less frequent basis. At the least, they would have to be done annually.

Providing incentives for good programming. One beneficial by-product of a rating system might be the provision of financial incentives for producing better programming. Public broadcasting currently has few such incentives. Producers, directors, and writers try to meet professional standards (enjoying the accolades of their peers and critics), but tangible rewards for better programs are rare. In part, this is because there is no agreement on what constitutes a better program. With a proper rating system, it would be possible to define a better program as one that reaches more of the audience for which it is designed and/or which satisfies that audience in greater degree. Then with a rating system, public broadcasting could introduce rewards for better production into its system.

One possibility that seems entirely natural — and long called for — in public broadcasting is a financial award or fee to be added to the cost of program production. Organizations or stations which produced successful programs could receive fees depending upon their degree of success. Perhaps a standard fee of, for example, 2 percent might be given to any production organization in addition to the costs of production and normal overhead. The organization might receive additional fees of up to 5 percent of the total budget depending on the proportion of the audience that is attracted or the success of the program in meeting other objectives.

A system of fees, while entirely foreign to the public broadcasting field, is normal in many other areas of enterprise — both public and private, commercial and nonprofit. The inclusion of a fee would give producing organizations some central funds to be set aside specifically for developing new programs or improving facilities. Program development is expensive, yet the experience of broadcasting shows that many more programs need to be developed than are actually televised. In the present system of public broadcasting, there is little room to develop new programs which can finally be discarded in favor of others.

The Cost and Benefits of
Special Interest Programming

Judging by present operating budgets, the average hourly cost of developing quality, special interest programming will be high — probably a minimum of $100,000 per hour, and perhaps higher. Can these costs be justified when they are not amortized over as large an audience as that reached by commercial broadcasting? The answer here depends upon the degree of success that public television has in satisfying its audience. If enough special interest audiences are defined so that when they are added together public television programming reaches most of the American public with an assortment of programs designed for diverse special interests, then public television will be serving its audiences in ways that commercial television does not, and cannot.

Experience with commercial broadcasting and experiments with subscription television show that the public is willing to pay for programs that meet its interests. Even though the per-hour costs of public television will not be low, they will still be relatively insignificant when spread over the sizes of audiences being considered here. Of course, only a fraction of the total program hours of public television would meet the interests of any one individual. But in the aggregate, the programming would meet the interests of a majority, and in this way a large and loyal audience for public television might be formed.

Such an audience would immediately transform a sick industry into a healthy one. Public support for public television could be expected to be translated into Congressional support, and the amount of money available for developing public television programming would be expected to increase severalfold. The costs of operating public television would not be greatly different from the costs of operating a commercial network, but the money would be spent quite differently. Given a large, loyal audience and sufficient funds, public television could then produce and broadcast certain other kinds of programming in addition to what would be the staple fare of the system — the special-interest audience programming. This other type of programming could include, for example, experimental programming, talent promotion programming, and local programming.

Experimental programming is especially important for the improvement of television. Experiments, however, are certain to involve failures, and it is unlikely that experimental programming can be expected to command much of an audience. Therefore, the cost of experimental programming could be regarded as a research and development expense for public broadcasting. It is an important investment for indicating new directions, but one that can be made only when both the audience and economic base of public television are more secure than at present.

The Future of Public Broadcasting

One of the major complaints about commercial broadcasting is that creative people do not have the opportunity to try new directions and to express ideas in their own ways through the broadcast medium. Many people from commercial television have turned to public television for exactly this purpose. It is important that public television continue to serve this purpose by providing an outlet for creative talent — actors, dancers, musicians, composers, writers, directors and producers. Again, it will be much easier for public television to support this type of programming when its audience and economic base are secure.

Finally, the development of a large, loyal audience will make it possible for public television to include local programming aimed at individual communities. While the above analysis shows that local programming cannot be the basis for securing a large audience for public television, local audiences do have legitimate interests that can be met by public television, and these interests should be served.

Reaching the Special Audience

Once special interest programming becomes the staple of public broadcasting, there will be some important implications for the entire broadcast operation. Under this scheme, most of the programs would be designed for particular special interests — tennis, money management, serious drama. There will be little reason to expect that one individual will have all or even many of these interests. It will be much more likely that an individual will find only an occasional program on public broadcasting which he or she wants to watch.

Public broadcasting stations will certainly attempt to schedule programs at times when most interested individuals can see them, but the audience in a given evening is likely to change radically in composition from one program to the next. If a program for serious music lovers is on from 7:30 to 8:30 p.m., it is unlikely that that audience will wish to continue watching when the station then switches to a program on business administration from 8:30 to 9:30.

Because of this varied schedule, public television will tend to lose one of the important assets of commercial broadcasting — channel loyalty. People will not turn on their public television channel expecting to watch for several hours in the evening. Rather, the audiences developed for public television are likely to be much more selective, tuning in only when programs meeting their own interests are being shown. Public television will, therefore, have a greater need than commercial television to let its audience know when a program of particular interest is going to appear.

To reach and attract special audiences, public television will have to promote programs heavily. Advertising in other media, on television and on radio will become much more important. In the current development of public television, advertising has been used only to a minimal degree, and for the most part, it has not been used in very inventive ways. If in the future, a program for serious music lovers is developed for public television, it should be advertised not only in the general interest publications and newspapers, but in those publications and other media that reach the music lovers directly — magazines written for music lovers, the program guides to symphony concerts and operas, and FM radio concerts.

Advertising costs should be considered a regular part of all public television budgets. Perhaps 10 to 20 percent or more of the program budget for an individual show should be set aside for promotion. Reaching the special interest audience for which each show is intended will be difficult. It will take ingenuity in the expenditure of funds, as well as a consistent advertising program.

A second requirement for attracting an audience to public television is that programs be on regularly — with a frequency of at least once a week — in order for people to develop the habit of tuning in. If a program on money management is developed, people need to know that every Tuesday at 9:00 p.m. they can turn on their public television channel and watch the program.

Answering the Questions—A Summary

The answer to the question, "Does public television need an audience?" is simple. The answer is an overwhelming "yes." Without a large, loyal audience, public television will continue to flounder in the trickle of funds it has so far received. Moreover, it will continue to be fraught with ideological and political controversy. On the other hand, a plan to develop a large and devoted audience will at least give public television a consistent vision of its future. To the extent that this audience is attracted and satisfied, public television will emerge from its period of inadequate financing and internal strife.

The Future of Public Broadcasting

The prescription for successful future public television has three requirements:

The first requirement is that public television release its hold on the myth of localism. Local broadcasting is important and will continue to be important. However, the experiences of both commercial and public television indicate that local broadcasting can never win a large, loyal audience for public television. Audience preferences and economics both require that public television depend largely upon nationally produced programming. The myth of localism may have some political importance for public television, and it certainly gives the local station manager a rationale for what he is doing. But the retention of this myth is likely to do more harm than good. Continuing to cling to it can only divert public television from realizing its essential purpose in serving special interest audiences. And without this clarification, it is extremely unlikely that public television can begin to reach its full potential.

The second requirement is the development of a method to define special interest audiences and then to determine how well those interests are being met. What is proposed is an annual report on the special interests of audiences that might be served by public broadcasting, combined with a rating system to determine the degree of success that individual programs have in meeting the interests of those audiences. Developing these techniques will be expensive and will also demand a large investment of intellectual effort. This system, however, will show public television the way to improve itself, and it will show the American public how well public television is succeeding in its mission.

Public television must be at least as honest in its self-criticism as commercial broadcasting. The commercial rating systems give commercial broadcasting a relentless way of weeding out programs that are not up to standard in the current commercial context. Public broadcasting needs a similar system designed and constructively applied for its own purposes.

The third and final requirement for public broadcasting is the development of an incentive system for stations and production companies to create programs that meet the needs of public broadcasting. In the long run, it is not enough for the Corporation for Public Broadcasting merely to pay the costs for program production. Successful programming that meets the interests of large audiences should be rewarded. Payment of a fee, over and above production costs, and based on the success of the program, is an entirely appropriate way for public broadcasting to continue in a nonprofit framework and yet build in incentives for the improvement of its product.

Ingredients of this prescription are already at work in public broadcasting, but these ingredients need to be pulled together to give public broadcasting a consistent and coherent philosophy. Then public broadcasting must remain steadfast in pursuing that philosophy until it wins the audience it needs by satisfying special interests with high quality programming.

References

1. Robert T. Bower. *Television and the Public* (New York: Holt, Rinehart and Winston, 1973).

2. Gary A. Steiner. *The People Look at Television: A Study of Audience Attitudes* (New York: Knopf, 1963).

3. Bower, see note 1.

4. Hartford N. Gunn, Jr. "Public Television Program Financing," *Educational Broadcasting Review*, VI:5 (October 1972), pp. 223-308.

5. Presley D. Holmes. "Public Broadcasting Development — The Next Step," *Educational Broadcasting Review*, VI:6 (December 1972), pp. 423-433.

6. Wilbur Schramm and Lyle Nelson. *The Financing of Public Television* (Palo Alto, Calif.: Aspen Institute Program on Communications and Society, 1972).

7. Roger G. Noll, Merton J. Peck and John J. McGowan. *Economic Aspects of Television Regulation* (Washington, D.C.: Brookings Institution, 1973).

Specialized Audiences: A Scaled-Down Dream?

STEVE MILLARD

Public broadcasting has always suffered from a chronic inability to name its own mission.* There have even been pockets of resistance to the idea that a diverse, locally based broadcasting service ought to *have* a single overriding mission — as if unity of purpose somehow implied subservience to central authority. Anyone brash or naive enough to raise so fundamental an issue could expect in response only a vague reference to "excellence and diversity" or to "serving communities," depending on whether the speaker's personal orientation was national or local. Often, the words have been delivered in a tone that seemed to dismiss the entire issue as more rhetorical than real.

Yet the issue persists, and with good reason. For to inquire about "mission" is to ask a simple, blunt, and wholly appropriate question: "What are you trying to do?" From public broadcasting, of all institutions, one has the right to expect a coherent response. Uniquely among American communications media, public broadcasting styles itself as a service that exists to do something distinc-

Mr. Millard is director of publications at CPB. He was formerly editor and is now chairperson, Editorial Advisory Board of the *Public Telecommunications Review.*

*The views expressed in this article do not necessarily reflect those of the Corporation for Public Broadcasting.

185

tive and important. It is reasonable to ask for a measure of precision about what that "something" is, and to discern in its absence the sign of a fundamental problem.

Over the years, those who speak for public broadcasting or one of its factions have devised a number of ways not to address this issue. Three stand out:

- Some have, in effect, denied that there is an "it" called public broadcasting to which a uniform "purpose" may be assigned. Apparently, the idea is that public television and radio stations are meant to "serve," but that the definition of "service" will vary with each locality. The argument is overdue for retirement. Public broadcasting is, after all, a movement in which complex national coordination is a fact of life. It is a movement that seeks nationwide public support — and federal funds — on the basis of its existence as a *single*, identifiable entity. Whatever differences there may be within its ranks, those who associate themselves with the designation "public broadcasting" say to the world that a common professional thread runs through their diverse activities, and that what unites them is more important than what divides them.

- Periodically, thoughtful professionals and observers have joined to create distinguished committees whose assigned task it was to define "goals." Unlike the extreme advocates of "localism," these groups have at least realized the inherent unity of public broadcasting and have sought to articulate it. Unfortunately, their statements have always sounded precisely like the work of committees, and their conclusions are seldom concrete or clear enough to be of use in the real world.

- Some in public broadcasting, realizing that the deliberations of committees are often beside the point, have noted that the real need is for a shared professional understanding. Ideally, such understanding would be embodied in the words of the best minds within a profession (whether or not they happen to lead major organizations), accepted spontaneously everywhere, and internalized by all as a guide to thinking and practice. This perception moves closer to the point. An understanding of professional "purpose" grows from tradition and experience; it does not arise because someone or some committee retires to a corner and concocts a creed. Unfortunately, this insight is not so much a solution as an interesting re-statement of the problem.

These well-meaning evasions of the issue are recurrent in the history of public broadcasting, but they are not the whole story. There have also been some conspicuous, though less than successful attempts actually to face and answer the question "What are you trying to do?" In recent years, one such answer has been heard frequently enough to deserve special attention. The answer is this: "We are trying to serve a series of specialized audiences, with the programming that each needs most and loves best. We are trying to reach all of the people — some of the time."

"Serving Specialized Audiences"

At first glance, that answer might appear to be a simple and fairly traditional way of contrasting public broadcasting, which seeks "specialized" audiences, with commercial broadcasting, which serves a "mass" audience. But it is much more than that.

What distinguishes this version of public broadcasting's purpose from most others is that it begins — and nearly ends — by defining purpose in terms of the intended *audiences*. All definitions of public broadcasting's mission contain two inseparable elements: (1) a conviction about the kind of programming that ought to be offered, and (2) a conviction about the kinds of people for whom the programming is intended. Previously, however, many conceptions of public broadcasting's mission began with some idea about programming, and then from that idea a sense of the intended audience was derived. By contrast, the doctrine of specialized audiences has few presuppositions about programming, but it aims to be quite precise, even scientific, about the audiences themselves.

The spirit behind "serving specialized audiences" is that public broadcasting — beginning at the local level — will devote its attention to establishing, first of all, what true specialized audiences *are*; that it will try to ascertain in detail what the audiences need and want; and that its programming will be tailored to meet those expressed needs. Whereas commercial broadcasting aspires to give the public what it wants, public broadcasting will give the *publics* what *they* want. It is assumed, however, that this philosophy — unlike commercial broadcasting's — will, by definition, produce good programming, because the programs will be attuned to the needs of active, knowledgeable, devoted groups, not simply tossed out to a passive audience. The theory is founded on diversity, not excellence, but it assumes that serious diversity demands excellence.

The idea is quite different from several other publicly expressed versions of what public broadcasting ought to do and be. In particular, it is different from the notion that public broadcasting's task is to provide the excellence that commercial broadcasting cannot or will not provide on a regular basis. This idea — heard more often outside public broadcasting than within it — represents a challenge to go out and shame the commercial networks with courageous and intelligent programming in such well-accepted "categories" as public affairs and drama. Gradually, these partisans hope, public broadcasting will draw attention and audiences away from commercial broadcasting (though it will never have a "mass" audience by commercial standards), and, in the process, the public programming will set a standard for all of American communications.

This viewpoint is not completely opposed to the idea of serving specialized audiences — either could accommodate a "Sesame Street" — but there is a crucial difference. This difference is not, as some apparently believe, that each viewpoint implies a certain "structure." The crucial difference is that the argument for what might be called "conspicuous excellence" begins with a programming hope and assumes that, if the programs are properly scheduled and promoted, appropriate audiences will follow.

Public broadcasting has taken great pains to disassociate itself from this notion, since the whole idea of conspicuous excellence sounds like head-on competition with the commercial networks. "Serving specialized audiences," on the other hand, has been heard more and more frequently and is vying for a place as *the* standard statement. It is invoked with approval by many of public broadcasting's leaders. It is evident in the widespread tendency to hang labels on real or potential audiences — labels ranging from "women," to "lovers of chess," to "blue-collar audiences." It is accepted enthusiastically by influential supporters of public broadcasting. Newton Minow noted, for example, that public television does not obtain high ratings "by the very nature of a program philosophy which seeks to serve many different audiences instead of a single mass audience."

The most extensive and influential reflection on the subject is offered by Lloyd N. Morrisett, president of the John and Mary R. Markle Foundation. In a long and thoughtful essay that highlighted the foundation's 1972/73 annual report, Morrisett notes that "public broadcasting must be justified on the basis of serving an audience," but that, for a variety of practical and philosophical reasons, it cannot compete directly for a mass audience. He concludes that public television "must then attract its primary audience by presenting material aimed at special subgroups of the population that share special interests." In fact, Morrisett notes *"this direction for public television has already been proclaimed, although the results* have been mediocre" (italics added).

Much of what Morrisett has to say is outside the scope of this article. He offers a lengthy critique of the "localism" concept, for example, and he speaks of the need to establish ratings and systems of incentive that are appropriate to public broadcasting. What matters in this context is simply his affirmation of the "specialized audiences" concept. That affirmation adds strength to an assumption that was already becoming wide-spread.

As public broadcasting's recent history has unfolded, gallon after gallon of ink has been spilled over organizational questions, especially the Station Program Cooperative. But there has been relatively little notice taken of the philosphy — not a "philosophy" really, but a single pervasive assumption — that accompanies these developments. The reason is probably that "serving specialized audiences" has such a ring of obvious truth about it that many take it for granted.

Certainly, it is simple good sense to insist that a public broadcaster — or any other serious communicator — be in close, effective touch with community needs. It is also logical to distinguish commercial broadcasting from public broadcasting not by the particular people that each serves, but by the way that each chooses to address *all* people. Finally, the commitment to serve special audiences seems to have its roots in that secular Scripture, the Carnegie Commission report, which speaks approvingly of service to many different audiences. With so much apparent logic and tradition on its side, the concept sounds like a leading candidate for the status of established truth.

It *is* a good idea — up to a point. In an enterprise that is often accused of being narrow and elitist, it is good to see an expressed concern for hard, close, effective observation of all people's needs. The trouble arises when "serving specialized audiences" is lifted from its natural place as one goal among several and is held aloft as *the* purpose of public broadcasting. Taken in isolation, as it often is, the concept raises serious questions — about what it means, what it implies, and where it leads. That the questions are not even being asked is a sure sign that something is being taken for granted. And nothing so clearly defines the problems of a movement as the things its participants take for granted.

Some Unexamined Assumptions About Specialized Audiences

Service to specialized audiences is sometimes taken to mean that the broadcaster programs for those with a sophisticated interest in public affairs and drama. Theoretically, it could also mean that the broadcaster programs for those who are deeply involved with canasta or the Roller Derby. Which will public broadcasting do?

According to a strict reading of the special-audience concept, public broadcasting will program for every audience in a way that respects the keen, devoted interest of that audience. Thus, there will be programming for the drama lover, programming for the student of public affairs, and programming for lovers of chess — or perhaps even checkers.

But which audiences deserve most attention, and why? The commitment to serving specialized audiences offers no criterion for making that decision. (It could be argued, for example, that *more* people are really interested in public affairs than in certain hobbies — although that is precisely the wrong argument, of course, because it introduces the same standard that governs commercial broadcasting.) The most likely response is not really an "argument" at all, but a gut reaction and an exasperated growl:

"Of course public broadcasting would run drama or public affairs before it would run someting trivial, because —" Because what? "Because — well, that's what public broadcasting is *for*. It's supposed to do *good* programming."

Of course it is. The greatest unspoken assumption about public broadcasting is that, whatever else it may or may not be, it is committed to excellence. The point seems too basic and too obvious to require comment — until one notices it disappearing altogether in the comprehensive concern for "serving specialized audiences."

It is instructive to consider the Carnegie Commission's treatment of the subject. The commission had a clear answer to the question, "Should public broadcasting serve specialized audiences?" — and the answer was a resounding "Yes." In the course of frowning on standard "networking," for example, the commission said that networking "presupposes a single audience, whereas public television seeks to serve differentiated audiences."

But the commission did not stop with the idea of specialized audiences — or, to be more precise, it did not begin there. The entire Carnegie report is permeated with the conviction that there is too little of consequence in commercial broadcasting, and that public broadcasting is uniquely equipped to raise the sights and widen the horizons of its viewers. One could quote any number of passages. Perhaps the best one of all comes not from the commission itself, but from a letter that E. B. White wrote — a letter that was used to set the tone for the Carnegie report:

> . . . noncommercial television should address itself to the ideal of excellence, not the idea of acceptability — which is what keeps commercial television from climbing the staircase. [It] should be the visual counterpart of the literary essay, should arouse our dreams, satisfy our hunger for beauty, take us on journeys, enable us to participate in events, present great drama and music, explore the sea and the bay and the woods and the hills. It should be our Lyceum, our Chautauqua, our Minsky's, and our Camelot. It should restate and clarify the social dilemma and the political pickle.

This passage radiates "diversity," but not the carefully calculated diversity that springs from a desire to "give the publics what they want." What is memorable in White's few words is the way that concrete, eloquent expressions of diversity flow naturally from a gifted writer's prior commitment to excellence, to "climbing the staircase." The issue is far more than a verbal contest between "excellence" and "diversity." The issue is what motivates public broadcasting as a total service.

Realistically, of course, public broadcasting continues to attract talented people who can and do produce individual programs of distinction. But if the appearance of these programs on the air is to be more than a lucky accident, there must be some workable set of priorities which affect the total pattern of activity. We have already seen that the focus on specialized audiences yields no priorities of its own. The obvious question, then, is whether exhortations about excellence are any more helpful.

The notion of serving specialized audiences at least has a ring of practicality and objectivity about it. Merely to mention excellence, on the other hand, is to induce slumber among the pragmatic. Excellence, we are told, is subjective. Excellence is vague. Excellence is probably elitist. Excellence is for commencement addresses.

The first response to these points is that excellence can be translated into words that are clear enough to give a sense of direction. The second response is that "serving specialized audiences" is far less clear than it sounds. What is a "specialized audience," anyway? There are stock answers: Children's programming (for various age groups), "serious" drama programming and public-affairs programming are among the broader ones; yoga, chess and cooking programs are narrower; programs for minorities or women are among the more sensitive. But the wild diversity of these categories — the fact that one person could belong to almost all of them and that several of them are found on commercial television — suggests that it may be futile to carve up the world this way.

To prolong the sense of futility, consider this example: Is "public affairs" for a specialized audience? Some argue that it is. After all, only a certain number of people have a continuing and active interest in the subject. A heavy dose of public affairs, such as coverage of the state legislature, will draw only a modest audience by television standards — though the audience would be far larger than any that saw the legislature in person. At the same time, consider the number of people who watch network news regularly, or who will watch a special report such as coverage of the Nixon resignation. With those figures in hand, it is reasonable to question whether the audience is at all "specialized."

The point is not that there is *never* such a thing as a specialized audience. The term can be sensible and productive when an audience simply cannot be reached unless one pays attention to its unique

192

characteristics — level of childhood development, for example, or language. It makes sense when applied to a particular "hobby" or "craft." There are also cases where a definable social group might have specific programming needs, although it would be questionable to call the group a specialized "audience." For example, a program on consumer topics might be genuinely useful to blue-collar families (*as well as* to others), just as a program called "Sesame Street" is demonstrably useful to young minority children — *and* to others.

The problem is that sometimes the expressed concern for "specialized audiences" gets in the way of simple understanding. Practically everyone has *some* interest in public affairs, *some* shared personal needs, and *some* level of response to all the human activities that go by the name "the arts." Moreover, in each of these fundamental areas, commercial broadcasting is doing less than is needed. It follows, then, that the *first* service public broadcasting could perform is to address these more general needs with programming that is good enough to matter, occasionally controversial enough to have bite, and imaginative enough to reach a wide audience.

The first fact about communication is not that there are thousands of discrete particles called "interests" and "needs," waiting for someone to come along and meet them. The first fact is that there are human beings in the world with a few definable needs and an endless variety of personal histories, levels of attention and biases. One individual's commitment to public affairs is exhausted by 10 minutes of the local Happy News team; another individual would like nothing better than a serious discussion of international monetary affairs; another would find that discussion heavy going, but has an honest interest in learning *something* about the subject. One individual's devotion to "the arts" is best illustrated by "Ironside," another's by "King Lear." But no one of these horizons is fixed, or even readily definable. There is always room for discovery.

That was always the problem with the idea that commercial broadcasting "gives the public what it wants." The problem is not that the idea is false — people do watch, after all — but that it is smug. It assumes that whatever exists now is *all* that most people want, or all that they *could* want.

Specialized audiences? It would be more accurate to say that public broadcasting was meant to address a special quality in every person. The individual who notices, who questions, who wants to grow — each of us is that individual in certain moments of our lives, and public broadcasting was intended to address us in those moments. It was meant to be "excellent" — in a special and definable way.

The Meaning of Excellence

Recall some of public broadcasting's best programs — the ones that, taken together, are the medium's most conspicuous claim to distinction. They share an important characteristic, and that characteristic is not the discovery of a unique "category," or the meeting of a need that no one else had happened upon. The programs share an excellence that begins with a seriousness of purpose, but goes beyond it — an excellence in the *how* of communication, not simply in the what. They are successful because they bring truth to life — because they get something across to people who might not have grasped it otherwise. The point was made rather well by Huw Wheldon, managing director of television for the BBC, in a televised conversation with Bill Moyers: "Programs should be truthful in their different ways. If a program is funny, well, then¡ it should be a good program that is funny and a funny program that is good. If it is a serious program, it should be truthful in its own serious way."

Many of the best public broadcasting programs — a disproportionate number, in fact — owe their excellence to the presence of a single, dominant individual, such as Bill Moyers or Kenneth Clark or Fred Rogers. Others, like "Sesame Street" or "All Things Considered," have a different kind of chemistry. But in each case, the end result is a special excellence in bringing truth to life. There was nothing terribly specialized about the topics (Learning to read? America in the seventies? The development of Western civilization?), and the closest one could come to a definition of "specialized audiences" is that some of the programs were meant for a particular group of children. But each of these programs, and others like them, shared the ideal and the achievement of excellence.

Attention to specialized audiences — or simply to audiences — is an essential part of this process. How can one know how to speak to people, except by involvement with them and their concerns? And specific programs for specific sub-groups are a part of what public broadcasting ought to be doing. But this is far from all that must be expected of public broadcasting. The concept of diversity, by itself, is a dead end. What can public broadcasting do for specialized audiences that might not be done better in 10 years by a combination of the marketplace and new technology — unless public broadcasting has a unique substantive commitment of its own?

Only a focus on excellence allows an unambiguous criterion for distinguishing public and commercial broadcasting. There is nothing elitist about this idea — not if excellence is clearly linked to the goal of bringing truth to life. Better to start with a commitment to doing great things — opening minds, widening horizons, raising hell — and to attract an audience for that, than to begin with an empty vessel called "interests and needs" and then try to pour programming into it.

The emphasis on specialized audiences is one more example of the tendency to confuse means with ends, tools with edifices, conditions of success with success itself. And when public broadcasting itself is confused, others will also be confused. Far less confusing was one of the many letters that Bill Moyers received when he left public television — from a man whose praise was expressed in these words: "You helped me to see what I mean." There could hardly be a finer tribute, or a better description of what public broadcasting ought to be doing every day.

The Role of Human Judgments

Yet the question remains: How does this understanding of excellence yield priorities? The answer is that it does not. Nothing "yields" priorities. The core of public broadcasting, or any other form of communication, is *value judgments* by particular human beings about what subjects matter most, which audiences need special attention, and which programs have special distinction. Research, testing, and "ascertainment" may inform these judgments but will never replace them.

A fundamental weakness in discussions about serving specialized audiences is that they obscure this truth under a veneer of "objectivity": The arguments for specialized audiences claim to imply certain priorities, but they can never substantiate that claim. By contrast, a clear focus on excellence has the fundamental virtue of acknowledging, and indeed highlighting, the central role of unscientific, human judgments. Unfortunately, as an institution, public broadcasting seems to have spent half its life in flight from the acknowledgment, let alone the highlighting, of this plain truth. Only reluctantly, amid discussions of "systems" and "processes," is human judgment mentioned at all.

To understand this reluctance, one need only consider the role of rhetoric in the practical world. Whatever meanings a statement of purpose may have within a profession, its external function is to *justify*: to persuade, to set a tone, to provide a framework of understanding that helps win support for an institution. If a growing number of influential spokesmen are attracted to "serving specialized audiences" as a rationale for public broadcasting, it would seem likely that — whether consciously or not — they find the words a convenient device to disarm criticism, to soothe influential nerves, and to clear a path for the safe progress of public broadcasting as an institution.

The typical *applications* of this rationale of specialized audiences suggest that the idea is used too often as a protective device. For example:

- The argument for serving specialized audiences is frequently cited as a justification for small audiences, even when a program is meant for and clearly hopes to attract a sizeable number of viewers.

- The argument is used to justify all types of programs. There is almost nothing that could not be called a "program for a specialized audience" if the words simply mean, as they often seem to, that some people are interested and some aren't. Consider, for instance, "The Way It Was," which looks remarkably like just another sports program, but which some public broadcasters have welcomed because it may attract a "blue-collar" audience.

- The argument is the most convenient, least abrasive way of distinguishing public from commercial broadcasting. To keep peace with its funders and to ensure its own growth, public broadcasting must (and does) exhibit a concern for serving all the people. But if it appears overly bold or competitive, it can always hedge by saying, "Of course, we are interested in serving them in small packages only."

Lloyd Morrisett is straightforward about this last point. Direct competition between public and commercial broadcasting "is simply not in the tradition of private enterprise in the United States," he says.

> It would be vigorously resisted by commercial broadcasters as well as by many others who would consider such competition plainly wrong. More important, perhaps, is that this is not the role that Congress or the Federal Communications Commission envisaged for public broadcasting. It is not the concept that has been used to justify public television to the American people.

This argument would be entirely justifiable if public broadcasting were to "compete" with the commercial networks in the same way that CBS competes with NBC — that is, if public broadcasting were to seek large audiences simply for the numbers, with no commitment to distinctive or alternative programs. But this is not the case, and Morrisett is not arguing that issue. What he is really saying — and he is candid enough to say out loud what others say quietly — is that public broadcasting, in the interests of its own survival and growth, cannot afford to match or even to approach the audience numbers of commercial broadcasting, regardless of the purpose or the quality of its programs. In short, the idea of "serving specialized audiences" can be an honest expression of concern for real and varied needs, but it is as likely to be a formula for establishing a safe distance between public broadcasters and whatever forces may threaten their existence.

If public broadcasting and its critics agree on anything, of course, it is that the system is not "competing" right now. The irony is that many of those in public broadcasting attribute this state of affairs to their concern for specialized audiences, while some critics argue that specialized audiences are precisely what public broadcasting is *not* serving. Unfortunately, the debate is being conducted on almost entirely the wrong ground, because the critics have focused their attention on public television's Station Program Cooperative, which the broadcasters in turn feel obliged to defend. The critics argue that the cooperative tends to yield "safe," even "mass appeal" programming and to neglect the daring, the different, the boldly specialized.

It is true that many, probably most, of public broadcasting's programs are not "specialized" in any meaningful sense, though that by itself is no criticism. But what the critics are really saying, in almost every case, is that public broadcasting lacks a clear set of priorities — a nucleus of programs designed to do something excellent for a wide audience, and an accompanying list of programs carefully tailored to particular needs. If that is so, why blame the cooperative — which is simply a mechanism for translating demands into programs (and only one of several at that)? Why not focus on the priorities themselves?

A more basic analysis of the problem might read as follows: Public broadcasting's first priority right now is not a program priority at all, but its own progress as an institution. Locally, some stations and state networks generate distinctive styles and priorities. As a nationwide entity, however, public broadcasting appears to be trying to respond to any and all influences that are not inconsistent with its goal of building wider "support." It will at times program for "specialized" audiences, particularly those whose demands are loudest. It will also frequently program for general, if quite limited, audiences. What it will *not* do, apparently, is chart an independent and adventurous program direction which is informed by detailed knowledge of its audience, but inspired by a commitment that precedes the accumulation of "facts."

The opening paragraphs of this article refer to public broadcasting's traditional confusion over its own mission and the signs in that confusion of a deeper problem. We can now see that the deeper problem, in its present form, is the classic ailment of institutions — a turning from external goals to preoccupation with survival. The notion of "serving specialized audiences" is not the only evidence of this preoccupation, but it is among the most basic and least recognized pieces of evidence. Public broadcasting is now beginning to be *defined* by this preoccupation with survival.

Of course, many people in public broadcasting reject "serving specialized audiences" as a statement of their purpose, and others who support the concept would not knowingly participate in the confusion it has created. Nevertheless, the confusion exists, it affects the entire institution, and it ought to be eliminated. We might begin with the following propositions:

> To hold up the notion of "serving specialized audiences" as *the* goal of public broadcasting is to wrench the idea of diversity away from the idea of excellence. It is to hold as gospel an idea that is descriptively incorrect, logic-

ally untenable, normatively inadequate, and sometimes politically motivated. Public broadcasting has no reason to exist on those terms. It has meaning only when linked to the idea that excellence is its goal; that its particular brand of excellence is inseparably connected with bringing truth to life; that success may mean large audiences, visibility, and controversy, all of which should be accepted without apology; that diversity and specialized service are by-products of excellence, not excellence itself.

Perhaps public broadcasting will follow a safe course and settle for a safe niche. But if that is to happen, let us at least be explicit about its true goal, so that we may gauge the distance between what it is and what it ought to be. Let us at least be able to say, as Huw Wheldon did in his conversation with Bill Moyers: "The game is not avoiding failure at all costs. The game is giving triumph a chance, isn't it?"

Public Broadcasting Audience & Program Research: Problems & Possibilities

JACK LYLE

Research, in the context of public broadcasting programming, is confined here to the somewhat narrow idea of studies of the content and of the viewers/listeners of public broadcasting fare. There are other kinds of research within the public system — technical/engineering studies, for example, or the compilation and analysis of a wide variety of systems data. However, we are concerned here only with activities intended (1) to help identify and rank programming possibilities, (2) to help maximize the potential of programming to achieve specific objectives among the audience, (3) to evaluate programs and schedules in terms of the number and types of viewers, and (4) to measure behavioral and/or attitudinal reactions of viewers to specific programs.

Students are told that, in addition to being effective, research should be parsimonious and cumulative. These goals are particularly desirable in an organization like public broadcasting, in which resources are always short. On the other hand, these goals — and research generally — seem to be particularly difficult to achieve in public broadcasting. To explain why and to offer some possible solutions or compromises is the function of this article.

Dr. Lyle is director of the East-West Communication Institute and former director of Communication Research for CPB.

The Future of Public Broadcasting

The major components of any broadcasting communication system are three:

1. The *content*, the programs distributed by the system.

2. The *distribution process*, which includes such activities as scheduling, promotion, and the provision of auxiliary materials.

3. The *audience*, that aggregate of persons who make use of the programs.

Each of these components requires appropriate research support.

Content. Research support in the content area can be provided at several stages. First, there is the selection of specific subject matter from the universe of possible topics. What things might interest people? What needs might be satisfied? Once topics are decided, research can also provide information which is helpful in selecting among different possible treatments for the development of the subject matter.

Broadly speaking, this is called *ascertainment research*. The FCC requires certain activities by commercial stations to "ascertain community needs" and has announced its intention to expand the requirement to public stations as well. However, the requirement amounts to little more than soliciting statements from a broad range of "community leaders." Many if not most commercial stations have been able to get by with little more than a *pro forma* compliance.

Sound content research would go far beyond these minimal and very general FCC requirements, of course. For instance, program ideas can be obtained from monitoring such indicators as public opinion polls, the subject index of the *Reader's Guide to Periodical Literature*, or the circulation figures and economic trends of special interest magazines. Surveys, either of the general public or of specific groups, are also useful in providing indicators of public needs and preferences. These indicators can then be refined and developed in more depth through discussions with panels or focus groups. A further survey might be used to validate the panel results.

Once program topics are selected, research can be helpful in deciding which of several possible treatments would be most effective in developing the topic. For example, "story board" testing with panel groups can provide insights at the pre-production stage, while experimental testing of programs or program segments during the production process can validate the potential effectiveness and attractiveness of the material.

Distribution. Careful analysis of production research and/or of past "performance" data for individual programs can help in the distribution process (scheduling, promotion, etc.). The point of scheduling is, of course, to provide the optimum opportunity for a program to reach the appropriate audience. Various types of monitoring, as well as experimental pre-testing, might be used in this research operation. The same type of research could also help those charged with the promotion of programming or with the development of nonbroadcast auxiliary materials.

Audience. Several techniques — diaries, telephone surveys, set meters, etc. — can provide estimates of the number of viewers. Many of these are available from commercial services, which will also provide some standard data on *who* is in the audience. Questions of audience response or program impact are somewhat more difficult, but they can be answered through special applications of field research. For instance, in-home viewing panels can be established, with post-viewing telephone interviews as a part of the procedure.

On a more sophisticated level, audience response can be obtained using two-way cable systems. Unusual programs which feature audience-response mechanisms — the telephone reference service of "V.D. Blues," for example, or the series "Feeling Good" — can offer special opportunities for setting up a system for monitoring and recording audience responses. Such procedures can be especially useful in providing information to the development staffs which have the responsibility for building financial contributions from viewers.

Structural Constraints on Public Broadcasting Research

Commercial broadcasters regularly use the aforementioned research techniques to pre-test content and to estimate audience size and composition. Naturally, advertisers are always very concerned about any research procedures that will reveal the impact of programs and their commercials. Over the past 15 years or so, public broadcasting has also come to focus a considerable amount of energy and money on research activities, but the overall research picture within public broadcasting remains largely fragmented and unsynthesized.

At least four major factors contribute to this confused, discouraging state of affairs:

- First, public broadcasting is a decentralized system. On the commercial networks, both the selection and scheduling of programs are central decisions, and there is little deviation by individual stations. In public broadcasting, however, the individual stations retain the prerogatives of selecting and scheduling the programs distributed by the Public Broadcasting Service (PBS). Indeed, both PBS and the Corporation for Public Broadcasting (CPB) are specifically enjoined from being directly involved in program production units, and both are extremely sensitive to anything which might be viewed as interference with their creative freedom by the two national organizations.

- Second, whereas all commercial stations have the same basic structure and goals, public broadcasting is quite diverse. The community public stations, which are operated by nonprofit community groups, are considerably different in both structure and goals from the educational stations, which are splintered into university, local school board, and state educational authority licensees. As a result, there is a wide variation in the organization structure and the operational goals of the public broadcasting stations.

- Third, public broadcasting aims to provide "alternative" programming, but there is no consensus within the industry (or outside it) as to what type of programs would meet that definition.

- Fourth, "alternative programs," of whatever type, probably imply relatively small or specialized audiences, and such audiences are difficult both to identify and to reach.

The impact of these four factors of research is cumulative. Decentralization, for instance, is compounded by the diversity of the stations. The relationships between CPB, PBS, National Public Radio (NPR), the individual stations, and the independent production units are hampered by friction points which all too frequently burst into flames of conflict of interest. Note that PBS stands for Public Broadcasting *Service*, not *system*. PBS has no authority to impose its individual programs or its schedule upon the stations. Indeed, during the 1974-75 broadcast season, PBS did not even have a regular weekly report of the carriage of PBS programs by the stations.* Obviously, this situation introduces great difficulty for research organizations in obtaining national audience information.

The diversity of the stations and their support bases also affects their programming goals — the "alternatives" they seek to provide. The various types of stations are trying to do different things for different people. These differences, in turn, affect what each station perceives to be its needs both in ascertainment and evaluation research. For the present discussion, these differences can be categorized into three general groups: (1) the "fourth network" philosophy, (2) the "instructional" philosophy, and (3) the "public access" philosophy. Many if not most stations operate on a basis of compromise between two or all of these philosophies, but the attempts to stipulate the optimum balance between them continue to be a major source of tension for the public broadcasting system, its supporters, and its critics.

The "fourth network" adherents see the role of public broadcasting as one of evolving into an American BBC First Service, working to transform what Newton Minow termed "the vast wasteland" of commercial television in this country. "Alternative programming" to this group means scheduling not only programs like the British imports which constitute the fare of "Masterpiece Theatre" but also "Monty Python's Flying Circus," tennis matches,

---

*The staff at PBS understandably seeks audience information to help make operational decisions, but since 1974, PBS has been dependent upon CPB for the provision of rating data. However, the CPB research staff puts considerable emphasis on the collection and use of these figures for "accountability" purposes, not for audience or programming information *per se*. The divergence of these approaches to the data produces tension and certainly reduces the practical utility of the data package to PBS. This difference has been narrowed recently with changes of management emphasis at CPB.

and hockey games. They justify these programs (to their own satisfaction if not to that of their critics) because the programs are in fact "alternatives" to the programs offered by commercial stations in their signal area within a specific time slot. The selection of such programs is also heavily influenced by the knowledge that they usually are more successful than the average PBS program in attracting viewers *and* viewer contributions.

At the other extreme are those who claim that public broadcasting should be basically a "public access" channel, providing an opportunity for ethnic, cultural or philosophical minorities to obtain public exposure via the broadcast media. They argue that this is a particular responsibility of public broadcasters because these broadcasters receive funds from the federal government.

Finally, although most school board stations today divide their programming emphasis between daytime instruction and evening entertainment and public affairs, there remains a cadre committed to specifically instructional programming. They can point to the fact that almost all public stations utilize frequency allocations which were withheld from would-be commercial operators because they are "reserved" by the FCC for educational purposes.

Such diversity — one might call it chaos — makes it extremely difficult if not impossible to have a coherent, cost-efficient central research program satisfactory to the entire system. The problems for researchers are exemplified by the divergent reactions within public broadcasting to a CPB publication which attempted to summarize audience data, *The People Look at Public Television — 1974*. Warm praise was voiced by many program managers, but at least some development people (those in charge of attracting corporation underwriting for program production) felt that the publication undercut their attempts. Indeed, it has been seriously proposed within CPB that different versions of audience data be prepared for distribution to underwriters, to ethnic groups, and to members of the Congress.

There was nothing dishonest in this suggestion. It was simply an awkward approach to the resolution of a very frustrating situation. The nature of public broadcasting's audience is very complex and very difficult to describe concisely. Yet impassioned members of pressure groups have little patience to hear out the whole story. Simple, direct answers to one group have the potential of becoming critical ammunition to be used by those of different viewpoints for an attack on public broadcasting. Although the proposal for distinct reports to different groups was never formally implemented, operationally it has been followed on an *ad hoc* basis in responding to specific requests from the various interest groups. The results have been extremely embarrassing charges that public broadcasters play a rather loose game with their audience data.

Still another research problem is created by the concept of alternative and/or minority programming. Within the context of America's polyglot population, members of most minorities have multiple group memberships or identities. This means that while they may be a "minority" with reference to one characteristic, in other characteristics they may be members of the majority. The genius of commercial network programming is the establishment of broad common denominators with which people from so many backgrounds can identify and find enjoyment. Thus, alternative programming designed to appeal to a highly specific group must, in the end, compete with the commercial programs for the attention of members of that group; for the group may well be attracted to the popular network shows as well.

This means that, in most instances, public television programs will have small audiences. But "small" is a relative term. In a nation with over 200 million viewers, where commercial network programs are expected to attract 20 million viewers or more, an audience of even 10 million is "small." Public television programs have seldom attracted audiences even that large, although in the 1975-76 season it achieved some "breakthroughs." For example, "The Incredible Machine" produced a shock throughout the television world when it attracted about one-fourth of the nation's TV homes, more than were tuned to the programs featured by two of the major networks in the same time period. But this was an exception. Most public television programs continue to have audiences more in the range of 1 to 5 percent of the nation's TV homes. Public radio's audience is even smaller. Still, these "small" audiences do include a lot of people.

Two aspects of this relative "smallness" are important to the researcher in public broadcasting. One is size *per se*, and the other is the nature of the individuals in an audience for a specific program series. If the alternative program is intended for a very specific group within the population, a research staff may be able to create a sophisticated stratified sampling from which members of that group — and that group alone — can be identified and measured far more effectively than through general national random samples.

However, as the alternative programming becomes less directly related to fairly standard socioeconomic and/or ethnic characteristics, such refined data become more difficult to obtain.

The overall problem for research is even more complicated, since from the standpoint of a public station's total schedule, we are not talking about one alternative program, but a constellation of such alternatives. The various programs within that constellation probably are intended to serve different specific groups. Thus, the researcher is in need of either multiple sampling frames or vastly increased general random samples which can assure sufficient numbers of each group for analysis. Either procedure is expensive, far more expensive than the comparatively small and simple samples which can adequately satisfy the requirements of the commercial networks.

Given these costly requirements, plus the overall problems of decentralization and the tensions which exist on and below the surface, public broadcasting research is unlikely to achieve a high degree of parsimony easily or quickly. At this point, the goal of making the research efforts *cumulative* seems more realistic, although decentralization poses hurdles for that goal, too. The various local ascertainment studies could be a useful beginning in compiling indicators of needs and desires that cut across the nation. The materials would have to be used in cumulative fashion, of course, which means that considerable central coordination would be required.

Possibilities for Cumulative Research

Any consideration of what the public broadcasting research program should be must relate to the nature of the system. At present, there is only one major research budget available for the entire system: that provided within the administrative budget of CPB. Children's Television Workshop (CTW) has a research budget rivalling or surpassing that of CPB, but those funds are devoted primarily to CTW's production activities. Some individual stations, production units, and regional networks also have their own research resources, but as in the case of CTW, they are devoted specifically to the needs of the parent organization. Thus, with few exceptions (primarily CTW), the resources available for general research in public broadcasting are extremely limited.

It makes good sense, then, that public broadcasters would share and cooperate in their research resources and efforts. But cooperation is hard to achieve. To use standardized techniques, even common questions, frequently means sacrificing the local specificity which a station staff rightly or wrongly feels is essential to the information they want. Production units also hesitate to share because they are competing for funding. Academic researchers, whom many stations depend upon, are noted for their zealous protection of their individual freedom. Good will, good sense, and proper persuasion can help build cooperation and exchange. But, inevitably, a central resource facility will be required as well. The suspicions which plague public broadcasting entities might suggest that this facility be an "outside" agency, but practical considerations argue that it should be provided by and within CPB.

Content research. Ascertainment is a good place to begin discussion of how the various units of public broadcasting could do research individually, yet cooperatively, and how CPB would relate to such a strategy. Although the FCC has not yet required public stations to perform ascertainment of community needs, many public station managements have already undertaken such studies, and the rest should want to. Individual stations have the responsibility for ascertainment within their own markets, but CPB can provide dissemination of techniques (a) by circulating reports of individual studies, (b) by supporting workshops organized, for instance, by the NAEB, and (c) by providing additional advice and direction. CPB has already underwritten the production of a handbook of possible ascertainment methods.

CPB should not involve itself in the actual field work or analysis of the individual studies; and whether or not it should provide actual dollar support, outright or on a matching basis, is debatable. Given the number of stations in the system, it probably is not practical for CPB to provide direct financial support for research efforts. On the other hand, stations can finance such studies out of the Community Service Grants (CSGs) which they receive each year from CPB. Indeed, some stations have already done so. (It is appropriate to note that some of the stations have done so with no prior knowledge on the part of the CPB research staff — still another example of the decentralization which plagues the industry.) Thus, a first goal might be to persuade stations to coordinate their research efforts with the CPB research staff and to provide the staff with a copy of the results.

Because it is the only agency with a budget for system-wide research, CPB is also the logical agency to provide for national "ascertainments." This task might mainly require the central coordination of local studies. However, in addition, CPB should commission some studies which seek information on programming needs and interests within the national context. Such studies should probably involve preliminary group discussions followed by a survey of national scope to provide broad-based tests of the ideas generated from the discussions.*

CPB involvement in formative research during production would be of questionable propriety under the present law, and there are plenty of persons who would jump at the opportunity to point an accusing finger. However, there are ways in which CPB could provide research support at this point without running the risk of being accused, either by Congress, producers or pressure groups, of trying to interfere with program content. For example, for each new project, CPB could provide a budgetary line item specifically for program development research to be administered and funded by its own research department. Producers submitting proposals to CPB for pilots or series could also be encouraged to build an appropriate reserach component into their proposals. In this way, if the proposal were approved, its research component would then be referred to CPB's research staff for study and a separate decision as to the funding of the research plan for the program.

Such a procedure would have several advantages. First, the producer would be given the burden of formulating the research needs for a program proposal. This could help ensure a real commitment to the research. Second, the procedure would enable producers with production funding from other sources to apply to CPB for research support. Third, by having the research funding considered separately from that for production, the producer would be less likely to feel that scarce production funds are being diverted to research. This is an important advantage in a situation where

---

*It should be noted that the John and Mary R. Markle Foundation has been supporting preliminary efforts toward this end. Also, in recent years, the TV Activities staff of CPB has attempted to establish a priority ranking of program areas on the basis of an informal review of the current American scene. They select a few areas which they recommend to the board for program possibilities to be disseminated to the stations. To date, this form of ascertainment research has not been as finely focused as it might be, but CPB's research department has been moving in the direction of refining its definitions of needs and interests within certain areas, particularly with reference to specified "target audiences."

production budgets are small and fragmented among many production units. Finally, this plan guarantees that CPB cannot be charged with interfering with content through research activities; and at the same time, it gives CPB the opportunity to assure the high quality of research by prior review of the plan and resources. The results of the research would be available to the CPB TV Activities staff when they ultimately faced the decision of funding a full series or a continuation of the series.

Still another benefit of this procedure is that it would help CPB focus its programming goals. In recent years, the CPB staff has attempted to make would-be producers stipulate the goals of their program proposals. Obviously, the more precise such stipulation, the more effectively research can be used for program evaluation. Perhaps out of recognition of that fact, many would-be producers have attempted to make this section of their proposals as vague as possible so that they will have (or think they will have) several options to use in arguing their case. Having to think through a detailed plan of research in support of their production would help producers to increase the specificity of their goals and to better meet their commitment to "alternative" programming.

Measuring audience and program impact. Audience impact research must inevitably include some estimates of audience size. With public broadcasting, however, this is a touchy issue in the present situation. Ultimately, the question of whether or not PBS is or should be the fourth network must be faced and answered. At present, there is equivocation from every direction. Congress doesn't help when its members deride public broadcasting for seeking mass audiences and then the legislators turn around and ask public broadcasting to prove its worth on the basis of how many people watch and listen.

In the first several years of its existence, PBS purchased weekly ratings of the programs in its schedule from the Nielsen Company. Later, with the help of the Ford Foundation, special analyses of the Nielsen data were done by Statistical Research, Inc., because the weekly figures of Nielsen seemed of doubtful use. Since 1974, PBS has not had a budget for buying ratings and has had to depend upon CPB for its information. CPB purchased a much-reduced research package, including individual program ratings for only about eight weeks out of the year, plus data for various cumulative time periods.

No matter how they are obtained, national ratings are expensive. They also have some methodological deficiencies in dealing with small audiences for individual programs. These deficiencies are particularly a problem in the case of public broadcasting, where there is no firm national schedule and programs may be repeated within and beyond a single week. Thus, given the present size of public broadcasting's audience, public broadcasters should find it both costly and dangerously misleading to use national ratings on a weekly basis for individual programs. On the other hand, at present, there is probably no more cost-efficient way to obtain current estimates of the *total* reach of the public broadcasting system than that provided by the cumulative figures of the rating services.

Other useful types of estimates, not related to individual programs, are also feasible. For example, under CPB sponsorship, Dr. Natan Katzman has experimented with compilation of figures using the individual reports of major markets. Since this procedure provides a larger aggregate sample than weekly national samples, demographic cross-tabulations can be made for individual programs. In this way, we can get an indication of what a program does under maximum conditions and without the reception handicaps which continue to plague public broadcasting on a national basis. Further, with the Katzman procedure, program performance in each market can be related to scheduling idiosyncrasies. From an operational standpoint, this type of analysis should cover the operational and accountability needs of both CPB and PBS and is far more valuable — and probably cheaper — than the weekly national ratings.*

Obviously, the standard commercial rating services cannot provide appropriate research information on the highly specific audiences for narrowly defined "alternative programs." To the extent that public broadcasting *does* provide such programs, it must also provide research contingencies for mounting special studies. This was one of the goals of the CPB/Ford Foundation "Public

---

*The Katzman analysis does not provide as estimate of the national audience of individual programs, however. This is a problem mainly for the people working to secure corporate underwriting for public broadcasting programming. These people always stress the "network" aspects of PBS programs, and both they and the representatives of the underwriting corporations ask for and feel entitled to national ratings. The solution seems clear. Until the public broadcasting programs are able to regularly attract significantly larger audiences, those concerned with underwriting should be made to understand at the outset that public broadcasting is different from the commercial networks and that national ratings are not appropriate tools for evaluation. This will create grumbling, but it is the only honest approach. In the long run, this approach should also help to develop a more positive attitude on the part of the corporate underwriters.

Television Survey Facility," which operated from 1972 to 1975. The goal was never fully realized, although some preliminary developmental studies were completed.

The major problem with this kind of research (as noted earlier) is that of constructing appropriate samples. The task could be commissioned from either commercial or academic sources, but both would require special funding. Thus, at the same time that approval is given for a new "alternative" series, there should also be planning for the research design and for its execution — including funding.

For those series which are funded by CPB, financial responsibility for the research should be assumed by CPB. If the series is funded by other agencies, such as the Office of Education, the National Endowments, private foundations, or commercial institutions, the underwriter should be given a clear understanding that if it wishes that type of information for evaluation, it must provide funding for the research. With proper central coordination by CPB and cooperative work by the research agencies, it should be possible in this way to achieve economies for everyone involved.

This plan should also apply to research to determine the impact of a program — that is, its success (or failure) in achieving stipulated program goals. We can anticipate that sponsoring agencies will be reluctant to pay for such research. Like the producers they support, these agencies are reluctant to reduce what all-too-frequently is a poverty-level production budget. The public broadcasting entities have felt so starved for content that they and funding agencies have agreed again and again to accept goal-oriented programming without any provision for obtaining the evaluation that everyone agreed the programming needed. Frequently, funding agencies have cut the research provision with a prayerful suggestion that perhaps other sources of money could be tapped for the purpose.

This approach has perpetuated a great deal of production which deep in our hearts we have known to be not merely ineffective but downright bad. The fact that so much of the content of public broadcasting is just plain dull can also be attributed in part to this situation. Production agencies and stations have been allowed to develop bad habits. Without research evidence to "prove" it, however, we have been able to avert our eyes from what, in effect, have been serious and continuing failures.

The Future of Public Broadcasting

In any area of research, it is important that research results are collated, synthesized and shared throughout the system. Given the decentralized nature of public broadcasting, synthesis and cooperation take on still greater importance, and CPB ought to provide this service for the system.

The CPB research staff has taken some steps in that direction. "Focus on Research," a frequent insert in the *CPB Report*, is an attempt to summarize in pragmatic terms the research on specific questions. Another effort of the CPB staff has been a compilation of different wordings used in research questioning and in comparing results. This project is not yet completed, but it will be of great help to stations trying to do local studies with limited resources. It should also aid the stations in making local research results more clearly comparable and cumulative.

These efforts by CPB are useful, but there is still an urgent need for analytic sifting through the data which flows in (or should flow in) to CPB from the various sources. At the present time, there is no one source for even the most basic information on programs and audiences. CPB and PBS staff members frequently are embarrassed to find themselves quoted with conflicting figures. Even more embarrassing are the occasions mentioned earlier when different sections of the same organization publicly contradict one another. Sometimes this reflects tension in the public broadcasting system, but most often it is the result of persons trying to do their jobs without access to a central data bank.

The Need for Management Decisions

Public broadcasting has had and continues to have many problems, probably more than its share. The evolution from "educational" to "public" broadcasting introduced new diffusion into its operation. Stations once firmly committed to using the potential of broadcasting for educating the public are tempted by the "fourth network" philosophy and the prospects it seems to offer for increased audiences and funding. On the other hand, as nonprofit "community stations" now receiving federal monies, the big city "fourth network" stations find themselves under increased challenge from politicized minorities. For example, the black member of the

FCC, Benjamin Hooks, has accused them (and public broadcasting generally) of overemphasis on programs for the rich at the expense of services to the poor and underprivileged. Thus, the long-sought financial relief provided by federal appropriations has increased pressures for a *quid pro quo* in programming policy.

PBS is a membership organization. Since that membership is diverse, it is not surprising that PBS's management decisions have reflected considerable equivocation. CPB's board has also been less than decisive, at least partly as a result of the considerable political buffeting in its eight-year history. Given this situation, perhaps it is not fair to expect that the board should have evolved a strong policy. But fair or not, the point remains that the key agency responsible for administering the millions of dollars provided annually by Congress for public broadcasting has spent most of its energies reacting to competing pressure groups on an almost *ad hoc* basis rather than on the basis of a firmly established statement of policy and goals. While such an unequivocal statement inevitably would be subject to criticism by some sectors, it would at least provide an unshifting framework from which to operate and seek public support. Without a real operational policy, CPB will continue to suffer from a lack of public identity, as well as the more serious confusions (even within broadcasting circles) concerning its nature, its functions, and its goals.

Among the debilitating results of this unfortunate situation is the fact that researchers, particularly at the central agencies, have found themselves being asked to provide primarily tactical support for short-term problems which continue to change. If public broadcasting's multi-headed management structure can come to firm decisions regarding program goals and policies, the prospects for effective research will be much improved. These prospects will also be enhanced (1) if agreement can be reached concerning the delegation of responsibility for various research operations, and (2) if pressures can be brought to bear to reduce confused duplication of research activities and of the reporting of results. Public broadcasting is too fragile an institution to continue to endure the confusion and internal conflicts which have plagued it since the passing of the Public Broadcasting Act of 1967. Indeed, it is not unreasonable to suggest that if this confusion and conflict persists, there may be something basically unsound in the structure which the present law forces on the institution.

Research and its synthesis can be useful in decision-making

but it cannot substitute for sound policy. Making decisions and policy is a management function. Thus, until there is a long-term strategic concept guiding public broadcasting, it will be impossible for its research arm to develop a coherent operation which has those desirable characteristics of parsimony and cumulativeness. And what is true of research will inevitably also be true of programming.

A Future Vision
of Public Television
Programming

ROBERT KOTLOWITZ

We in public television exist in several futures simultaneously, and we seem to be learning to accommodate all of them with reasonable ease. There is, for one, the immediate future, that imminent set of daily crises and endless imponderables known as the "upcoming season." It is always upon us, always there lying-in-wait like a nagging conscience that cannot let go. It demands our best work, nothing less. The programs must be superbly provocative and filled with profound ideas and answers to everything, with gorgeous tributes to Culture in all its varieties, with odes to self-help and analysis, and with captivating ways of keeping the kids glued to the set while turning them into premature Ph.D.s. All of this, of course, is rightly expected to be dolled up with production values sophisticated enough to ensure that the novelty-sated adult audience will also stick with us, just like the kids, once they tune in. All of this must also be ready to be broadcast tonight or tomorrow or next week.

For producers and public television stations — for all television stations, in fact — the immediate future also demands the bulk of any working day at any given time, the largest slice of funds available, and the maintenance of a subtle, constant balance between

Mr. Kotlowitz is vice-president for Programming at WNET, New York.

the needs of creative energy and the reliable management of talent, money, and production schedules. This means the establishment of a flexible line, visible to all, along which both sides of the often opposing forces can work with some collaborative equanimity and in non-adversary positions. For public television, the immediate future also involves the daily involvement with the mechanics of our system. By that I mean the scheduling negotiations with the Public Broadcasting Service, the daily, welcome interchange of ideas and problems with both PBS and the Corporation for Public Broadcasting, and the necessary maintenance of friendly relations and productive problem-sharing with all of our colleagues at the 250 or so stations in the system.

This "future" is beyond belittling. It is the reality we deal with every day. It is with us all the time, in the harassing preparations and extensive research required to develop a valid set of program proposals that will make up a suitable list of entries into the Station Program Cooperative at the very moment that the upcoming season is opening. (By suitable, I mean a list that fits the needs of the system and its growing audience as well as each station's sense of its own self as a producer — and there, as we all know, vanity, to say nothing of self-interest, both play a certain role.) It is with us in the long, bracing, and, some think, debilitating acting-out of the SPC mechanism, which takes six months from first catalog to climactic vote for the placement of programs in the national schedule. It is with us in the local struggle to act on one's responsibility to the countless constituencies that make up the public television audience everywhere, in the careful, crucial building of a daily schedule for one's own station, and, most of all, of course, in the demands of a producing effort — the demands for making good programs, or acquiring them, through the shared energies of hundreds of people, half of whom may be unknown to the others. There, in the studio or on location or in the editing rooms, is where the real crisis of the immediate future always comes. That is where our most serious needs are defined. Those needs are good programs, better programs than can be found anywhere else on a television set.

This future, the season that is always upon us, the program that goes on the air tomorrow night, next week, or in a month, takes twelve hours a day to deal with. It also provides the rich, basic, adrenalized excitement that gives television its special nature and keeps most of us with it — that restless, dragonfly quality which allows us to skim with a hopeful, buzzing intelligence over the

218

surface of the world and which, by reflecting that surface on the home screen, authentically creates something far more than each individual picture might suggest. For in television — in television that deals with real events at least — the whole is always far greater than the parts. We all suspect by now that real events are perhaps the real nature of the medium. What will we ever do, in terms of authenticity, to match Jack Ruby's brief, still-incredible moment in Dallas, or the sense of the occasion that our Congressmen brought to 1974's Judiciary Committee Hearings, or the bloody, hostile struggle between witness and questioner during the Ervin Committee's probes? Perhaps we can do little beyond developing the patience to try to deepen all our understanding of such momentous public events — events which we share with each other through a unique and powerful medium that is new to the nation and the rest of the world in our time.

The second future lies just twelve months ahead and is embodied in the following questions: What will we be producing for next season? Where will the money come from? What will our fellow-stations be producing? Together, will it all make a schedule, something so urgent in the lives of our viewers that they will be forced to think about it and act on it daily? And, beyond those questions, how will we maintain the size and range of the staff we have so carefully put together, and so craftily assigned to this project or that, in a God-like attempt to match talent with project, skills with programming needs, the right person with the right idea? How can we continue to cliff-hang from day to day over revenue (federal and otherwise), while the public expects us to meet the programming promises which we ourselves have worked so hard to establish in their minds as an annual hope? One price of even a little success is an increased appetite for more success. Bigger and better every year is what the public wants, and perhaps rightly, for it is what we have always told them they will get.

This second future is no less demanding than the immediate one, and it is inextricably bound up with it, overlapping at many points. Often they must be dealt with simultaneously: in the stomach-dropping gaps that sometimes open up within the course of a conventional day between crises, chronic decisions, temper tantrums, funding difficulties, and the problems of this unit caught in a three-day rainstorm on location in New England (which will cost perhaps ten thousand dollars in budgetary penalties), or in the behavior of a state legislature as it decides the economic future of the world's largest city, while expensive public television mobile units lie in the streets outside the capital building, purring away thousands of dollars each hour, or in a program that is not going to make its six-month deadline, for any one of perhaps a dozen, perfectly reasonable reasons or countless other factors which all go to make up the stuff of daily television.

And these two futures are dealt with. Somehow, beyond the twelve-hour limit of the normal day (always stretchable, of course, to fourteen), that is still within the energy capacity of most of us, those problems are solved and the questions of next season's programs — what do do, how to get the money to do it, and all the rest — are met, faced, and even solved. But already some improvisatory load has been imposed upon the decisions — some more-than-necessary whim, some margin of excessive and perhaps false energy. These hourly crises, which are exacerbated by the limitations of our personal talent and stamina, can take a subtle but relentless toll of our own best intentions, and can sometimes turn us into crabby, complaining creatures of circumstance, as sour as our worst imaginings can dream up. We have all had this experience. We have shared it all our working lives. It is a commonplace in print journalism, in all media, and nowhere is it more commonplace than in television, where the urgency of deadlines is the whip that moves the beast along. Yet the extent of man's ability to softshoe his way through the most pressing crises and demanding decisions is astonishing. And nothing is more astonishing than how often it works, how often we actually make it through. Nevertheless, we continue that way at our personal peril, at the peril of all our colleagues, at the peril of the quality of what we do, and at the peril of acting, beyond our will, in bad faith to our audience.

Which brings the third future in sight. In that third future — how we conceive it, how we meet it and act on it — lies the heart of our problems. We know how to get the "upcoming season" on the air. We even know how to deal with next year. But that other future — that is, the future as expressed by the number 1980, or 1982, or 1990 — is the real target date for all of us, and how we learn to develop the techniques to meet its demands and fill its needs will take the measure of all of us. Perhaps by envisioning that future in specific terms, by describing what it might be like (indeed, should be like), we can find our way to a programming checklist that might prove useful. For the moment, I would like to set up the ideal — for me — modus operandi for WNET/13, which is the only station operation I know intimately. I understand that there are many public television stations that have less, rather than more, in common with us. However, I also believe that there is enough in WNET's situation to allow an imaginative projection into the future that might be generally valid. Such a projection would contain some extrapolation of shared hopes and goals (ideals even) that we all automatically assume and act on simply because we are working together in public television.

In any case, my dreams are greedy, like everyone else's, and I presuppose, for the purposes of this chapter, that they will be paid for. For WNET/13, then, I dream of a system, shared by all our fellow-stations within the larger system (and already partially in operation at a few stations at this moment), in which we have all emerged from the conventional notion of "station" and have grown into larger entities known as "Communication Centers." The components of these centers would be: 1) a VHF channel, 2) a UHF channel, 3) an AM/FM radio channel, and 4) a publishing arm, which would enhance the station's broadcast schedule by publishing a serious monthly journal of ideas and issues, as well as books, pamphlets, and other print materials designed to deepen and reflect our own programming and, in the end, create a source of additional income to be used for program development. Public television then literally becomes public broadcasting, and public broadcasting, in turn, becomes public communications.

There is nothing novel in all this, as we well know. The BBC has been at it for many years and on many levels, though often with considerably more mixed daily results, hour by programming hour, than we might imagine from the superb quality of the BBC importations we air on our own national system. Nevertheless, the BBC has constructed a model, and it is probably the most successful of its kind in the world. But the BBC model exists in another, highly centralized context which could not be more foreign to our own hopes, given our legal governmental definitions and the cherished independence of all American public television stations. It should probably be added at this point that, while the bureaucrats of public television talk more and more about decentralization, there is always a real, centrifugal force in Washington moving toward a centralized bureaucracy with ever-increasing powers. Bureaucracy, by its very nature, and sometimes even despite its own best intentions, cannot help its own thrust toward such power. Power, like nature, abhors a vacuum, and television bureaucracies, by the same rule, abhor functions without studio capability and the opportunity to produce programs.

In any case, the BBC model is useful to us only as a source of professional guidance. There is no way we can duplicate its organizational mechanism on a national level in this country, nor should there be. So my fantasy of communication centers must be projected on an individual, station level, with certain technical support systems maintained by the centralized PBS-like system, and perhaps the national distribution of books and other publications which might emerge from such a structure.

But *what* do we communicate? Having developed this vast wired network of transmittal capability, electronic and print, what will we in fact transmit?

First, let's try to deal briefly with the question of what we should *not* be concerned with. This would seem to be self-evident, but it is not always so. Like the commercial networks, we often become pleasurably ensnared in the honeyed trap represented by audience figures, overnights, and numbers in general. And our tendency — confirming the fact that we are all human in quite specific, greedy terms — is to pay attention to those numbers when they spell out conventional success for ourselves, for our colleagues, and most of all, for our potential funders. But that is my definition of a losing game. We cannot compete on that level, with anyone, for anything. Even our highest-rated programs, with rare exceptions, are laughable as "success stories" to the commercial networks. And when they do pay serious attention and try to imitate those successes, "Beacon Hill" is the result. We can take certain statistical information as clues, as signals; but once we develop the habit of depending on it for our essential thinking about programming we will have become another breed.

So, it becomes necessary to state the obvious: we will not be concerned with programming that deals with violence as a substitute for action. Nor will we be concerned with programming that, while passing itself off as entertainment, actually is still another device for promoting the worst aspects of the worst aspects of our own national culture. Every producer who has not made it at NBC, CBS, or ABC, every producer who is temporarily unemployed, or without a show of his own, is on our doorsteps with such proposals, in one variation or another, and they are sometimes able to argue seductively, indeed. We need quiz shows, we need rock shows, we need acid rock shows — it's the spirit of the times and we're missing it. We need fashion, we need show business gossip, we need a nest of talkative celebrities who look beautiful and share a hyperbolic vocabulary of one hundred words or so with each other nightly on everybody's network air. Our audience demographics, we are told, indicate that at least half our audience is over fifty, or even older, and we shake (a little) at the prospect, as though we have suddenly stumbled on a new, wholly American taboo involving doddering untouchables. We must learn to target (as though programs are weapons), have clear objectives (as though *anyone* wants a muddy presentation), use audience meters to make our decisions, and broadcast "comedy" programs simply because we have, at present, no comedy programs. In short, we must touch willy-nilly all the already-tainted points at which the rest of television has failed us, themselves, and the rest of the country. (This 1975-76 season has already come to look like bitter trench warfare in the no-man's land of commercial television, in which new programs have a life expectancy of about three weeks.)

The point is that there are no lessons for public television in the success of "The Beverly Hillbillies." Nor are there any lessons to be learned from "Hawaii Five-0," from the new NBC nightly newscast, from "Beacon Hill," from afternoon soap operas, from "Let's Make A Deal," or from "Cher." There are only warnings and road-signs to point us in another direction. We must take all our cues from ourselves and each other, from our sense of our own audience and our role in terms of that audience. We all know what our audience thinks of us; they let us know at the slightest provocation. So we must have the arrogance of our own programming convictions, and part of that arrogance rests in the firm assumption that the audience is really smarter than we are.

Now, I am not speaking of education. I am speaking about intelligence. Our experience in New York is that our audience will share our failures with equanimity and extreme tolerance, as long as these failures do not exceed a reasonable limit of excess, either in number or in substance. Our audience will share the pleasure of our successes and pay for it in the bargain, and they will participate with considerable critical detachment in our experiments. They are not mere numbers to us, not a set of demographic figures, not a curving line on some abstract graph, but a real body of highly individuated responses existing in all-too-human form. In short, they are ourselves and our neighbors, in growing numbers and growing loyalty, and they know that we are not in the business of selling them to advertisers as targetable markets.

So they have a share in what we do, beyond their role as viewer. To a great extent, their concerns are ours, and ours are theirs. They had better be. And when we find that we are not sure of those concerns, we have means of making contact, of personally touching their worries. This process is called ascertainment and it is shared among the entire organization at WNET/13, extending far beyond the limits of programming alone. Our lawyers attend ascertainment sessions, and so do our underwriting and development people, media service experts, publicity and promotion, all the representatives of all the aspects of the station. It is true that ascertainment has often been perceived as being used for political purposes, as a means of satisfying the demands of both local and federal agencies. But when used correctly, with both real interest and some reserve of shared skepticism, it can and does provide us with a list of possibilities, a center for surfacing public concerns, a technique for periodically making the attempt, in public, to find out what people care about.

Once these concerns are uncovered, we must then create programs, at our discretion, to satisfy them. But we must turn aside the tyranny that is the main threat of ascertainment. We must ascertain and then lead, rather than ascertain and then follow, as so many seem to believe. Ascertainment provides source material, not programs. The programs must come from us. We can use ascertainment as a kind of dowsing rod to help us uncover the community's concerns. However, by itself, ascertainment cannot make programs, or even shape them.

On our UHF channel, we will provide instructional television: classes for credit (and pleasure) tied in with local educational institutions, informational courses, and guides to specialized skills. From this UHF channel, the viewer will learn how to speak Spanish (and English), will study American History in fifty-two hour episodes (or seventy-five, or one-hundred, whatever the need may be) which will include lectures, discussion groups, filmed materials, slides, and specially-prepared art work. The viewer will learn how to cook in many styles, sew, keep house, give basic medical treatment in an emergency. He will learn where the local cultural action is, what local neighborhoods are up to, how to deal with local government, how to deal with taxes, what his rights are in terms of retirement pensions, Social Security, and other matters. He will have an annual medical report on the state of his health, in terms of his neighbors, and a guide to what treatment centers are accessible to him for his special medical needs. He will learn how to type and take shorthand. He will learn where to vote and where to register. He will have weekly access to a job market report that will tell him where there is work in his area, where there is not. All this information will be supplemented by texts, study materials, and pamphlets from our publishing center, which will work in close collaboration with the educational institutions involved in specific programs. All courses with an academic orientation, of course, will provide college credits; but everyone matriculates.

On our UHF channel, we will also provide total access to the working processes of democratic government, on the local, state, and federal level. This means coverage of public hearings. This also means the right to bring cameras into the legislative halls of government, to televise the legislative proceedings, as well as the work of investigative committees. I am aware of all the arguments against this, but none of them are as powerful as the ordinary right of citizens to observe their elected officials at work in their elected capacities. That is where accountability lies, and, as we learn periodically with great pain, this country can only maintain its unity within a system of open, shared accountability. With whatever degree of respect, every public official understands that now and, I hope, with due anxiety.

The UHF channel must also provide an outlet for public access. This means two hours every day in which the public, in terms of its special interests, has a place in which to demonstrate those interests. Public access is one of those peculiarly American concepts, at the heart of which lies pure democratic idealism. Everyone, this ideal says, should have a place on the air; everyone should have a chance to be seen and heard. But our experience with public access on cable television in New York, to date, is extremely problematic. Everyone does have a chance, as long as they have sufficient funds to produce a tape. And everything goes, everything is allowed, in the name of uncensorable freedom of expression. The result is an arbitrary, untrackable mess of primitive techniques, often offensive content, and open-ended self-promotion for some of the more energized marginal figures of urban society, rejects from the Warhol factory assembly-line. Soft-core porn, second-rate disco openings, one-man masturbatory fantasies all vie for public attention with other, sometimes lively, political cultural programs. In other words, there are no standards at present. All you need to get in is money. The whole concept of public access must be reexamined, but there is little question of its basic validity or of its place in television.

So then, our UHF channel will educate, inform, demonstrate,

and serve as public access forum, in some sort of controlled environment. But so will our VHF channel. The VHF channel will beam its powerful signal during evening prime-time hours, beginning at six and going to midnight, and provide six hours of original programming daily, including: 1) a full hour of news, balanced between local and national, with analysis and discussion using the finest intellectual resources of the community for comment, accompanied by filmed-and-tape reports of the continuing issues of the day, 2) a weekly documentary study on public and cultural affairs subjects, to be broadcast nationally over PBS, 3) a weekly science report, and 4) the best drama, films, and music, including once a week, fifty-two weeks a year, a live performance, viewed by the entire country from one of the great international performance centers, using satellite for transmission. And, beginning at midnight every night, public television's museum-without-walls will open to the world: a six-hour, slow-moving tour of the art in the great museums of the world, room-by-room, work-by-work, a week or two each in Chicago's Fine Arts Museum, the Louvre, Boston's Fogg, then on to New York, Madrid, Minneapolis, Washington, London, and so on. These tours will be low-keyed and informal. They will provide pleasure and modest goals. Parts of them will be excerptable for daytime art courses. They will allow the restless sleeper to awaken to the sight on his public television screen of the Venus de Milo, or the View of Toledo, a Rembrandt self-portrait, or any of thousands of other great works. Commentary will be brief, but music will play all night long. And beyond all this, public television will offer a weekly, hour-long program of the best television from the rest of the world, from Tokyo to Mexico City, from Budapest to Moscow, from Tel Aviv to Montreal, from Edinburgh to Leeds.

All public television will be involved in the production of these programs. All the great production centers and all the growing stations across the county, now eager to show their capability for national production, will be part of it. Each station will measure its own needs and set a balance between local programming and national feed coming through PBS. And, as always, each station within the public television system will continue to formulate its own broadcasting schedule in terms of its local audience and viewing patterns.

The AM radio frequency, meanwhile, will broadcast the UHF channel's coverage of legislative activities and public hearings at other times during the day. This means that the viewer will have optional access to all testimony and debate. All of this will be shared with the broadcast of music on the FM station, all kinds, both in grand educational terms and in pure "concert" terms. At the same time, live performances will be aired on a regular basis from all parts of the world.

As for our publishing arm, it will act as an extension of regular programming. It will provide transcripts for every broadcast that has topical or historical value. It will develop its own publication and books to enhance the prime-time programs on the VHF channel. And it will, of course, create its own original books and monthly journal. (The BBC has been so successful at this that commercial British publishers, fearful of the threat the BBC posed in the marketplace, took them to court for exceeding their charter. The commercial publishers lost the case and the BBC continues to dominate the British best-seller lists with such books as *Civilisation*, *The Ascent of Man*, and various others.)

Of course, all of these ideas are meant to be suggestive, as is the idea of Communications Centers. But I am serious about each one. They represent real hopes, real possibilities. And I have tried to be specific because I believe that there has been quite enough rhetoric (including my own) about public television during its short life. Such rhetoric protects the flanks, of course, but in the end who can be held accountable for it? Nevertheless, at this moment and at all moments in the future, only one thing really counts: what appears on the screen, what goes out over the air. All our relentless struggle to create a system, all our necessary involvement with technology — both urgent needs — all our attempts to battle the politicization of an institution that, by its very charter, was politicized at birth, cannot make good programs for us.

The problems couldn't be clearer. They involve money, the quick smooth flow of ideas, an atmosphere in which creative energy can be released without too much wastage, a continuing search for a way to program for an entire system that, station by station, does not always share the same problems. Of all these problems, money is the most urgent. By premising my dreams on the assumption that they can all be paid for, I know full well that I have avoided the most basic hard reality of public television. Old sources of funding are disappearing; we are trying to create new ones as energetically as possible. Individual memberships, commercial corporations, federal funds, small foundations — we try them all. Yet with each new opening, we discover a new set of constraints, a new set of problems.

The Future of Public Broadcasting

For one example, the very concept of "discretionary funding" seems hardly to exist any longer. Most programming grants are made for specific program ideas in which the grantor perceives some return, either in public favor, in good will, or in the fulfillment of some internal organizational mandate. Commercial corporations rarely fund public affairs programs, which is the programming area most sorely beset by funding problems. Consequently, we must devise a way in which public affairs will be funded on a consistent, ongoing basis, and, at the same time, will remain shielded from all externally imposed strictures and interference. There are no signs — none — that this can or will be done, but it is an essential priority.

And there is an additional problem that we are just beginning to face up to. That problem is how to make a home for and find a way of creating our own professionals. Talent must be invited into the system; we must learn how to take chances with people; we must make it worth their while to stick with us and give them a chance to expand. No one is ever really prepared for how hard television is, for how complicated and difficult it is to make a bad program, much less a good one. And public television is harder than anywhere else.

Well, it scarcely needs to be added that public television lives in the real world. We must sustain studio operations, staff, the up-coming season, next year's season, a broadcast operation, minority training centers, consumer help programs, nerve centers that feed into and out of our own communities. And we ourselves must raise the money to do it all. But we do have a constituency, one that cares, that is involved, that believes in us. No commercial network can say that. Not NBC, CBS, or ABC. All they have are faceless audiences about which they know almost nothing — except numbers, which they use to sell their audiences in prime-time like futures in grain. Our own future, whatever its form, lies in the heart of that constituency. That is where our most important signals come from. And for that constituency, only the best will do.

Meanwhile, television, now nearly thirty years operative, continues to search desperately for its real substance. I do not think it is excessively prideful to insist that public television act as point in that search.

Public Television Programming and the Future: A Radical Approach

RICHARD O. MOORE

The words have been cited over and over again:

> Noncommercial television should address itself to the ideal of excellence, not the idea of acceptability — which is what keeps commercial television from climbing the staircase. I think television should be the visual counterpart of the literary essay, should arouse our dreams, satisfy our hunger for beauty, take us on journeys, enable us to participate in events, present great drama and music, explore the sea and the sky and the woods and the hills. It should be our Lyceum, our Chautauqua, our Minsky's, and our Camelot. It should restate and clarify the social dilemma and the political pickle. Once in a while it does, and you get a quick glimpse of its potential. — E.B. White, in a letter to the Carnegie Commission on Educational Television.

Mr. White's vision is broad-scale. It is also a revolutionary vision, in that it is addressed to the proper uses of television. It describes a potential service for *all* of the American people, and it

---

Mr. Moore produces programs for both commercial and public broadcasting. He was formerly the general manager of KQED in San Francisco.

implies a *primary* rather than a *supplementary* public service television system. It recognizes the importance of popular as well as more elitist programming. In short, Mr. White states the purpose of a television service as a national sociocultural instrument rather than as a corporate enterprise on behalf of stockholders. Regrettably, what is happening today in public television makes White's vision an improbable dream.

The question to be considered here is whether public television can be expected to play a measurably more significant role in our national life in the 1980s than it does today. Many people within the public television establishment tend to think that the answer depends primarily on whether greater federal funding is made available for station operations and programming under a decentralized system. They assume that if only public television were to become financially secure, the programming generated by the system would not only be good for all of us, but good also in the sense of attracting the attention and support of the American people.

I disagree. In my opinion, the future development of public television is directly related almost solely to its ability and willingness to serve a *national, mass audience* — that is, to provide programming that will attract and keep viewers in mass numbers. Furthermore, the size of that audience and the quality of that programming depend *not* on federal funds, but on two variables only: (1) the nature of the institutional structures that generate public television, and (2) public television's definition of its role with respect to its audience.

A History of Neglect and False Priorities

The history of public television's domestic production over the past 20 years reveals that the ostensible priority of good programming has been illusory. Apart from the predictable and dreary disputes over "eastern liberal bias" or, if you prefer, "ideological plugola" and "elitist gossip," noncommercial television has seldom taken the subject of programming seriously. What *is* taken seriously is the issue of control and participation in the hierarchy that makes the programming decisions. And even in these disputes, the issue is never really programming and audiences, but rather the distribution of available monies for the purposes of institutional survival.

As noncommercial television approaches the first quarter century of its existence, it is still making messianic promises and then defaulting on delivery, while the true believers continue to battle over who is to control the priestly hierarchy. Public television has even developed its own Pharisaic class that pretends to divine the true intent of the Carnegie Commission Report and the Public Broadcasting Act of 1967 or the latest press release or memorandum from the Ford Foundation and the CPB Board of Directors. The summa of this new scholasticism is to be found in the unwieldy but wholly consistent computer logic of the Station Program Cooperative. Noncommercial television has built a system but has failed to produce the great awakening that its adherents continue to promise.

In the beginning, there was a national production agency (NET) funded by the Ford Foundation. NET had no production facilities and no assured access to noncommercial stations. Although the actual history of broadcasting in the United States and elsewhere in the world has been one of centralization and networking, United States broadcast law underlines the responsibility of the individual licensee; that is, the local station. As a result, the stations very quickly began to realize the power of "the switch." Even though NET programs were offered "free" to the stations, the programs remained on the shelf unless the stations chose to accept and broadcast them.

A battle ensued between NET and the stations, and although the dispute was couched in the language of licensee responsibility, the real issue was not programming but money. If a program is meaningless without being broadcast, should not the first priority be economic assistance to the stations? Would it not be better if the stations were given the money to produce programs which they could then exchange with other stations? From the moment the stations voiced this argument, NET's days as an independent and primary production and distribution agency were numbered. The question of how to attract the best talent and produce programs in an optimum cost-effective manner became merely a masquerade for the real issue of station survival and system building.

The Carnegie Commission on Educational Television was a direct outgrowth of this first struggle for power and money in what was soon to be called public television. The Public Broadcasting Act of 1967 and the creation of CPB and PBS represented the reformation of educational television based on the principles of decentralization. A collective expression of these principles, the Station Program Cooperative, was next in the chronology. And now a new battle seems to be brewing between CPB, PBS, and a third force represented by the larger producing stations.

The struggle is the same old struggle for the control and distribution of monies. The fear is the same old fear that the ghost of NET, as an independent production agency devoted primarily to programming, may return under a new set of initials. The one heresy that public television cannot tolerate is the emergence of a strong individual or group with the resources to generate imaginative and popular programming, free of the extraordinarily dense filtering system represented by the sum of stations.*

A System That Guarantees the Second Rate

The development of new programming is always the most frustrating problem faced by a broadcast system, commercial or noncommercial. There is simply no set formula for a successful program. Historically, excellence in television programming has been associated with strong leadership in highly centralized organizations. Only such organizations seem capable of establishing an environment in which individual judgment and creativity can flourish. Television programming is always the result of teamwork, of course, but the generation and execution of an outstanding program concept is usually the work of an exceptional individual.

Public television has devised a system wherein the power rests with a collection of institutions and boards. It is a system that guarantees the second-rate in the name of localism and system survival, and it does so while serving, with our tax dollars, an inexcusably small percentage of the American people. Programming decisions tend to be made either wholly on an economic basis, in order to fill out the schedule, or on the "safe" basis of striving to create new versions of last year's "standards." The idea of innovation and the breaking of new ground — not in the narrow experimental sense, but in terms of all the objectives set forth in E. B. White's statement — is not even a priority. With 50 percent and possibly more of CPB's funds "passed through" directly to individual stations, the financial condition of each station becomes the determining factor in what passes for program planning and decision making in public broadcasting.

At the root of the problem is the policy throughout public broadcasting of lumping local broadcast operations and program

---

*The Children's Television Workshop represented a tolerable heresy, in that it began by tapping funds hitherto unavailable to most stations and then giving away a much needed and popular product. However, now that a substantial proportion of CTW's costs have been shifted to the stations — plus the fact that the organization is branching out into other than children's programming and is competing for foundation support, corporate underwriting, and CPB funds — CTW may well become the new principal heretic within a system based on decentralization, localism, and majority rule programming.

production into the same institutional package. Among other things, this means that program production budgets must reflect the overhead factor for the whole institution. As a result, the budgets tend to be unnecessarily high (the overhead frequently approaches 40 percent of actual costs). One of the early arguments in favor of contracting with local broadcast stations to produce national programs was that it would enable stations to increase staff and facilities and to attract talented people. Basically this attitude remains dominant today, except that stations now compete with each other for production contracts as a means of maintaining existing staff and covering overhead. It is not surprising that somewhere in this shuffle, programming objectives get lost!

It is a painful dilemma for which there is no simple resolution. Current policy in public broadcasting, in FCC regulation, and in forthcoming legislation stresses decentralization, localism, and station-based production. However, this approach is demonstrably more wasteful and, at the same time, woefully inhibiting with respect to innovation and risk-taking in programming. Public broadcasting will continue to be dominated by political rather than programming interests so long as the "integrity" of public broadcasting is identified with a system in which the collectivity of the bureaucracies, as represented by the sum of the licensees, has the controlling voice in national programming policy.

The subsidization of local operations in the name of programming is also, in my view, a self-defeating policy. Granted that without this policy on the part of the Ford Foundation and CPB, the development of public broadcasting might have proceeded at a much slower pace. However, it can also be argued that if the monies spent on station development and "survival" had been invested instead in programming that was effectively competitive with commercial stations, we would be much nearer to the goal of a public service television system consistent with the "ideal of excellence" described by E. B. White. I am convinced that public television can hope to develop into a mature and stable broadcast system only by offering a product that the U. S. television audience will watch, applaud and then support through subscriptions or contributions to their local station.

A New Role for Public Broadcasting

I propose that public television, as a model for our efforts at the improvement and refinement of television *per se*, can become the *dominant system of broadcasting in the United States in the*

1980s, superseding both commercial and the presently financed public television system. This is a fairly bold statement considering the present state of affairs. But it could be an accurate prognostication if public television proves willing to redefine itself with respect to the changes taking place in the United States as a whole.

Television is a function of the society as a whole; it changes as the society changes. Predicting the state of this nation, even over a five-year span, takes a kind of clairvoyance that no one has as yet reliably demonstrated. Nor can we be any more certain about what kinds of television programs will be broadcast in the next decade, or how the electronic media will be incorporated into our lives. It is nevertheless a certainty that the nature and quality of television will change in the next few years, and one does not have to be a "futurist" to recognize some of the fundamental technological and social changes evolving in our post-industrial society.

We can reasonably presume, for one thing, that we have come to the end of the "economy of abundance" based on increasing production and increasing consumption of materials and energy sources. It also seems reasonable to say, then, that as the society continues to shift from an energy-exploiting, producer-oriented system to an energy-scarce, consumer-oriented one, commercial television will become less viable. Commercial television, whose priority is — and has to be — profit-making, depends upon expanding industrial production and extensive consumption of products and services. It can not and will not see itself primarily as a service dedicated first to the needs of its audience. It has never demonstrated any flexibility in responding adequately to new cultural, social, and class demands or in developing new media institutions.

The future issue, in my opinion, will not be whether the commercial system will further the development of a "better" society or a society bereft of present-day values. The question will be whether or not the commercial system can sustain itself at all in the changing circumstances. Commercial television may well be a reflection of an era we are by necessity leaving behind.

Noncommercial broadcasting, on the other hand, could be on the ascendent. As the population's dependence on television increases and the financial base of the commercial system weakens, the notion that people will be more willing to pay directly for television — as they would for a public utility — becomes a possibility worth serious consideration. It depends, of course, upon whether public television will be able to gain a foothold and then maintain itself as a responsible source of information and a popular source of entertainment.

To my mind, there is only one way that public television can begin to achieve that goal: The system must redefine itself as a *service* enterprise, independent of political interests and obligations and self-consciously dedicated to the sole purpose of delivering entertainment and information to the American people. I distinctly do *not* mean a public broadcast system that achieves a modicum of political stability and rests there, or one that congratulates itself with providing " an alternative" to commercial broadcasting or with "serving special-interest audiences." I mean a system composed of institutions that continually determine how best to serve the entire American television audience and then set out to do just that.

But can a new and dominant (in the sense that the commercial networks are now dominant) form of broadcasting emerge out of what we now know as public broadcasting? To many, it may seem that there is no feasible alternative to our present system of broadcasting, in either economic or political terms. It would be politically absurd, of course, to suggest a revival of the old private versus public ownership debate, and it is equally absurd to suggest that a communications system can develop without an adequate economic base. But to stop there is to limit one's thinking. Granted, it may be difficult to imagine another kind of broadcast system becoming dominant in this country. However, not many years ago, it would have been equally difficult to imagine the collapse of the major film studio system and the rise of independent production companies. A different institutional pattern emerged to meet the existing market.

"A name without a concept." Public television, as it was originally conceived, grew out of two principles sacred to American political and social ideology: the importance of education, and the importance of local sovereignty. Both have in effect restricted public television to a supplementary role with regard to commercial television. The "new public television" proposed by the Carnegie Commission Report a decade ago was anything but new. Its system model was no different from the theoretical model for commercial television (a system based on local stations, with the admission that some national programming is desirable), and its key funding proposal (a manufacturer's excise tax on sets) was wholly unrealistic politically.

Five years after the Carnegie Report and the Public Broadcasting Act of 1967, there was still no agreement on the appropriate role of public television either with the ETV enterprise or among the general public. In 1972, an Aspen Institute Program on Communications and Society conference formally asked the questions again:

Is Public TV a complementary, supplementary or competitive broadcast system? How is program content distinctive from commercial TV? Is it possible to build a viable broadcast schedule from widely varying minority audiences?

Such questions just haven't seemed to bear fruit. To me, they seem too narrow; they subliminally regiment public television to a secondary role. Within the framework of these questions public television continues to be, as Les Brown described it, "a name without a concept."

Let me reiterate that, in my opinion, the specific matters to be addressed are audiences and programming, not the old political and ideological disputes and definitions that never resolve themselves into constructive, creative changes. To be sure, the nature of a broadcast institution determines what that institution is capable of in the way of programming. But the capability for programming does not necessarily suggest how the American people may best be served via television.

These very distinct concepts — capability and service — must be considered together. The institutions generating public television must determine not only what they *can* do, but what they feel must be done, irrespective of the existence of an in-place commercial system which reaches at least 95 percent of the total households. The real necessity is for effective leadership and a clear operational philosophy defining why, how, and for whom public television should be developed.

Television as process. I am of the opinion that if we are to make a serious effort to conceptualize and develop a television service in the United States, in which the public interest takes precedence over the private interest of stockholders, we must begin to develop a systematic understanding of what the medium is and how it functions in social terms. Once we reach that understanding, and not before, we can concentrate on the next two factors crucial to a viable and responsive public television: the ideal nature of the institutions generating public television, and the ways in which society can afford the enormous cost of television. First, then, what is needed is no less than a comprehensive body of knowledge about the television medium, apart from its purely technical aspects.

Although classic communications theory originated in this country with Paul Lazersfeld and others, there has been very little theoretical examination of how the medium actually functions as a communications phenomenon. Marshall McLuhan has raised questions that challenge the whole of traditional communications theory as applied to the television process. His general theory of media is much more inclusive and explanatory than the "content" theory of television, which holds that "the process is the same whether the signs are broadcast on a television wave or whispered by a young man into his sweetheart's ear."[1] McLuhan, however, is a man who uses fireworks to light his way through a dark place. The illumination is intermittent and distracting, and we need a more constant light to be sure that what we have seen is what we need to see in order to make our way from here to there.

There is also a vast missing acreage in the McLuhan territory. Any study of process must include an awareness of all of the agents that impinge on that process, and institutions are the agents of TV as much as frequencies, scanning, and the matrix image. Indeed, the initial agent of the television process is the corporation which causes the switch to be thrown. Neither the moral character of executives, nor program content of itself, will generate television into viewers' homes. The priorities of the institutional agencies in control initiate the process that must be studied, and the nature of the process is determined, at least to some extent, by the nature of these priorities.

For example, there have been a number of excellent studies of television journalism and of the relationship between electronic journalism and the government. But with a few exceptions (the books of Fred Friendly and Edward Jay Epstein come to mind), there has been very little study of the limits imposed upon "the search for truth," or whatever you choose to call it, by the corporate structures that currently dominate the electronic medium. What is "the truth" with respect to advertisers' priorities? What would be "the truth" with respect to a service-oriented broadcast system? Until we have a real understanding of the process by which information is transmitted to and received by viewers, we will have no real answers to these questions.

We are also shamefully deficient in any systematic evaluation regarding goals, consequences, successes, or failures in television programming *as it affects audiences*, including children. There are gross measurements — the industry lives by them — as to how programming affects advertisers, but most of the so-called audience research is directed toward something quite different from the meaning and consequences of TV for specific audiences. McLuhan is unconventionally lucid when he observes, "Political scientists have been quite unaware of the effects of media anywhere at any time, simply because nobody has been willing to study the personal and social effects of media apart from the content."[2] Program strategies based on an evaluation of the content of a program, as measured on a social, moral, or cultural scale of values, may have little or nothing to do with the effect the program will have when it is broadcast. Put another way, the meaningful exercise of social, moral, and

237

cultural judgments in television may well require a wholly new understanding of the television process.

I'd like to return now to the questions asked at the 1972 Aspen conference with regard to defining the role of public television. Those questions were:

> Is Public TV a complementary, supplementary or competitive broadcast system? How is program content distinctive from commercial TV? Is it possible to build a viable broadcast schedule from widely varying minority audiences?

To these questions, I propose the following answers:

- Public TV must see itself as competitive with commercial TV if the intent is to serve the public interest and to play any significant role in satisfying the six-hour-a-day viewing habit in U. S. households.

- Program *content* is the wrong question. It reveals a lack of understanding of the viewing process. The aim should be to provide programs that people watch.

- The concept of minority audiences may be an illusion. The least served minority is the better educated sector of the population, which expresses dissatisfaction but watches what everyone else watches.

The real battleground is for *television*, not public versus commercial television. We must find the best institutional and economic means to make high quality, popular television programming available.

A "genetic code" for change. What fascinates me as a possibility is that certain aspects of present-day public broadcasting may contain the "genetic code" for the new broadcast institutions that must evolve in response to changing conditions in our national life. In fact, I am convinced that there are a few — a very few, but enough — factors within the present system to provide a practical ground from which to build public television into a dominant system. What I have in mind, however, has nothing in common with most aspects of the present system and the existing stations.

Two factors presently operating in public television give promise for the future. One is institutional: the existence of nonprofit community PTV corporations, as distinguished from state, municipal, or college and university institutional licensees. The second is both attitudinal and operational: an increasing trend toward identification *of* and programming *for* audiences, combined with a growing understanding of direct audience support as a means of providing income.

The independent nonprofit corporation, free of the limitations and annual budget appropriations of university, state and municipal educational bureaucracies, is the most flexible and responsive institutional form for public television. Although these corporations and their boards of directors have evolved in a fashion similar to the organizations that control local museum, symphony, and other cultural activities, they nonetheless remain open to change and to a broader vision of their responsibilities as trustees of *all* the public's interest.

With respect to identifying audiences and determining what they will watch, the problems are more complicated. Any discussion of audiences seems to make public television advocates uneasy. In the 1973 Annual Report of the Markle Foundation, Lloyd Morrisett concludes that, "after examining alternative arguments and on the basis of simple common sense, it seems that public television can be justified only on the basis of serving an audience." In very convincing fashion, Morrisett takes public television to task for what he describes as "the myth of localism." He proposes research to identify special-interest audiences; programming designed for audiences thus identified; intensive promotion of these programs; the development of a rating system to measure the success of a program; and, finally, an economic incentive plan to reward successful producing stations and production companies. He suggests that, as a measure of its success, a public television program should reach 50 percent of its target audience. The argument is capped by the reminder that "Sesame Street" was designed for a special-interest audience.

Although one cannot deny that pre-school children constitute a special-interest audience, it should be noted that, by definition, one cannot design a children's program except *as* a special-interest program. The same does not hold true for prime-time programming. A substantial percentage of day-time programming on commercial television can be described as programming for special-interest audiences; but with the evening hours, and with the whole family as potential viewers, it is a different story. Who is to control the set? The youngest, the oldest, males, females, the best or the least educated? In our enthusiasm for providing the potential viewer a smorgasbord of choices, we tend to forget that there is a scarcity of plates in the home. Even in multi-set families, joint viewing is still the predominant pattern.

I remain very skeptical of proposals that put forth minority or special-interest programming as the goal for public television. True, well-researched and well-produced and promoted special-interest programming would in all likelihood increase public television's present audience. But it would also lock the system, once and for all, into the role of a supplementary television service. We must keep in mind that the American people are not in revolt against the present dominant system of television, nor are they seeking out public television as a means of filling felt needs.

A concentration on program content is simply not enough. In fact, in light of the existing evidence, it does not seem to make very much difference what programs are available to viewers. Researchers have discovered some very interesting — in some cases, astonishing — facts about the attitudes of the American people with respect to television. Dr. Gary Steiner's study in 1960, *The People Look at Television*, and the 1970 study by Dr. Robert Bower, *Television and the Public*, are particularly useful sources. Bower summarizes the changing attitudes toward television between 1960 and 1970 as follows:

> The population of viewers in 1970 found television less "satisfying," "relaxing," "exciting," "important," and generally less "wonderful" than had the population of ten years earlier. This decline in regard to television was found among all subgroups of the population. Even the enthusiastic black audience was not quite as enthusiastic as its brothers and sisters had been 10 years before.[3]

However, one should not jump to the conclusion that the television audience is disenchanted and about to tune out. The study also revealed the following:

> People were watching more television than ever in 1970. Not only that, they seemed to be enjoying more of what they saw. When we turned, for instance, from how people felt *about television in general to how they liked the programs they viewed*, on the whole, we found a higher assessment of the programs as "somewhat enjoyable" or "extremely enjoyable" than Steiner had found ten years earlier.
> . . . if we can believe the response at all, we might conclude that people were finding more programs among which they could choose than they had before — thus improving the chance they could watch many things they really enjoyed, even with a diminished respect for tele-

vision's fare as a whole. Whatever the reason, the public's generalized attitude toward television (as defined by the measures employed in the two studies) *did* decline during the same period of time when much of the content of the medium was picking up new adherents — more people enjoying a larger proportion of the programs, more applause for the performance of the news departments, and broad approval of the changes that were observed over the decade.

Most surveys of public television audiences have revealed that the preponderance of adult viewers are from the better educated, more affluent sector of the population. The Bower finding that the better educated viewers tend generally to hold the television medium in lower esteem and say they are more apt to be selective in their viewing would appear to indicate that they have substantially different viewing habits. This, however, is not the case:

There is no more reason to suspect the educated viewer's expressions of attitude and preference than those of anyone else, but there does seem to be something in the act of television viewing that prevents him from behaving quite as one would predict after listening to him talk. We have seen that he watches the set (by his own admission) just about as much as others during the evening and weekend hours . . . the educated viewer distributed his time among program types — comedy, movies, action, information and public affairs, and so forth — in just about the same proportion as did those with less education; and even when he had a clear choice between an information program and some standard entertainment fare, he was just as apt as others to choose the latter.*

The fact that measurable differences in attitudes about television did not produce similar variations in the time spent watching it prompted Dr. Bower to raise a number of questions:

---

*Predicting what kinds of audiences will watch particular types of programs has long been a dream of television executives. The Bower study does not offer much hope in this regard. Although there are some differences in attitudes toward television in terms of the education, sex, age, and race of viewers, these differences do not apparently have a significanct effect upon viewing habits. (The study revealed only that the young, regardless of education, are much more inclined to accept programs dealing with social unrest; "nowhere else in the inquiry do the age groups differ so markedly.")

The lack of correspondence between determinants of attitudes and viewing behavior, which such·findings suggest, leads one away from attempts to explain viewing as a phenomenon associated with socioeconomic status, and toward some more universal explanation. Has television become so psychologically essential that it must be watched the prescribed number of hours a day no matter how much one would like to ignore it, like a hospital meal taken intraveneously? Or is it universally useful in the modern world in some more pragmatic sense? Is it a necessity of life, without substitute, for the twentieth century man who would keep up with the events of the world around him, engage in social intercourse with family and friends without the embarrassment of ignorance, and find easy recourse to easy moments of relaxation? The automobile as a means of getting around would be another modern example of such a necessity. The amount one uses it probably has little to do with how one feels about the appearance of the front grill or about the economic policies of General Motors.

On the basis of Dr. Bower's evidence we can speculate more intelligently about the future of broadcasting in general. It is inevitable that by wires (CATV), by cassette, and by satellite, additional television services will be made available to the American home. Although this may not measure up to the ideal of the so-called "television of abundance," there can be no question but that the viewer will be confronted with additional image sources delivered electronically. But it is wholly speculative to suggest that present viewing habits will be substantially changed as we move away from the present situation of a relative scarcity of channels. There is little or no evidence to suggest that viewers are demanding or will demand a wider variety of choice in television programming. In fact, choice on a basis of "quality" and "content" may have little to do with the actual viewing process.

Again, the obvious conclusion is that public television must determine for itself — with no help from outside institutions or audience demand — how best to serve the American people. The role that public television plays in the near future will inevitably be determined and limited by where the money will come from. Public television has received some good news recently: Longer term funding appears to be assured. This gives the system, as well as the individual stations, a slight purchase on the future. The bad news is that this apparent security could inhibit and possibly prevent

242

the development of a truly innovative and independent public television system in the United States.

This is not to suggest that innovation and independence are outgrowths of financial starvation and the garret life-style. Money and what it can command in talent and facilities are necessities in television. But financial control from the outside clearly results in policy control, particularly in an enterprise that at present has no clear definition of its own fundamental nature.

Consumer-Supported Television

The problem, then, simply stated, is this: Is there an economic base for broadcasting other than government funding, philanthropy, and the sale of air time? Quasi-commercial support in the form of corporate underwriting is already a major factor in the funding of public television programs, but the majority of public television stations are supported from tax monies. The one promising exception to the kinds of funding that would inevitably inhibit public television from becoming a dominant service is the growth of direct audience support in the form of audience memberships or subscriptions — a kind of voluntary pay TV. Although income from this source presently represents only a small percentage of the total system income, the growth rate is impressive. Station income from memberships and subscriptions amounted to $16.5 million in fiscal 1973, an increase of 59 percent over the previous year.

In recent years, this growth rate has been even more phenomenal, due in large part to the Station Independence Project, which has been aimed at increasing memberships or subscriptions or other voluntary income-producing sources at the local stations. In 1975, the SIP's three-week campaign, known as "Festival 75," produced $5 million; in 1976 a similar campaign is expected to produce $10 million. There are now in excess of 2 million subscribers to public television stations throughout the country, and by 1977, that figure is expected to rise to nearly 4 million. In 1976, the newly appointed president of PBS, Lawrence Grossman, described another important advantage of this growing public membership: "If we have 5 million members or subscribers paying $20 a year, it not only represents substantial income but considerable political clout. I don't think politicians would want to oppose it."

Such terms as "free TV," "pay TV," and "tax-supported TV" are confusing and inevitably arouse powerful emotional responses. But in our increasingly consumer- as opposed to producer-conscious society, the idea of paying for television should no longer be as "threatening" as the commercial television and motion picture companies would have the public believe. We will have to educate the public to the hard fact that no matter how the money is transferred, all TV is paid for by the people. We pay for "free TV" when the cost of advertising is added to the price of the products we buy; we also contribute our share to the tax dollars that go to the support of public TV. Of all the possible methods of paying for television, the user- or consumer-supported method is the most direct and has the closest "demand" relationship to the source of "supply." It is also more consistent with American traditions than is tax-supported television.

The usual complaint about an audience-supported, noncommercial television system is that, inevitably, only a few actually pay for what others can receive without paying. A discouragingly low 2 percent of the households within reach of public television stations with membership plans are paying members. A very few stations (KQED in San Francisco, for example) have memberships of more than 10 percent of the households within their signal area. Nationally, the average subscription rate in 1973 was $21.89 per member. Still, when one considers the inequalities in the tax system and the fact that the poor must pay the same high and sometimes higher prices for the necessities of life as the affluent, the prospect of "freeloaders" within a voluntary audience-support plan for television is not a convincing argument against the idea.

Another objection to direct audience support is that programming would reach for "the lowest common denominator" and would become indistinguishable from commercial television programming. In part, this view rests on the "content" theory of television and has little practical relation to what actually happens in television viewing. It also assumes that there is no difference between advertising agencies and the general public, a view which I find hard to accept.

What the audience sees on commercial television is what advertisers decide they want to sponsor. The Nielsen figures indicate which programs people are watching (and, therefore, which ones the advertisers will continue to support), but it doesn't necessarily follow, reversing the logic, that these same programs are the *only* ones that people will view.

If, in fact, commercial television programming represents "the lowest common denominator," it is a product of the caution and conservatism of the broadcast and advertising corporations, not of the audience. Programming is anything but an exact science, and the networks are constantly being surprised by the popular acceptance of show X over show Y. Within the commercial complex, the only formula for success is the imitation of an existing successful program. The occasional breakaway success in a new season always represents a departure until imitation turns it into a standard formula. A service agency that sets itself to determining how the selecting and viewing process works would stand a good chance of coming up with a more sophisticated idea of what audiences will watch. Furthermore, an audience that is paying directly for the television service would undoubtedly make itself heard.

For years, people in public television have been saying that the system can't compete with the commercial networks. The fact of the matter is that if a program is good enough, and, of almost equal importance, if the program is adequately promoted, television is television and people are going to watch the program. The public is already finding public television when there is a superior program —witness the success of the National Geographic's "The Incredible Machine." This raises another point. If public broadcasting is to focus its energies on high quality, *competitive* programming, what will stop the commercial enterprises from imitating the successes of public television and ultimately stealing its new audiences back?

The answer involves the economics of programming. If, as I assume, the advertising base of commercial television begins to falter, the newly successful system will be that which can achieve maximum cost efficiency in delivering the product. The nonprofit corporation has the advantage here. If a corporation is in the business of returning income to stockholders, it has one priority: profitability. In contrast, the responsibility of the nonprofit corporation is to direct all available income into its product. Furthermore, the nonprofit corporation enjoys the benefits of a much lower overhead.

Another advantage of consumer-supported television is the insulation it provides for controversial fare. For example, public-affairs programming which is subsidized by tax dollars, no matter how "laundered," will always be suspect. Fred Friendly, in testimony before Senator Pastore's Commerce Committee Subcommittee on Communications, suggested that no government money should support that part of public broadcasting devoted to public affairs programming:

> . . . even a dedicated federal trust fund, insulated from annual appropriations, may not be independent enough for the sensitive area of news and public affairs programming. Public television should not have to stand the test of political popularity at any given point in time. Its most precious right will be the right to rock the boat.

The Future of Public Broadcasting

Certainly, it is much healthier for the free marketplace of ideas to seek its support in the free marketplace of direct consumer support than to be threatened with the withdrawal of support because its programming displeases whichever party is in power. Independence from outside pressures could best be achieved if television were developed, in both its information and entertainment modes, as a service paid for directly by those to whom the service is made available.

The institutional expressions of this idea are the nonprofit broadcast corporation and the nonprofit program-producing corporation. They would differ from present televison practice in that their programming would be "sold" directly to the audience, not packaged for advertisers or provided "free" through tax funding. Usually this audience-support idea is dismissed lightly as impractical, but my response to this is that the idea has never been put to a serious and practical test. In public television, the prospects of substantial federal funding has always dominated everyone's attention as the easier and therefore more attractive alternative.

I don't advocate a quick reversal in funding policies for public television. Obviously, if all funding other than that received directly from the audience were to be withdrawn from public television, the entire enterprise would collapse overnight. The present funding mix is generally a good one so long as it doesn't get out of balance. Certainly, the federal government will continue to play an important role in public television as will the corporate underwriter. The difference in my proposal is that there will be a radical increase in the role of the voluntary subscriber. It is important, however, that all options — and particularly the option of developing consumer support — be kept open with respect to the long-range development of PTV. In my view, tax-supported public television would not be sufficiently responsive to replace a weakened commercial system, but consumer-supported television stands a chance. If commercial networks and local stations come to be truly threatened financially, consumer support for relatively low-overhead, nonprofit broadcast institutions will gain a new significance. And the prospect of several nonprofit broadcast institutions operating, in many instances, on channels now licensed to commercial corporations could prove to be a much healthier situation for the consumer than the present situation, wherein the three networks sell air time clustered around remarkably similar programs to the same set of national sponsors.

I'm certainly not suggesting that school stations or, for that matter, any commercial stations that can manage to hold on will have no place in the new television spectrum. I think they will. I also think that we will probably move more in the direction of the so-called "television of abundance," with multiple channels and fragmented audiences. Even so, for all the reasons I've cited, from cost efficiency to political clout to membership loyalty, the community-supported station offers the most flexibility for successfully entering this new television age.

Again, my emphasis is on what might evolve from the present situation. In the absence of a use tax dedicated to a public corporation, consumer-sponsored broadcast institutions would have to prove themselves in the marketplace one by one. With the exception of public education (and most people still think of their public broadcast station as "the educational station"), this has been the route followed by all product- and service-based corporations and utilities.

It will not be dissatisfaction with commercials, but the loss of advertisers altogether that will make the voluntary-payment idea possible. And it will not be so-called "good programming" as opposed to popular programming that will prove attractive to viewers. Because the "break-even" point for a program under voluntary sponsorship is lower than that for a program run for advertisers, the nonprofit production agency offers the potentiality for a wider choice and less slavishness to formula. The agency would also be less dependent upon immediate popular success than the commercial networks are now, and it would be under less pressure to follow the imitation formula. It would exist for the sole purpose of meeting the needs of the audience and would therefore concentrate on defining and interpreting those needs. And it would hopefully abandon the notion of television as a conduit for "good programming" and begin to investigate television as a broad-scale but little understood process which involves and affects almost all U. S. households.

The present leadership in public television appears to be moving closer to these goals. For example, PBS president Larry Grossman stated in 1976: "We should have no ambivalence and no shame about going after audiences. We operate with public funds. We ought to reach out to the widest possible number of people." Grossman also stresses that unlike commercial television, which is tied down to a single source of revenue — advertising — public television, with its much wider source of funds, should be able to offer a much wider spectrum of programs. Public television should begin to compete for audiences in measurable terms, in the same way that commercial television does. He notes that it is a questionable use of the public dollar to serve merely a small minority of the American audience. On the other hand, Grossman cautions, ". . .we're not simply another market for an unsold commercial project. We have to be certain that what we broadcast is something quite special. But public TV is where the real opportunity lies for creative television."

Research and analysis at least as comprehensive as the Carnegie Commission Report is needed to establish marketing data and strategies and specific objectives relative to the regulatory, legislative, and other changes that would be required by a consumer-supported television service. The research required for an on-going analysis of the viewing process would be monumental. But adapting to changes in society has always been hard work. It should not discourage serious folk from asking serious questions about what kind of television will best serve the American people in the substantially different world that lies immediately ahead.

References

1. Wilbur Schramm. "Communications Research in the United States," Wilbur Schramm, ed., in *The Science of Human Communication* (New York: Basic Books, 1963), p. 6.

2. Marshall McLuhan. *Understanding Media* (New York: McGraw Hill, 1964), p. 323.

3. Robert T. Bower. *Television and the Public* (New York: Holt, Rinehart and Winston, 1973), p. 177. The subsequent Bower quotes are taken from pp. 178, 179, and 182.

Program Funding
in Public Television
and the SPC

NATAN KATZMAN *with* KEN WIRT

Nearly 50 million dollars were spent for national public television programs distributed in the 1974-1975 season. These funds come from a variety of sources: direct grants by the Corporation for Public Broadcasting, appropriations from federal agencies and the National Endowments, contributions from nonprofit foundations, grants from private corporations, and the newest source of national production funds, the Station Program Cooperative (SPC). The current form of the Station Program Cooperative has its roots in various proposals and antecedent organizations, but the immediate impetus for the SPC experiment was undoubtedly Hartford Gunn's article, "Public Television Financing," which appeared in the *Educational Broadcasting Review* of October 1972. Gunn was president

---

Dr. Katzman is director of Research and Programming Services, an independent research consulting company. Since 1972 he has been involved in a variety of research activities for public broadcasting including analyses of public television and public radio content, community surveys, and reports on public television audience patterns. He is the author of the 1976 report, *Program Decisions in Public Television*. Portions of this paper are based on that report and a previously written analysis of the first Station Program Cooperative. Mr. Wirt, a doctoral candidate in the Mass Communication Research Program at the University of Michigan, is chief research associate for Research and Programming Services.

of the Public Broadcasting Service at the time, and the *Educational Broadcasting Review* (now renamed the *Public Telecommunications Review*) was a universal forum for the industry.

In Gunn's plan, local PTV licensees were to be the system operators "in every respect," working on their own and "through their designated agencies." In this way, national production would be the product of a consensus of all participants, rather than the decision of a small number of program planners and national agencies. One reason for the proposal was the insistent opposition from the Nixon White House and its Office of Telecommunication Policy to the idea of a more centralized public broadcasting system. In Gunn's words, "once the specter of centralist programming is removed," the seriously endangered prospects for long-term federal financial support for public broadcasting would once again become a possibility.

The cooperative under the original Gunn plan was to provide three levels of services. First, there would be the basic membership, which provided use of an interconnected system of program distribution, a tape library, promotional services, and voting rights in the program cooperative. The second level of activity for Gunn's SPC proposal involved the "basic cooperative program service." The third level of service would be the "optional program services," which involved another set of fees for additional materials not included in the basic service. There would also be "bonus" programs, underwritten with outside funds and free to all members.

The second level service — the cooperative program service — deserves some note since it differs considerably from the system that was later instituted. In the original plan, the membership fee (based on the same factors that were used to determine federal grants to stations) provided each member with (1) "a minimum number of program hours . . . selected by the stations for its use *from a pool of programs developed jointly by the stations*" [emphasis added] , (2) interconnection; and (3) the minimal color tape equipment required by each station. Stations would not have to use any or all of these services, but their fee payment would give them that right. Gunn also noted that the fee "must be sufficient to provide financing for that minimal level of service which the preponderance of the stations deem necessary and appropriate for their use."

Gunn's "market plan" (from the idea of a free market for program purchases) was given significant impetus at the annual PBS meeting in the Spring of 1973. By a vote of 124 to 1, PBS in effect became a station cooperative. The change meant that PBS no longer served the stations; it *was* the stations. The stations became members of the Public Broadcasting Service, and the PBS staff and officers now represented the stations and served at their pleasure.

In December, the producing stations were asked to submit their program proposals. Then, on January 21, 1974, PBS member stations held their annual meeting in Washington and passed a resolution that outlined the principles of a "station program cooperative" for the coming year. The PBS staff was authorized to develop a plan to provide "national programming funding and [foster] autonomy and future growth of the stations." By the spring, a policies and procedures manual was sent to all the stations, the proposal was ratified, and the Station Program Cooperative was officially in business.

The following major procedures and policies were specified within the first SPC manual sent to each station:

1. Program proposals should be generated in response to national needs. The proposals are evaluated by vote of the stations, and then the PBS Programming Committee, using station preferences and "other considerations" creates a Program Catalog for use in the cooperative. Concise information about various aspects of each proposal is to be included in the catalog. Producers are encouraged to provide pilot material for their proposals.

2. "Program Selection Rounds" of voting — using a computer-assisted process — will be employed to eliminate programs receiving no bids (or bids only from the producers of the programs).

3. "Elimination Rounds" will further reduce the number of offerings and allow station purchases of some of the offerings.

4. (a) If 80 percent or more of the stations bid on a program, and the price to each station does not go up, the program is to be declared purchased. The bidding stations are then committed to purchase it.
    (b) If less than 30 percent of stations bid for a program, the PBS staff must determine whether the bidding stations are willing to pay up to 80 percent of its cost among themselves. If they are not willing, the program is to be dropped.
    (c) During these voting rounds, producers are allowed to absorb some of the program cost and thereby

lower the price to bidders. However, Programming Committee consent is required, and the price change data must be communicated to *all* stations.

5. "Purchase Rounds" of voting will determine what other programs will be purchased through the SPC. So long as the price to the bidding station does not increase, bids during these rounds are binding and purchases are irrevocable. Potential price increases may be eliminated by subsidy from the producer or by other underwriting, subject to the approval of the Programming Committee.

6. Stations may not use programs they do not purchase, and they may not use purchased programs if they are behind in their payment schedules.

The key to the proposed SPC operation was DACS (Dial Access Communications System), a computer-controlled teletype network which already connected PBS to all PTV stations. The DACS system provided the mechanics for "votabs" tabulations on any issues (including ratification of the SPC) which required a vote of PBS members. The basic DACS hardware was ideal for station voting on programming choices and for automated computer processing of the results. A grant from the Ford Foundation paid for the creation of the new computer software and equipment that would process the SPC data.

The cost of the programs to individual stations was determined by two factors: (1) a "pricing share," and (2) the number of other stations purchasing the same program. The pricing share was determined by a formula that reflected station size. Each station was assigned a percent of the total price of any program. If, for example, station **A** had a pricing share of 0.5 percent, it meant that if all stations purchased a $100,000 program, station **A** would have to pay $500.

The most critical factor, though, was the number of stations that wanted a given program. Actual price to a station was determined by that station's pricing factor, divided by the total of the pricing factors for all purchasing stations. If only half of the stations wanted a $100,000 program, the price for station A's 0.5 percent share would be $1,000 (0.5% divided by 50% equals 1%) for the program.

The Outcome of the First Two SPCs

After the first two years of operation, the SPC mechanism financed a total of 63 programs. The evidence indicates, however, that the programs purchased through the SPC reflected at least one or two and often all three of the following characteristics: (1) prior national or multi-station exposure, (2) a low price and/or an exceptionally good value per unit time, and (3) a "bandwagon effect." In other words, the chances of success for ambitious (that is, expensive and/or innovative) new programs were very slim. The price per minute for programs purchased through the SPC averaged about a third of the price per minute of rejected programs. The purchased programs also tended to offer a better value to the stations, because an average of 40 percent of their production costs had been underwritten with funds from outside the SPC.

Because the selection of a program is based on the number of stations bidding, the programs which receive few votes become proportionately more expensive to potential purchasers. This creates the "bandwagon effect." If a program receives few votes in the opening rounds, its cost to a given buyer makes further votes for that program prohibitively expensive. Programs that were eventually purchased in the past two seasons have averaged over 75 votes in the first round (out of approximately 150), while programs that were rejected averaged 30 or less. There has been no proposal with low initial support which has eventually been purchased by a large number of stations.

As the figures in the following table demonstrate, the SPC failed in its first two years to finance untested, high-budget programs:

	SPC - I		SPC - II	
	Purchased	Rejected	Purchased	Rejected
Number of programs	25	68	38	94
Prior national or multistation exposure	72%	26%	76%	18%
Underwriting as % of average production cost	42%	22%	44%	7%
Dollars/minute cost to SPC	$294	$1063	$348	$823
First-round votes	79	18	86	30

The rejection of expensive and/or new programming is not really a fair indicator of the mood of the stations, however. Rather, it is primarily a by-product of the voting procedure. If 15 new programs are each supported in the voting by 10 stations, none of the new programs would be purchased even though the 150 stations all wanted something new.

The Search for Alternative Funding

Public television must look for alternative sources of funds if it wants to encourage the creation of innovative materials. But who will provide the money? The following list describes the division of the nearly $50 million spent on programs distributed nationally by PBS in the 1974-75 season:

Local station funds . . . . 5 percent
Direct support from CPB . . . . 10 percent
Foundation support . . . . 14 percent
Federal projects . . . . 21 percent
Corporate sources . . . . 25 percent
The SPC . . . . 25 percent

It is clear that the SPC is by no means predominant. The list is also somewhat misleading in that the percentages more accurately reflect the *division of authority* under which the money was spent, rather than the actual *sources* of the money. In fiscal year 1975, for example, three-fourths of the 25 percent spent by the SPC came from Ford and the CPB, and the latter got almost all of its money in turn from the federal government.

The CPB is in a difficult position in regard to the financing of national programming. It is under pressure from PBS to contribute more toward SPC development, but it also faces pressures from outside public broadcasting. For example, the Advisory Council of National Organizations (ACNO), originally founded by the CPB in order to provide a wide range of advisory opinion regarding public broadcasting, tends to focus its concerns and programming pressures either on services to various target groups or on projects that have an educative value. The CPB also receives considerable congressional feedback regarding alternative programming and minority issues. Partly as a result of these outside forces, more than half of CPB's national program funds in 1974 went to educative projects ("Feeling Good" and "Nova"), while another 11 percent went toward "Interface," a target-group program. In 1975, CPB became even more heavily involved in target-group programming with Hispanic, black, women's, and elderly projects.

The major contributor to national production funds, either directly or through the CPB and the National Endowments, is the federal government. Several federal agencies provide direct support for broadcasting projects which fall within the scope of their operations. For example, HEW continued to support "Sesame Street" and "The Electric Company" through 1975, and the U. S. Office of Education contributed over $4 million to "Carrascolendas," "Villa Alegre" (both bicultural children's programs), and a project to rebroadcast the ABC news with written captions for people with impaired hearing. The National Endowment for the Arts and the National Endowment for the Humanities have also committed significant funds for national PTV programming over the past five years. Whatever the source, the federal grants are generally limited to two spheres: cultural offerings in the arts and humanities, and support for specific target groups and educational projects. Happily, these limitations are within a range that pleases public broadcasting; and although some quarters of the federal government, especially HEW, may be decreasing their funding efforts, federal contributions in general will undoubtedly increase in the future.

Corporate underwriting provides an important source of support for the production of high-budget PTV programming, but underwriters generally restrict the types and subject matter of the programming they will support. Corporate underwriters tend to look for noncontroversial programming with mass appeal, although they have also given significant support to children's and educative programming. In 1974, more than two-thirds of all funds for cultural programming came from outside underwriting sources, and 20 percent of these funds originated with three oil companies: Mobil, Exxon, and Atlantic Richfield. Since public broadcasting executives and development directors have no hesitation in presenting corporate public-relations departments with information about the "opinion leaders" reached by underwriting credits before and after each program, it can be expected that in the future, corporate underwriting will continue to play a major role in financing drama, music, and even some types of documentaries ("National Geographic Specials" were underwritten in 1975/76 by Gulf Oil).

The educative and target-audience programming which CPB supports, and the cultural programming supported by corporate underwriters and the National Endowments, are important segments of the public television schedule. There is, however, another important category of programming — public affairs — which tends to be neglected by these sources of support. In-depth, intensive analyses of news, politics, society, and current events is what many people envision as the type of alternative service that public television is mandated to provide. However, the public broadcasting industry is somewhat uncomfortable with federal support for such programs, fearing political interference. And corporate underwriting is seldom extended for public affairs because of its potentially controversial content. As a result, funds for new, high-quality public affairs materials are scarce.

The SPC offers program managers from individual stations the chance to fund any type of material they choose. Although new public affairs proposals are desired by many managers, and although such programs have been offered in the SPC, few new proposals have succeeded in the first two years of the cooperative. The SPC has tended to purchase only those public affairs series which are well-known from previous airings on public television. Thus, in the 1974 season, the SPC provided 45 percent of the support for national public affairs programs, including such PTV staples as "Firing Line," "World Press," and "Washington Week in Review." But because of the limitations the SPC imposes on expensive new material, the cooperative was not inclined to fund any ambitious new public affairs proposals, and it purchased only one new program, the nightly "Evening Edition" for PBS. (Actually, the series was not new; it had been running on many Eastern stations for several years.)

Where will new public affairs series find support as older series come to the ends of their natural lives? At present, the best answer seems to be foundation funds. In fiscal year 1974, foundations — among them, Lilly Endowment, Ford, Martin Weiner, Anderson, Rockefeller, and the National Economists Club — supplied $3 million for public affairs programming. That sum represented 34 percent of all the dollars spent by public broadcasting on programs of this type. The $3 million also represents 42 percent of all foundation contributions for national programming (this excludes Ford's matching funds to SPC). Corporations provided another 10 percent of public affairs funding, and CPB contributed 4 percent (exclusive of its SPC matching funds).

At present, the reality of public television is such that it is possible to make a strong case for both a significant increase in funds for local operations and a significant increase in national production funds. Local stations are under-equipped, understaffed, and underpaid in comparison to the commercial television industry. They also require a great deal of money simply to remain on the air. On the other hand, the staple of local public television stations are the high quality national productions fed by PBS. (Only 11 percent of all air time is local material.) Thus, an additional dollar for national production has greater impact than an additional dollar for local operations. Each national production dollar eventually affects most of the stations; a dollar for local operations will affect only one broadcaster.

At current funding levels, decisions to produce expensive national series, such as "Theater in America," "Nova," "Bill Moyers' Journal," or "Zoom," are difficult to make. The most attractive national programming tends to be expensive British material which has been purchased at bargain rates. It is to the credit of public television that high quality American-made programs are appearing with increasing frequency. But there are still many ambitious projects which are not begun because the funds are simply not available.

Given the restricted national production budgets in the public television industry, it is important to establish a set of priorities that will determine which programs should, and which should not be produced. At the moment, there is only a kind of *de facto* ordering of priorities which occurs as each of the various interacting organizations — funders, producers, and local stations — responds to its own interests. A control is missing in an affirmative sense: "What programs do we need, and how can we get them?" It is also absent in a negative sense: "We don't need that kind of program even if there is a corporate underwriter ready to pay and one of our stations wants to make it."

CPB is supposed to fill the gaps left by other funding sources with material that will provide a "balanced" group of programs. But it, too, is subject to insistent pressures for specific types of programming which do not necessarily balance the national schedule. Since each of the outside sources of production funds is likely to continue supporting mainly the kinds of programming it now supports, public television needs some form of unified authority to exercise control over the overall pattern of program availability. Can the SPC, as just one segment of the funding mechanism, provide this authority and improve the overall configuration of PTV programming? It seems unlikely, unless there are major changes.

Looking Toward the Future

It is difficult to imagine a scenario in which the SPC voting procedure can ever support much innovative programming. In fact, it is difficult to imagine how this procedure can do much more than sort through old programs and proposals to repackage material produced elsewhere and to determine which stations want which.

The Future of Public Broadcasting

A single decision-making entity, or a deliberative body meeting face-to-face, might ponder questions of balance, diversity, innovation and quality. But the accumulated decisions of 150 entities create a statistical force toward the known, the safe, and the cheap. It is a case of the sum of the parts adding up to less than the whole.

Given the limited funds and the built-in bias of this noninteractive* participatory system, it is difficult to see the SPC as anything more than a "meat and potatoes" purchasing agent. (And there are some who wonder just how much meat is coming along with all those potatoes.) This situation may not inhibit the growth of quality and diversity in public television, but it will certainly not help very much. Clearly, first-year funding for "Sesame Street" and "Nova" would never have been drawn out of the SPC. Imagine the typical response at 40 or 50 stations: "Millions of dollars for this wild idea for preschool kids — are you kidding? We still don't have enough color equipment, and meeting the payroll is already a day-to-day crisis!" The steep price of these series to each station voting for their purchase would increase even more, and finally too few stations would be willing to support the project.

The present operation of the SPC also has a potentially dangerous effect on the prospects for long-term corporate underwriting. If McDonald's pays for half of "Zoom," it wants all the youngsters in the country to have a chance to tune in. But when more than 40 percent of the stations did not carry the new "Zoom" episodes from SPC-I because of the expense, the hamburger people were encouraged to *avoid* the SPC altogether. After all, the point of such partial outside underwriting is to lower the purchase price of expensive and especially worthy programs. Indeed, the key to much of the quality programming that was found in the SPC purchases of the first two years was outside underwriting. If the present system is not modified, this partial outside funding for SPC proposals is certain to decline.

Producing stations, too, have learned that they cannot afford to gamble development money on the hopes of an SPC purchase. Currently, producers receive only production costs and overhead for their programs. This gives them no incentive to spend local money to develop pilots or program concepts. Nor, considering the track record of the SPC, should they.

What's the prognosis? Left unchanged — with limited funds,

---

*The system is "noninteractive" in the sense that decision makers do not communicate with each other. The "interactive" computer system is no more than a sophisticated abacus which tallies votes quickly.

no central planning, no contingency money, poor interstation communication, low incentives for partial underwriting, a single PBS interconnection line, and a voting system that precludes innovation at the national level — the SPC may hinder improved national service. Indeed, too many low-budget programs could also create a downward spiral.

Consider, as a possibility, the following scenario:

A large number of inexpensive and/or "target audience" programs leave no room on the schedule for repeats; therefore, ambitious projects can only be shown one time, and the cumulative audience for an expensive program is low (that is, its impact is low). The justification for funding ambitious projects declines and fewer such projects are funded. The audience then declines in the face of weaker material. Finally, nothing is left but a few professors in swivel chairs talking via television to a few elderly intellectuals sipping wine in front of their sets.

Clearly, the system will not be allowed to fall to such a state, but adequate planning is preferable to emergency reactions. After the first two cooperatives, program managers found that they did in fact have a bit too much material on their hands at certain times of the year.

In the best of all worlds, the public television system would be quite different. A voting procedure similar to the current SPC mechanism would re-fund and upgrade popular programs for those stations that wanted them. Underwriters, the CPB, foundations, and federal agencies would continue to support a vareity of program types. A *representative* executive body, deriving its authority from the stations, would finance projects for quality, balance and innovation across the schedule. Program quality would be consistently improved, and there would be a corresponding growth both of audiences and of impact on society.

The most likely future for public television is somewhere between these two poles. The SPC will probably continue to support the solid core of successful programs from prior years (the meat and potatoes). Public affairs materials with low budgets (depending on total SPC funds available) will continue to predominate. Outside the cooperative, corporate underwriting will be the key to programs in the arts. These programs may be of high quality, but it is also fairly certain that they will be "safe." Government agencies and foundations may add funding for a significant number of "goal"-oriented programs — history, humanities, health, and minority content; and secondary producers will be able to upgrade a few local series ("Black Perspective," "Consumer Survival Kit") to national status.

The major producing stations will develop outside sources for their first-year funding and will look for SPC support only *after* their series have become an integral part of the public TV schedule. Unless member stations are willing to pay considerably higher dues and/ or overhead charges to PBS (and neither seems likely at the moment), the Public Broadcasting Service will merely operate an interconnection and plan a feed schedule. It will be able to exercise a minimal veto power over unacceptable material funded outside the SPC, and it will have some power by virtue of its scheduling responsibility. But PBS will be unable to *lead*, in any sense of the word, despite its status as a station-run organization.

It is ironic that the SPC system, which was designed to place programming decisions at the local station level, will actually have the effect of transfering the most important decisions outside station hands. Producers with new ideas will learn to shun the SPC until their series have run on public television for a year or two. The stations will merely ratify and continue broadcasting materials that are developed with funds provided by other corporate entities. Exxon, Mobil, the federal endowments, and CPB will become far more influential than stations in determining the quality and diversity of programs on public television.

The role of CPB *vis-a-vis* an unmodified PBS and SPC will be crucial to the future success of public television. An unchanged PBS and SPC will leave a vacuum of programming leadership (in quality and innovation) into which CPB, corporate underwriters, and government agencies may or may not choose to enter. The CPB, in particular, will remain as the only entity in public broadcasting that can innovate, balance the schedule, and fund expensive projects of high quality. After evaluating both SPC purchases and all underwritten projects, the CPB is the organization that can fill the programming gap if it chooses. It has the opportunity to supplant talking-heads with documentary public affairs material. It can be the source of funds for programs relevant to neglected minorities. It can sponsor creative video artists. It can promote dialogue, stimulate the unusual, pioneer unexplored realms of television. In short, if it chooses, the Corporation will be able to exercise considerable programming leadership. On the other hand, CPB can sit back and safely hand over its limited funds to "worthy" projects that have negligible effects on the social, intellectual, educational and cultural fabric of the nation.

It has been argued that additional — and *insulated* — money will allow the SPC to go beyond "buying programs by the pound" and enter the realm of innovative, high quality materials. It is quite true that more money is needed, and that additional funds can help improve the system. However, more money is a necessary, but not a sufficient condition. The ideas of well-negotiated contracts, more efficient and effective fund raising, and "insulation" from outside interference have come to overshadow the fact that TV programs and their effects are the reason public television exists.

Money alone — without system modifications — will not change the statistical forces responsible for the purchase of well-known, non-controversial, inexpensive series and the neglect of a balanced, high quality schedule. Additional funds in the first SPC probably would have allowed more stations to buy "Zoom," "Assignment America," "TV Theater," "Black Journal," and "Animation Festival." Several of the unsuccessful offerings, such as "Advocates," "Day at Night" and "Opera Theater," might also have been funded. However, the effect of these added programs would not have significantly improved the quality of the season. In the second SPC, additional funds would not have provided additional quality and diversity. Indeed, there is some evidence to indicate that many stations had more money to spend but found nothing additional that they wanted to buy.

Some Suggestions for Improvement*

Two broad and general suggestions might improve the overall public television system: First, *more money is needed for national program production.* Fifty million dollars is clearly inadequate for a national service that seeks to provide a wide range of high quality materials. Second, there is a need for some central authority to ensure a proper balance between funders, producers, the government, and the public interest. Too often public television content is determined by available funds or the interests of pressure groups. Both of these ideas may be farfetched in the short run; but they should not be forgotten, since they may be the key to a future for the SPC and for public television.

If and when more money becomes available to public television, there will be at least two questions of policy which will have to be resolved in an effort to create the best possible system. The first issue concerns the proportion of programming money that should be allocated to local versus national production. Although local stations are crying for funds to use in local production, it seems that at inter-

---

*This section was written prior to the plans developed for SPC-III, which introduced significant changes.

mediate funding levels, the stations would be better served by a stronger national service which appealed to more viewers and therefore had a greater potential effect.* The principle here is simply conservation of limited resources. There are too many local stations for public TV to be able to afford a local daily *Newsroom* at each one. (More than half of all licensees have total operating budgets below the budget for KQED's famed local news program.)

Furthermore, most local public television stations are not capable of producing more than an hour or two per week of strictly local prime-time material. Even with two playings of everything, this amounts to no more than one-seventh of the weekly air time between 7 and 11 p.m.* Thus, local production, although it is the heart of community service, is relatively minor when compared to programming that has been prepared for wider use. Unless hundreds of millions of dollars become available for local production, the national service (the PBS-interconnected feed) must be seen as the core of the evening schedules. Local public television schedules are diverse not because of any significant amounts of strictly local material, but because of the varying patterns of *acquisitions*.

The second issue in the event of greater funding will revolve around the question of the proportion of national programming monies to be allocated to the SPC. This is a difficult problem, because the SPC is still in a state of development. If the system seems to offer possibilities for innovation and a mechanism for balancing the schedules and filling national needs, then a higher proportion of national programming funds should go to the cooperative. But if the developing SPC seems to offer little incentive for quality and diversity, then a lower proportion would be in order. The need for a central authority to ensure balance, quality, and innovation in public television becomes increasingly clear as current national funding sources display their particular interests. Such an authority need not take the form of the dreaded "network" that many in the industry fear. However, whether the form is an extension of the cooperative concept, an outgrowth of the current PBS organization in Washington, a derivative of CPB, or some other entity, it will

---

*A pattern of growth among community-supported stations clearly depends on national programming. Attractive programs bring in viewers; viewers become station supporters; contributions from supporters provide the funds for local production.

*During 1974, local production accounted for a bit more than 12 percent of prime-time hours. This figure includes the creations of the major stations — WNET, WGBH, KQED — which offer more than average amounts of local material. Local origination is typically in-studio public affairs material, and there is good reason to believe that the availability of more money for local production would lead mainly to *improved quality*, rather than an increased proportion of local offerings during prime-time.

require men and women of courage. Any group given the responsibility for creating a high-quality, balanced public television schedule will inevitably find itself embroiled in conflict with producers who want their programs to be funded and aired; it will irritate people who do not share the judgment or values of the key decision-makers; and it will occasionally bring down the wrath of politically motivated organizations that wish to see public television become a vehicle for their messages — regardless of viewer interest.

An additional general suggestion is that public broadcasting institute a second interconnection channel. Some activity in this direction has already begun with the announcement of plans to make use of satellite technology. Almost 37 percent of the U. S. population could be served by two PTV signals if all licensed stations were operating at full power. Three considerations would be important in the introduction of such a service. The first would be the need to provide service of equal quality to all time zones. The second would be the problem of what to do in the communities with more than one PTV station. The third consideration would be the PBS goal of promoting local scheduling flexibility.* This desire may nor may not be a good thing, but local autonomy is a philosophical principle with widespread support. "We are not a fourth network" is a potent rallying call in public broadcasting.

On the other hand, is there any intrinsic need to have "Evening at Pops" shown at 8:00 Monday in one community and 8:30 Thursday in another? Local program managers can flex their muscles; but are the two communities better served by these managerial idiosyncracies? The fact is that the communities and the stations are probably a bit worse off, because national promotional efforts are disrupted. National promotion is a powerful and cost-efficient factor which is consistently undermined by haphazard scheduling by local stations.

In addition to more money for national programming, a "balancing" central authority, and a second interconnection, a number of specific changes can improve public television. These suggested changes are divided into four groups, presented in order from what is probably the least controversial proposal to what may be the most controversial. Virtually all of the suggestions also center around a

---

*The Eastern Educational Television Network provides useful background information. Members of that regional network are served by two interconnections. They receive the regular PBS feed and the EETN feed, which provides alternate air times for PBS materials along with additional acquisitions made by the regional network for use by participating stations. Scheduling flexibility is enhanced, and even now EETN members are using the second interconnection to fill "holes" created when stations have not purchased SPC offerings.

single proposal: *The SPC system would be improved by a shift from what might be called participatory anarchy, with a limited information base, to a participatory/representative democracy, with fullest internal communication.*

Activities external to SPC operations:

1. *Arrangements should be made for negotiation and cooperation among stations with overlapping signals.* The negotiations should also involve PBS, in order to determine optimal price factors. In some cases, a single price for the whole market might be appropriate; in others, it would not be. The initial pricing formula had both WNYE and WNYC — which are completely overshadowed in New York City by VHF-WNET — paying more for a program than WETA in Washington. In fact, there were only seven licensees that had to pay more for programs than these secondary and tertiary outlets. The situation in Los Angeles and in other overlapping markets present similar problems, and there are enough of these markets to make the matter important. Community size and station budgets must be balanced in an equation for setting price formulas for stations with overlapping signals.

At the present time, the relatively poor communication between PTV stations with overlapping signals wastes a valuable resource for public broadcasting. The problem is no secret, but perhaps it will take an outside agency to convene the necessary open discussions between such stations. Cooperation among these stations in SPC voting could lead to far greater diversity of programming in a given market. Channel 13 should tell its viewers, "Our next program is going to be . . . and if you tune to Channel 31, you can see . . ."

2. *CPB should use its funds to encourage development of programs needed to fill the gaps left by the SPC.* Although the Corporation now expends funds for new program development, more attention should be given to the purchase of programs to produce a *well-balanced*, attractive national schedule. An appropriate approach might be for CPB to study the SPC results and the available underwritten programs. Then, the Corporation might issue requests for program proposals, specifying goals and production standards. At that point, interested producers could submit ideas for evaluation.

This is a more active approach than the simple evaluation of unsolicited proposals. It would stimulate program production and implement a planned programming philosophy which would add needed programs to SPC purchases. At present, the Corporation theoretically acts in this fashion. However, its list of "needs" seems more a product of target group pressures than the outcome of an examination of what "quality" public television should be doing.

Improvement in SPC communication structures:

3. *Stations and producers should participate in a two-way evaluation process for many versions of proposals.* There were preference votes in the second SPC year, and these votes were a first step. However, in the future, a producer should be able to offer several versions of the same basic proposal, with each version featuring different costs, different formats, and different lengths. Stations could respond by voting and by explicit comments via DACS. Producers and SPC catalog editors would then know what is desired and why. Several such cycles of offer, response, and counter-offer would approximate the negotiations that take place between typical funding sources and producers. The goal would be to have catalog offerings fit best with station needs and wants.*

4. *PBS should evaluate each proposal in the catalog and rate the proposals as to quality, need, position in schedule, and value for cost.* Staff evaluations could be submitted to the PBS Programming Committee for approval and then transmitted as an integral part of the SPC catalog. Thus, a well-informed group of professionals — *employed by the stations* — would provide the information that is needed for thoughful station decisions. The procedure might also enhance the possibility of high quality new programs being purchased by the SPC. That is, favorable evaluations by the committee might produce the essential core of support in first-round voting. As things currently stand, new programs cannot succeed in the SPC unless they are either well known, largely under-written (and this is no guarantee), or very inexpensive.

Clearly, specific evaluations would arouse controversy and debate. However, we must assume that there are some standards of quality, value, and utility that can be applied to program proposals. Furthermore, a bit of controversy would be a small price to pay for keeping SPC voters well-informed and for giving new programs a chance to succeed.

5. *After each voting round, producers should be provided full*

---

*SPC-3 adopted a variation of this idea. The initial catalog included variations of some initial proposals. In addition, small group sessions at the 1976 PBS meeting provided useful feedback among purchasers and to producers.

lists of votes for and against their programs. * This is essential to the formation of coalitions to purchase programs after predetermined price drops. "Would you buy the program at half its current price?" is a fair question. By knowing whom to ask, producers might increase distribution of their programs while lowering the cost to each buyer. The criticism that too much salesmanship would be introduced by this procedure ignores the nature of any purchasing cooperative. If somebody is buying, somebody else is selling; and if the decision is in the hands of 152 voters, producers must be able to promote their wares with *each* of them.

6.   *The DACS system should continue to be available for uncensored, limited-length messages among the producers between voting rounds.* This procedure, introduced in the second SPC season, is far less expensive and far more effective than using the telephone for negotiations. PBS should be allowed to monitor all communications via DACS, so that it can issue amplifications or replies if necessary. Indeed, some of the debates and disagreements that occur in this way might profit from a public airing.

The thrust of this suggestion, and of suggestion 5, is to open inter-station communication channels, so that coalitions might be easily formed. Consensus could then be reached after interaction among voters, rather than through a series of blind votes. Once again, the goal would be to bring stations together to make decisions that reflect their interests as a group (or as a series of subgroups).

Modifications of financial arrangements:

7.   *Profits from sales outside the SPC should first be used to cover underwriting by producing stations. Additional amounts should be split on a fair basis between producers and PBS.* Foreign rights and nonbroadcast uses for programs have some value. Returns should go to producers as a form of incentive for further development and as a method of inducing producers to underwrite costs for the SPC. For example, if a producer is willing to gamble half the cost of a series on the chance that it will be sold to the BBC, the SPC price might be lowered and the producer would still have a chance to earn on his investment. Producers should also have a share of profits above production costs. Such income would support general

---

*In SPC-II, any producer could get a list of purchasers who agreed to release their station's name. This mechanism allowed for some feedback to the producers, but it was far from ideal.

station activities and strengthen production centers for further projects.

8. *After the close of voting, excess funds in the pool of matching funds should be proportionately distributed to stations that exceeded their spending limits.* The matching ratio would not be predictable for this rebate. Even so, stations would be encouraged to go beyond their limits to buy better and more diverse programs. The plan would reward stations which were willing to dig deeper into their coffers to finance high quality programming and a more diverse schedule. Since there would be no assurance that any matching money would be left, stations would have to commit their own funds. However, even a potential discount would probably draw more local money into national programming.*

Creation of a basic program service funded by member stations:

9. *PBS should arrange for funding of "Special Events" coverage with money from members, from matching funds, and from outside underwriting. "Special Events" would be provided to all member stations, and funding would be outside the voting procedures.* (Such a procedure could only be adopted with full agreement of the PBS boards and committees and with an overwhelming ratification by the stations.) Unpredictable preemptions must be available to all stations. If events are important enough to be broadcast, they are important enough to be broadcast by everyone. A few stations (almost all of them in overlapping or non-interconnected markets) would have to take a service they did not want to buy during SPC's first year. However, the costs to this very small number of stations (which would be forced to duplicate a service already provided to their communities or to find local alternative materials) would be more than offset by gains and savings for the overall national system. Preempted material can always be held for later airings, and sequential series (for example, "America" or "Masterpiece Theatre") could retain their order. Regular public affairs series might skip a week of production, thereby saving some money for the system.

10. *PBS should arrange for funding of a small group of "must have" programs (such as "Sesame Street" and "Electric Company") with money from members, from matching funds, and from outside*

---

*A major change for SPC-III removed the "matching" concept. CPB and Ford supplied $5.5 million to be used for the first programs purchased by each station regardless of the total amount spent. Additional purchases would not use "discount" funds.

underwriting. These programs would be provided to all member stations, and fundings would be outside SPC voting procedures. This proposal is similar to that for the provision of "Special Events," but it is suggested for different reasons (all of which also apply to "Special Events" funding). SPC voting would be more of a decision-making procedure if the bulk of available funds were not taken off the top for "required" material. The current situation creates the psychological feeling that most of the money is gone before any "decisions" have been made. Thus, if a basic package of "must have" programs and "Special Events" were funded before the voting began, voters would feel more freedom of action among remaining offerings. This arrangement would also allow PBS to seek partial underwriting, with a guarantee to potential funding agencies that a particular program would be available to all stations.

11. *All programs purchased by over 80 percent of the stations should be declared purchased by the entire system.* All stations should be fed such programs, to use or not use as they saw fit. The price of the programs would be absorbed by the entire system. There are several reasons for a serious consideration of this proposal: First, it would make scheduling for the interconnection easier, while also avoiding holes in the schedules of nonpurchasing stations. Second, it would make possible the purchase of individual one-shot programs for use in a "special of the week" type of series. Because all stations get underwritten specials, whereas the SPC purchases vary among the different stations, the current SPC procedures work against single programs and specials, in that the planning for the current special is always difficult. The proposed 80 percent change might help this situation.

Third, there is reason to believe that actual costs to individual stations would not go up if all programs with more than 80 percent support were declared fully purchased.* In any case, gross costs

---

*Consider a simplified example: Ten stations (WAAA, WBBB, WCCC, etc.) are choosing among ten programs (#1, #2, #3, etc.). Each program costs $16,000 to produce. Each station votes for eight programs. Each program gets eight votes (80 percent support). Under current SPC procedures, the stations selecting program #1 would each pay $2,000 ($16,000 divided by 8) for #2, etc. Station WAAA might have chosen #1, #2, #3, #4, #5, #6, #7, and #8; and the total bill would have been $16,000. Station WHHH may have chosen #1, #3, #4, #5, #6, #8, #9, and #10. Its bill would also have been $16,000. All ten programs would be produced, each of ten stations would pay $16,000; and each station could use eight programs.

Under the proposed 80 percent rule, all ten programs would be declared purchased for everyone. Each station would pay $1,600 per program ($16,000 divided by 10). The total bill to each station would remain $16,000, *but all stations would be able to use all programs* (but, of course, they would not have to do so).

for all purchased programs do not go up. The only issue is redistribution of costs to individual stations. There is tentative evidence that if the 17 programs with more than 80 percent support in the first SPC year had been assigned to all stations, the lower price for already purchased programs would have balanced the added cost for previously underpurchased programs.* If stations did not want a program purchased under this 80 percent rule, they would not have to use it, and they would have spent no additional money.

In SPC-II, PBS attempted to create such a package without the legal authority to impose it. Stations were informed of the potential savings if they all purchased all the programs remaining after a middle voting round. The procedure probably saved some programs and gave wider distribution to others, but it was only a partial measure.

Proposals 9, 10, and 11 together define a basic program package. (Even if proposals 9 and 10 were not implemented, the 80 percent rule would probably produce the same basic set of programs, including "must haves" and "Special Events.") If stations wanted so little material that they would be harmed by this package (that is, they would have to pay more for the basic package than they would have paid for their specific selections), they could simply decline SPC membership and negotiate separately with PBS for the few programs they wanted. (Only two or three stations would be likely to fall into this group.) The 80 percent rule is essentially democratic and it is similar to many majority-rule situations (though the 80 percent is far more than a simple majority) in other types of purchasing cooperatives.

12. *A discretionary programming fund should be available for use by the PBS staff.* By decision of its boards and its Programming Committee, PBS should be able to complete funding of partially underwritten projects and purchase materials to balance the overall national schedule. This proposal would require the establishment of a PBS bank account and might imply the application of matching funds to PBS purchases. The partial returns from non-PTV income brought in by SPC programs might supply some money. Post-market purchases might supply more. However, the bulk of the funds will probably have to come either from the federal appropriation, via CPB or stations returning CSG money, and from any remaining Ford Foundation grants.

One approach for fund raising would be to increase PBS mem-

---

*PBS was interested in a computer run to check this hypothesis, but the data could not be made available in time for this paper.

bership dues. Another would be to create a surcharge on SPC purchases. A third would be to arrange funding from the CSG pool before it is distributed. However, these ideas are unlikely to be supported; and, in fact, the possibility of finding money for a PBS programming fund is slim. Nevertheless, the addition of such discretionary power to the body that represents the stations would clearly be another step toward implementing a responsive programming system.

A Fourth Network?

Given that other sources of national production funds have their own priorities, it is not surprising to find that the SPC is more likely to finance certain types of programs than others. Changes in current SPC operations should take the nature of all other funding sources into account. However, in order for this to happen, someone — an individual, a group, or several groups — must first be willing and able to define what is meant by "balanced" and "high quality" programming. For public television to fulfill its purpose, it must have both meaningful programming and large numbers of people watching those programs. The present system — corporate underwriting for "high culture," federal funds for mandated projects, CPB support for target groups, SPC money for renewing old series, and foundation grants for stations or specific projects — neither ensures balance nor guarantees uniformly high quality.

No amount of tinkering with the SPC will change the situation significantly if other aspects of public television program funding remain unchanged. The problems are problems of an entire system, not just one of its components. The common excuse is lack of funds. Yet lack of coordination, lack of freedom to innovate, and lack of opportunity to invest in new projects without searching for outside funds are probably more serious burdens. The redistribution of the amount of money now available might help the quality of national production as much as a major infusion of new dollars.

Does all this imply that a centralized fourth network is the solution to public television's problems? Not necessarily. The whole issue of whether PBS is a network has become a semantic exercise of minimal value. The proposals presented here seek only a responsive, high-quality system. Decisions are to be left in the hands of the stations and their designated representatives and employees. The basic model remains a representative grass-roots democracy. However, there are differences between a division of authority, a delegation of authority, and a dilution (or even avoidance) of authority.

More than money, public television needs a structure in which competent professionals can judge programs on their merits, not their sources of funds. Competent professionals should also have the ability to develop and create new series which are needed.

Many of the problems identified here were foreseen in Hartford Gunn's original article proposing station financing for national programs. Indeed, some of the suggested modifications come close to implementing Gunn's original plan. For example, the 80 percent rule and the automatic purchase of "must have" programs are quite similar to his "basic program service" providing subscribers with choices within a list developed by a consensus among member stations.

It is essential that the system establish better internal communications and a selection procedure which is more flexible and more responsive to the special demands of a medium requiring both long-range planning and rapid decisions. It would be asking too much if we were to expect 152 decision makers to keep fully informed of moment-to-moment changes. Nor could we expect all 152 of them to spend the time and effort required for adequate long-range planning for a total national programming service. But such responsibility can be fairly and easily delegated by the stations (who would retain the ultimate authority and power) to their chosen representatives on the PBS boards and committees. Certainly, station representatives (and their designated national staff) would be in a suitable position to consider and evaluate information and make decisions that truly reflected consensus (but not necessarily unanimity) at the local level.

During 1974, PBS provided 71 percent of all prime-time PTV hours, whereas local stations produced 12.2 percent of their prime-time offerings. These same proportions can be expected over the next five to ten years. The national service, then, is clearly the core of local programming (especially when local stations can choose among nationally provided alternatives). If this national service is carefully planned, and if member stations delegate some authority, PBS could provide itself with a responsive and efficient system of decision making which would be considerate of local desires, open to innovation, protected from outside pressures, alert to unexpected events, aware of minority needs, interested in a balanced schedule, and concerned above all with improving the quality of public television programs.

Public Television Production— "It Can't All Be Done By One Club"

HERMAN W. LAND

The achievements of "Sesame Street" and "The Electric Company" have been so striking and so visible that the Children's Television Workshop has lived another almost full-time career as a subject of study, analysis and emulation. The CTW formula for successful program development — research and professional counsel melded with creativity, adequate funding, and independent planning and decision-making — has been examined and effectively demonstrated. Observers of public television may have assumed that it would be only a matter of time before the lessons of the CTW experience were fully adapted and new independent production centers were built in its image.*

Things haven't happened quite that way. To date, PBS recog-

Mr. Land is president of the consulting firm, the H. W. Land Corporation, and of the Association of Independent Television Stations, Inc. (INTV). He was formerly an executive with Group W Westinghouse Broadcasting Company and with Corinthian Broadcasting Corporation, and he served as vice president and executive editor for *Television Magazine*.

*In 1971-72, the author undertook a study of the CTW under U. S. Office of Education auspices, producing a guidebook for would-be emulators: "The Children's Television Workshop/How and Why It Works."

nizes only two independent production centers besides CTW: Bi-Lingual Children's Television (BC/TV), whose target is the Spanish-speaking child, and Family Communications, Inc., created by Fred Rogers of "Mister Rogers' Neighborhood." Bi-Lingual Children's Television was reportedly on the brink of insolvency late in 1975, when HEW finally agreed to renew its support. Family Communications, not yet in production in late 1975, has been focusing most of its activities around an already existing library of syndicated programs produced earlier by Rogers. Even the future of the much-admired CTW may be somewhat clouded. The CPB and the Ford Foundation have phased out their subsidies of the two CTW series; and the U.S. Office of Education, which has been the stalwart backer of the CTW from the start, is apparently concerned about the size and the continuity of the commitment to "Sesame Street" and "The Electric Company."

While the concept of independent production *centers* seems to be making little headway, the opposite is occurring in connection with the idea of *independent production*. The public broadcasting system has begun to relax its access restrictions and to be more open to the works of independent production units — that is, producing groups which have no financial or managerial ties to the stations or to PBS. Nor does it seem to matter as much any longer whether these independent producers are public television veterans or whether they are commercial producers who have become sensitive to the possibility of new market stirrings. This trend, it seems to me, will continue through the second half of this decade, until multi-source program origination becomes the established practice in public broadcasting.

In this paper, I have taken on the task of informally examining some of the questions raised by the concept of independent production in a medium now going through a tortuous trial-and-error struggle toward a permanent organizational form. At issue is the kind of public television the American people should have. Should the system be completely self-contained and totally insulated from the commercial field, with the national programming schedule limited to productions by member stations and/or people from public broadcasting? Or should there be a substantial admixture of production from outside the public broadcasting system? Do the ultimate strength and vitality of the medium demand that the public stations enjoy exclusive access to federal and corporate subsidy? Or is there room in the financial and artistic scheme of things for independent production centers or other producing organizations which are not connected with the stations? Should independent producers be forced to make contact only through recognized stations or centers, or should they have the right of direct access through the PBS?

The Short-Lived Idea of
Independent Production Centers

We should begin, I think, by trying to clear away the semantic fuzziness surrounding the term "independent production center." The differences between an independent production center and other independent production organizations begin with the word "center," which suggests a physical *place*, a permanent institution with a production responsibility beyond that of a specific program. The CTW, for example, was conceived in national, *institutional* terms as an ongoing experimental laboratory with a "social mission" to carry out research and development as integral components of the programming it creates. The CTW was founded to educate America's children through television, not merely to produce television programs.*

Most important of the differences between independent production centers and independent producers and productions has been the special access of the former to the public broadcasting system. CTW, with its long-range workshop character, its serious social mission, and its careful research, was granted equal rights with the stations and NET for access to PBS channels. CTW became a kind of third branch of PBS, and its productions were accepted on the same basis as programs coming from a station or from NET. Presumably, any independent production center would enjoy this special access to PBS. Independent producers, on the other hand, must generally find a sponsoring "producing" station before their programs can be aired.

When I was consulting for the Corporation for Public Broadcasting in 1969, even before "Sesame Street" had reached the air, I had concluded (along with others) that the major challenge for the future welfare of the medium rested on public broadcasting's ability

---

*It is no accident that the three existing production centers are all devoted to the welfare of children. There was a vacuum in television service to pre-school children during the 1950s and 1960s. CTW and the other two centers came into being in order to fill that vacuum.

to build public and Congressional support. It also seemed clear to me that the key to this support was outstanding programming in the educational, entertainment and public affairs areas. The articulate passion of Joan Cooney and a few sample excerpts from "Sesame Street" had already begun to work their magic at a Congressional hearing as well as at gatherings of public television people. Thus, with the obvious promise of the CTW concepts, and with the example of commercial television, I thought that the road to programming excellence could best be found by concentrating the slim resources of public television in a few production hands and by accepting the realities of the Hollywood-New York talent and facilities axis.

Even in this period, there had been considerable discussion of moves in the direction of multiple-station production centers, but the idea seemed to me premature. Whatever the philosophical and political advantages of decentralization, I felt they would be counterbalanced by a dispersion of energy and resources that could only delay significant national development. It was my contention then that regardless of the desires of many stations for a station system, the brute facts of program life in the United States would sooner or later lead the medium into a network-like pattern, though the system would probably look considerably different from the commercial institutions.

The success of "Sesame Street" and the CTW experience suggested that other similar enterprises might benefit the system. There might be an institution to develop public affairs programming, for example (The Ford Foundation and the CPB were already planning what came to be known as NPACT, the National Public Affairs Center for Television). Another independent production center might devote itself to science programming. (Boston seemed a possible location for such a center, and, interestingly, the NOVA unit of WGBH has since come to fulfill a good part of a "science" production center's mission.) Yet another independent production center might choose the goal of developing adult and other forms of educational programming. Dr. Cardenas and his associates had already begun studying CTW operations in preparation for launching Bi-Lingual Children's Television.

There were other possibilities. There might be room for a black-programming center, for instance, though I thought that the overall movement toward more cosmopolitan programming on television would make the black-center idea unnecessary in a few years. I could

278

also see room for one or two *general* production centers. One, NET or its successor, would be in New York; later, another might be founded on the West Coast.

An important concept in this scheme was the clear separation between national programming, conceived as such from its inception, and local production, which would be geared to the needs of a station's community and appropriate to its financial level of operation. There would be time, it seemed to me, to build the much-desired local-station production system. Meanwhile, the system should not rush ahead of the available national talent and skills. Public television had to compete with the best that commercial television had to offer every day and night of the week, year-in and year-out. Above all, it could not afford amateurism on the screen. This gradual approach was designed to retain the advantages of scale and concentrations of talent and resources while avoiding central dictation of programming.

The Increasing Dominance of the Stations

The system was moving in quite another direction, however. This is the time of the station. Within the ranks, the stations are perceived as the central element on which public television is to be built. The stations' future is the medium's future. Two boards of 25 each now control PBS, one consisting of station trustees, the other of station managers.

Station primacy has been further advanced recently by the Station Program Cooperative (SPC), which was introduced in 1974 to allow stations to "shop" and bid for programs submitted either by other stations or the independent production centers. In helping to found the SPC, the CPB was adopting a "seeding" policy of underwriting a new program (CTW programs included) for only *two years* and then letting the SPC marketplace decide the fate of the program. Up to 40 percent of the national schedule is now accounted for by the market procedures of the SPC. As a result, the producing stations and CTW are now in competition for the same scarce resources available to the public television system for nearly half of its national programming.

To appreciate the station frustrations, as well as the dilemma of the CTW, one has merely to consider, first, that the stations are paying approximately *one-third* of their severely restricted SPC budgets for the two CTW programs. Second, the CPB and the Ford Foundation are *temporarily* contributing a full 75 percent of the actual monies expended by each station in its SPC bidding. These grants are intended only to get the market process going among the public stations, not to support the SPC system indefinitely. Thus, some stations are concerned that they may now be spending a disproportionate amount of their slim resources for children's programming. They are also worried that the grants for SPC bidding will soon be eliminated or at least decreased, and that they will then be forced to sacrifice even more of their overall program needs in order to keep the very popular CTW products on the air in their regions.

Understandably, this situation can lead to charges that the independent production center, specifically the CTW, is overbudgeted and wasteful. A center, say its critics, is so institutionalized that it has the same large administrative and overhead costs as a station. Furthermore, the independent production center requires major financial support, not only to keep going, but also to undertake new pioneering efforts (an important aspect of its function, as we shall see later). Thus, station and center enter into competition for scarce resources. But the center, so goes the argument, is not equipped to spend as efficiently as the station, whose whole existence is predicated on its ability to make one dollar do the work of many.

A forceful exponent of this station point of view is, not unexpectedly, the president of KCET Los Angeles, James Loper:

> No more independent centers should be created. They pose serious problems of whom they report to and of how they fit into an integrated pattern. The system has to make relatively few dollars stretch as far as possible. Stations are more aware of the need to stretch than independent production centers. I am a centralist. I believe we must concentrate our dollars in a few centers. And I don't just mean studios. There is no incentive for a large station to go into national production unless there is a large base on which to amortize it. The station is the on-going entity, year in and year out. The system cannot support any more independent entities.

Others argue that production should be kept totally within

the station ranks because national production can serve a valuable purpose in helping to upgrade a station's programming skills. Lloyd Kaiser, manager of WQED Pittsburgh, says:

> The BBC has a production commitment to its own air. All its production genius and creativity are harnessed to its on-the-air goals . . . all channeled into one process. We won't develop the same internal strength until the CPB and the other funders are willing to support production centers within the stations. We want great things in PTV.

WGBH-TV president David Ives agrees:

> The system is still weak, the stations not yet strong. It's important to encourage the stations to engage in production. It helps to build their local capabilities. The local station is the bedrock of the system.

At the same time, Ives is aware that such production can be a mixed blessing:

> National production sometimes results in diverting attention from the local situation. We never undertake a national production of a program unless it's one we'd like to do for our audience. However, what may be of paramount importance locally may have no national interest.

At bottom, of course, the argument is about economics. National production keeps staffs and facilities active and provides financial underpinning for overhead and administration. There is a danger, however, that a station will become dependent on national production for the very same reasons. Once a heavy investment is made in facilities and staff and national production capability has been built, a station is under ceaseless internal pressure to sustain the national production level. Loper is quite justified when he argues that if the system expects a station to maintain such a capability, it must organize its funding accordingly.

Given the financial stresses in public broadcasting generally, it is unfortunate that "Sesame Street" and "The Electric Company" were entered into the SPC sweepstakes. The CTW programs hardly needed to prove themselves by forcing the members of the SPC to choose them over other entries. And in view of the very tight budgets of the stations, the situation was almost certain to generate new frictions between them and CTW. The stations gave little thought to the high cost of the CTW series so long as the programs were being subsidized by HEW and the foundations. The moment the programs became part of the SPC competition, stations inevitably began to mutter about CTW waste and self-indulgence.

As a result of insistent pressure from PBS, Joan Cooney agreed to a reduction of $200,000 from the original asking price for "The Electric Company" and to limit new production for the show to two years, thereafter moving "The Electric Company" into a four-year re-run period. Some observers consider the decision on "Electric Company" a rational compromise, in that the Workshop has probably learned as much as it reasonably can for the moment about how to use the medium for teaching reading. However, one could hardly extend this rationale and similar cutbacks to "Sesame Street." Our swiftly changing culture and ever-new generations of viewers demand continuing research and perennial renewal of content and treatment for the "Sesame Street" format. Nevertheless, some stations have been insisting — short-sightedly, I think — that "Sesame Street" should also cut down on original production and increase the number of repeats.

The Miraculous CTW

It strikes me that whatever the merits of the stations' arguments against the costs of CTW products and of the Workshop's overhead, they are overlooking something rather basic. In "Sesame Street" and "The Electric Company," we are not dealing with simply a pair of "good shows," but with extraordinary achievements which move them into a dimension far above and beyond the conventionally successful television program. They must be appreciated for what they are to our society: a major and historic breakthrough among social ventures. Had they appeared in the middle years of a mature medium, the CTW programs would have fully justified the great investments that have been made. Coming as they did in the medium's infancy, the programs must be seen as nothing less than miraculous. Four hundred years later, and still no second Shakespeare. Similarly, the magic that is "Sesame Street" may never be repeated.

Consider, also, the importance of "Sesame Street" and its companion to the development of public television. They are the system's brightest and proudest boasts, the living illustrations for the public, for Congressmen, for foundation trustees and corporate boards of what can be achieved for our society through communications. It may be time for the stations, and for CPB, PBS and HEW, to adopt as policy what they assume in practice: That for the good of the system as a whole, "Sesame Street" *just has to be preserved and supported*, regardless of the share of the total budget it may consume.

It would be tragic, foolish beyond description, to abandon or seriously weaken "Sesame Street" simply because it has been around and there are other new ventures, however worthy. As well abandon a great university, which has been lovingly built over generations, because it is a burdensome business to support it and there are new, untried institutions to be built. "Sesame Street" is, after all, a national educational institution which is doing a supremely important job in the nation.

I think that, for all of the complaining, the members of the public television fraternity understand the importance of CTW and will continue to support the CTW programs. Undoubtedly, they will also continue to press for lower costs, but they know better than anyone that programming is an expensive art, and that the trend of costs is inevitably upward as the system grows more ambitious. Cooney and company simply recognized this fact early and made up their minds to live with the reality.

A Promising Future for Public Broadcasting

It is probably difficult for public broadcasters to believe, but time is on their side. I find many other individuals in the field who share my conviction that we are destined to see more and more dollars flowing into the public broadcasting system. The fact is that there is now a tangible federal commitment to public television. The Corporation for Public Broadcasting, which began as a $5 million agency, is anticipating a five-year Congressional appropriation which will rise to $140 million in FY 1979. There is PBS and there are the 260 public television stations. Corporate underwriting has increased dramatically. And this is only a start.

The Future of Public Broadcasting

It is also well to remind ourselves that the birth of the new public broadcasting occurred at a time when our national life was being distorted by internal tensions and the Vietnam War. Its formative years coincided with a Presidential-media conflict unique in our history. That period is over. Predictions are hazardous, but it does appear possible that the next administration, regardless of party affiliation, will be disposed to look upon public broadcasting more as a national asset to be developed than a threat to be contained. With luck, social vision will return to the White House to inspire a constructive effort to realize the medium's potential. And even if this does not occur, or does so only in part, the long-term outlook for public broadcasting is far more promising than it was just a short time ago.

What is more unfortunate in the whole scene at present is the schizophrenic tendency of the government and the large foundations to hop, skip and jump rather than stick to what has proven its worth. As CTW chairman Lloyd Morrisett notes, foundations like to view themselves primarily as "seeding" institutions, interested in stimulating the new rather than sustaining on-going enterprises. Thus, Morrisett had no illusions about the longevity of foundation funding.* He assumed that grants of any significanct sort would come to an end relatively soon — and they have. What has been nerve-racking for him, and for public broadcasters generally, are the signs that even sustained government support is not to be taken for granted.

Naturally, government is also concerned with aiding the pro-

---

*Morrisett anticipated some of the future money problems for CTW and realized that the Workshop had to find a way to generate continuing income once the conventional funding sources had run dry. He came up with two plans — nonbroadcast activities involving publishing and merchandising, and finding new overseas markets for the programs. According to Morrisett's estimate, the total potential of these self-support efforts is now about $3 million.

In another scheme, a recent Ford Foundation $6 million capital grant has enabled the CTW to establish two new subsidiaries which would work in communications and apply their incomes to new Workshop projects. One of the subsidiaries, CTW Communications, Inc., is already active with cable enterprises in Hawaii and Dayton and is now looking for additional cable opportunities and radio stations. The other, CTW Productions, Inc., seeks revenue-producing opportunities in commercial television and theatrical motion picture development and production. Just what the financial potential of all of this activity will turn out to be is anyone's guess. The history of commercial television suggests that the road to riches may be quite tortuous.

mising *new* venture, particularly in connection with the educational media. In my opinion, however, it is time for a top-level rethinking of "seeding" as a proper policy, especially for government and for foundations as well. Isn't there something irresponsible about launching a new venture that proves its social value and then leaving it to founder on the grounds that one must pursue new dreams? While preparing this paper, I was reminded again that public broadcasting is a national institution today only because of the willingness of the Ford Foundation to stay with the system until the link with government was forged. On the governmental level, particularly, continuity is even more important. Monies allocated for proven enterprises with major social aims should be considered a given so long as the end product of the enterprise continues to maintain its quality and effectiveness.

CTW's dollar troubles are worth dwelling on; for they are the troubles not of just another organization, but of the great glory and pride of the system. They also lend credence to a simple and obvious generalization: *Independent production centers should not be casually encouraged into existence.* After the initial euphoria is dissipated and the original funding sources have turned to other projects, where does a successful enterprise turn for support? This is a basic question which should merit the time and thinking of the people and groups who have the interests of public broadcasting at heart.

I suspect that the other lesson to be learned from the history of the CTW is that before a center is established, there should be a demonstrable and over-riding social need which is not being met satisfactorily through existing institutions. Measured against this standard, I'm certain that many a proposed production center would be found less than absolutely necessary. As in the case of the Workshop, a successful center is most likely to develop when there is a coming together of need, money and human talent, all at the right time. When and if this happens again, the new project should be helped in every way to succeed. We will all be the richer for it.*

---

*I agree with Dave Davis, of the Ford Foundation, and David Ives, of WGBH-TV Boston, that the CTW is largely an accident of the right people at the right time. Ives believes independent centers are inevitable, though not necessarily in the CTW mold: ". . . I give Joan Cooney a lot of credit. She has tremendous drive and commitment. When someone else with a similar drive and ability comes along, then independent production centers may come into being. It's a function of individual people."

The Future of Public Broadcasting

The Benefits of Independent Production

In all the concern with the costs of "Sesame Street," it is easy to overlook what the CTW experience has amply demonstrated: that the independent producing organization has an important role to play in the system simply by virtue of its very independence. If only because its personnel are "free spirits," unencumbered by the burdens and pressures and practicalities of station life, the independent enterprise markedly increases the chances for true creativity, innovation, excellence. Such a view is expressed by William McCarter, who manages WTTW Chicago:

> Independent centers may be as good, if not better, than centers trying to work within the station. There is a mysterious ceiling on quality in a broadcast institution. We wear two hats: that of the traditional broadcaster and that of bedazzled production houses. We've rushed into production because of economics. The CTW is not in broadcasting . . . the animosity of the stations comes from the fear of losing dollars.

McCarter is pointing to one of the basic advantages of independent existence: the freedom to dream, plan and act undeterred by the constraints of station life. To do its job right, a station must provide services to a population made up of many subgroups. It must strive for balance in its schedule. It would be understandable, then, that in any given instance, a station's program judgment might clash with that of the production unit it houses. The independent center, on the other hand, sees its social mission as foremost in the scheme of broadcast priorities. It simply goes its own way and makes every effort to get its programs on the air.

There is also a *funding* constraint on the producing station. A station naturally turns wherever it can for financial backing — to the federal, state or local government, to corporate underwriters, or to the public at large. It is always necessarily making hard choices of what to seek funding for. Inevitably, the production center would sometimes wind up with the short end of the stick. In contrast, the independent production center, left to its own devices, is free to pursue its own underwriting. The center's fund-raising efforts would be competing with the stations in some cases, but at least it would not be in the awkward position of a station's producing unit, which might come into direct conflict with its own station guardian.*

On the question of submitting programs for entry into the national system, here again a station has to make difficult choices based on managerial priorities and financial risk. In the case of new ventures particularly, a station might not be willing to take the gamble and the effort necessary to introduce a program into national distribution. The problem does not arise for the independent center, since it presumably enjoys the right of direct access into the national system. Moreover, the sole purpose of the independent center is to produce programming for the national competition.

Yet another advantage of the independent center is its separate institutional existence and the undivided focus of its staff on the projects and the success of the center. Once the talented individuals who have been gathered together for the first project learn to function as a team and identify themselves fully with the organization, they cast their futures with it and proceed accordingly to plan and dream for the future, seeking new creative worlds to conquer. New challenges and projects become almost an emotional and psychological requirement, once the immediate challenges have been met and a project is set on a reliable course. For example, with "Sesame Street" successfully launched and entering its second year, the CTW management and staff set about developing their next project, which turned out to be "The Electric Company," an exciting (and equally successful) new approach to the national reading problem.

The Need for Independent Production

Whatever their reservations about new independent production centers, the decision-makers within CPB and PBS appear to share with me the growing belief that the health of the public broadcasting system calls for it to accomodate producers and ideas from outside the station fraternity. Listen to John Montgomery, PBS program vice-president, reporting a discussion which took place within PBS on this very subject:

---

*It is by no means unusual to have a manager wryly observe that in practice a public television station is not always very different from its commercial counterpart – both are in the race for dollars! This is what accounts for station insistence that all production come into the system through its good offices. It means both prestige and additional funding to a station, even if the production occurs outside.

In terms of quality and innovativeness, we have reached a plateau. We have had "Sesame Street" and "The Great American Dream Machine." These were breakthrough programs. But nothing since.

Like Montgomery, Donald Quayle, senior vice-president of the CPB, is unsympathetic to the idea of new centers, but he is convinced that *independent production* can greatly benefit the system:

> The concerns of the PBS and CPB are similar. We are charged with building a strong system. Strong production centers help the system grow and produce good programs. But we do not feel that national program production should be done totally within the station system. If a program is best done by an independent producer, well and good. We are interested in his being fiscally responsible, editorially responsible, and having acceptable production credits. In most instances, all other things being equal, we prefer to keep production within the system. But if the best idea comes from the outside, as in the case of CTW, we will fund it.

What, then, if the independent producer's proposal is turned down by a station, or if he prefers to deal directly with the PBS and the CPB? Should he have direct access to the system? In the opinion of John Montgomery, one of the values of station origination is that the station "warrants the standards of the system." Production should come through a station "unless there is a very good reason."

Nevertheless, the PBS governing boards have agreed to accept independent productions under unusual circumstances. "PBS is looking for ways to overcome the plateau while protecting the station centers," Montgomery observes. If the PBS staff responds favorably to a program, it goes to the program committee. If approved by the committee, it would presumably enter the system as soon as financial support had been secured. In Montgomery's view, the main obstacle in the way of a full-blown PBS relationship with outside producers is a shortage of PBS staff members qualified to oversee the independent productions.

A healthy eclectic pattern of programming sources is apparently evolving. The resistance of some stations, though quite understandable, will not prevail. Sooner or later, the nature of the public broadcasting system, as envisioned in the national legislation that gave it birth, will force it into non-restrictive access patterns. There is simply too much creative energy in this large, heterogeneous democracy for the stations to be able to foreclose others from the programming process.

An interesting project to watch is "Visions," at $10 million the most ambitious venture in the history of television drama. "Visions" might well have been launched in the form of an independent center project, but its funders — the Ford Foundation, CPB, and the Endowment for the Arts — chose quite consciously to lodge it in a strong station, KCET Los Angeles. To begin with, they wished to avoid what they felt would be the overhead and administrative costs of an independent organization. In addition, the policy of the Endowment for the Arts is to fund projects only, not institutions. However, the funders also insisted that at least 50 percent of all "Visions" programs must come from production sources outside the public medium.

As described by KCET president and manager Jim Loper, the project has been carefully designed to afford executive producer Barbara Schultz complete creative freedom:

> "Visions" has built-in autonomy. The lines are clearly drawn. Our role is host for that unit. It is based on facing the realities. We have financial accountability. There is no censorship. Barbara works through Chuck Allen, our program vice-president. It's a quite informal relationship. She is a very fine professional who has worked before in a major structure (the CBS Television Network) and knows how to function in one.

Another interesting area to watch is Washington, D.C., where NPACT, the National Public Affairs Center for Television, has been completely absorbed into WETA. Ward Chamberlain, the new WETA manager, believes that (1) the merger will represent a more efficient use of manpower and resources, and (2) the local news and public affairs effort will be vastly improved while the unit continues to make major contributions to the national scene.

What remains to be determined in practice is whether a station can truly function as a national institution on a sustained basis. To begin with, from the standpoint of a national production unit, the community to be served is the nation. Unlike nonproducing stations, a national unit cannot, and should not, be concerned primarily with the community of license. Quite properly, the unit will act from a *national* orientation. Moreover, the production scale is quite appropriately geared to national, not local, distribution. It is rare, even in the largest of stations, for a local documentary budget to come within shooting distance of the typical national budget. The discrepancy is even greater in the area of entertainment.

This national orientation also assumes special significance in the area of news and public affairs. The public broadcasting system may have recoiled, for political reasons, from the network concept. But "network" is not necessarily equivalent to "national." *Networking* refers to a form of operation involving a central decision-making body which distributes programming to affiliates. It stems from the patterns established by commercial broadcasting in this country. *National* programming, as we have seen, does not necessarily call for centralization on the commercial model. It does, however, call for a national *outlook*. It also requires *freedom* for national programming — that is, the producing unit must be able to function regardless of the home station's local constraints, whether they be governmental, business, or local establishment and pressure groups. A national news and public affairs producing unit must be free to respond to the national requirements of the moment, without regard to prior station commitments.

I come away from these considerations with the strong feeling that the concept of a truly national news and public affairs institution will sooner or later rise again for consideration. Just as Washington, because of its location, is the station most likely to grow in importance in the sphere of public affairs programming, so New York and Los Angeles are already moving with great speed to claim positions as the production giants of the system. There is no point in fighting this. So long as excellence remains the public broadcasting standard, the notion of multi-station production, however desirable ideally, is a dream of the future.

This does not mean, of course, that other stations should be shut out. Far from it. WGBH-TV must be allowed to make its very special and significant contributions. So must KQED San Francisco, WTTW Chicago, WQED Pittsburgh, and others. Nevertheless, when major-league production is required, the two coastal cities can be expected to dominate, just as they do in commercial television.

Direct access to the national system, whether from production centers or independent producers, will have to be limited in some fashion. Otherwise, chaos would result. If all outside producers were permitted direct access to PBS, the system would soon become an unwieldy tangle. Thus, there is much work to be done on the *how* of a direct access system.

It is difficult at this point to propose specific solutions without detailed study. It should be remembered that we are dealing with a medium still in flux. PBS is only a few years old; the SPC is of even more recent vintage. What is called for is a major inquiry in the very near future into both the goals and organization of the system. Certainly one of the main areas for investigation would be that of the optimum relationships between the national distribution system and the production elements.

In the meantime, I think it can be safely said that the future favors the emergence of the independent producer as a basic element of the public television design. It will be only a matter of time before the medium comes to agree that there is very little to be lost and much to be gained in opening the system to all who have the talent and genius to contribute. Public broadcasters would do well to overcome any reluctance to deal with the so-called "commercial producers." They should look on this group as representing program opportunities, not as potential competitors for dollars.

The proper distinction is between quality and its absence. Barbara Schultz came to KCET from CBS. It was from that same network that CTW drew its main production talent. Actually, sooner or later, the producer who has chosen to create independent productions for public television will find it mandatory for survival to do commercial work as well. Performers have been following this pattern for years, and there is nothing wrong in their so doing.

Donald Quayle, of CPB, sums up the issue well:

The CPB is willing to deal with commercial producers . . . This is good if there is competition in terms of quality and costs. There are problems with the health of the system. There should be more production done by independent producers (as well as) more within the system. It can't all be done by one club.

Public Broadcasting and the New Communication Technology

WILLIAM HARLEY

If public broadcasting were starting out today rather than some 50 years ago, we would certainly hold very different views of how it should operate, what it should do, who should govern it, and how it should be financed. The principal differences would undoubtedly be based on the remarkable contemporary developments in communication technology. Viewed from a 50-year-old perspective, the current public broadcasting system in most large communities — one single-channel FM station and one broadcast-television station — might be considered an indication of reasonable progress. Viewed from today's perspective, however, we can hardly be impressed with a public communication system which has the capacity merely to funnel educational and cultural materials through a one-channel distribution network widely available only in the metropolitan areas.

There are so many other distribution techniques at hand today that it is no longer necessary or even sensible for a broadcast transmitter to be the exclusive nucleus of a public communications plan. In addition to broadcasting, for example, educational stations might now be employing television cartridge or cassette systems, audio cassettes, FM radio multiplexing, the multi-channel Instructional

Mr. Harley is president emeritus of the National Association of Educational Broadcasters.

The Future of Public Broadcasting

Television Fixed Service (ITFS), satellite transmissions, and multi-channel cable hook-ups. Remember that each audio cassette and video cassette or cartridge can serve as a discrete channel of communication. Keep in mind, as well, that cable systems can provide not only a very high quality multi-channel audio and video distribution capacity but also the opportunity for numerous innovative services, including computer interconnections and print-out capacities between the various educational, informational, political establishments and between these establishments and private homes or offices.

It is possible to speak now of a broad-based public *communication* service, rather than just a public *broadcasting* system. And it is my opinion that today's public broadcasters ought to see themselves as the nucleus around which such services and capacities can wisely be developed. Indeed, they have nothing less than a social mandate to bring their organizations and services into a position where the full capacities and benefits of today's communication systems and techniques can begin to be enjoyed *today*.

The Public
Telecommunication-Center Concept

For some time now, I have been urging that public broadcasters expand their stations into *public telecommunication centers* for the design and production of educational, instructional, and cultural materials and for the transmission of these materials to homes, schools, libraries, and other learning, informational, and social-service centers. The means of transmission would vary widely, depending on which of the available electronic delivery systems would be most suitable for the program materials and the receiving center. For example, a telecommunication enterprise might use ITFS or microwave frequencies to interconnect with the head-ends of any number of educational CATV systems in the immediate area, with outlets in schools, homes, hospitals, libraries, community centers, store-front academies, governmental and private offices, prisons, and industrial plants. The center's library of audio and video program materials could then be distributed either electronically or physically to any head-end or sub-origination point in this localized system. Any original material could also be traded and transmitted to other, distant telecommunication centers through interlocking computer arrangements which would allow program planning, distribution, and evaluation at national, regional, and local levels.

Each of the telecommunication centers would have access to these computer-bank catalogs of information about available resources: talent, production facilities, schedule openings, taped and filmed materials, and evaluative data about programs aired in the past. Demographic and other data about audience groupings could be collected and analyzed in order to assess needs for which new programming or delivery systems should be undertaken. The telecommunication center computers would also be charged with the complex task of retrieving and simultaneously transmitting/distributing diverse program materials along multiple channels to the very specific, pre-selected audiences. Among other possibilities for service by the telecommunication centers would be the ability to "scramble" or otherwise give privacy to specialized programming; the use of dedicated video or audio channels to "index" offerings on the total system; and the opportunity for two-way communication — as well as high-speed, computerized facsimile transmissions — between various information centers and individual or institutional receivers.

For the telecommunication-center idea to become a reality, the educational and social agencies most benefitted by a center will have to join in new cooperative administrative units through which their financial resources can be pooled and their programming needs effectively assessed and categorized for the joint advantage of the educational communities they represent. The facilities for these cooperative enterprises need not necessarily be located in the same building or even on the same campus. Indeed, the community may be state-wide or even regional — as, for example, the South Carolina Center for Public Broadcasting or the University of Mid-America, the State University of Nebraska's open-learning project. The telecommunication center should be seen not so much as a specific entity, but as a concept — as any cooperative combination of facilities and resources that can make effective and economical use of all the modern communication technologies in order to meet the complete range of educational and public-service requirements in a community.

Expanded versions of today's public broadcasting stations would, in my view, serve as the logical cores for these education/communication consortia. In the first place, many public broadcasting licensees, particularly those in the metropolitan areas, already incorporate a wide range of community interest groups in their organizational structures, and are well-established as cooperating, coordinating *public* and *community* enterprises. In addition, through regular contact and consultation with local institutions and organizations, the public broadcasting stations have generally developed a deep awareness of community needs and desires. Finally, the public stations are able to build upon past experience and present expertise to exercise professional supervision over the planning, production, acquisition, distribution, utilization, and evaluation of the new and wide-ranging communications services to be offered through the telecommunication center's multiple facilities.

I also see a *completed* and satellite-interconnected version of today's public broadcasting *system* as the logical cornerstones of a cooperative *nationwide** public-service information/communication system. If most public radio and television stations at the metropolitan, state, or regional level were expanded into telecommunication centers, they would readily serve as the key points in the new system for origination and reception, switching and retransmission, storage and retrieval.† A few of these telecommunication complexes could then be developed as prime producing centers, with special equipment and large production and technical staffs, backed up by dependable financial support.

The Public Telecommunication Center and the New Technologies

Of the new communications technologies, cable television and communication satellites are potentially the most far-reaching and

---

*I prefer to call this concept a "nationwide," rather than "national," public telecommunications system, because the latter suggests an organization that is centrally controlled. The telecommunication-center system would be a cooperative enterprise in which no government unit could qualify as solely responsible for organization, support, or regulation. The system would, and must, remain politically, institutionally, educationally, and in every other way pluralistic.

†An unpublished 1971 NAEB memorandum, "Public Telecommunications Organizations (Some Projections and Speculations)," proposed a nationwide system of public telecommunication facilities located in 270 places: four in cosmopolitan centers, three in megalopolitan centers, 50 in metropolitan centers, 63 in large urban centers, and 136 in rural area centers.

the most important components of the public telecommunication-center concept. Critics of public broadcasting have frequently pointed out the "waste" of using scarce broadcast channels to serve comparatively tiny audiences via a mass medium. Cable, with its multiple-channel capacity, provides the stations with an answer. It is an efficient way to reach small target audiences with a greatly expanded diversity of programming, as well as a host of ancillary services. In particular, cable offers new outlets for feeding classrooms with instructional fare (at times convenient to school schedules) while reserving the broadcast channel for programming of more general interest. Cable's unique capacity for affording relatively simple two-way interactive service will also be extremely important some day, not only in the teaching/learning process but also in consumer and social-welfare services and perhaps even the political forum.

The communication satellite will be the other important element in the operation and services of telecommunication centers. Because domestic satellites are a more cost-effective means of signal transmission than long-lines or micro-wave relay, they should be widely used for the interconnection of public broadcasting stations. The satellite-transmitted programs might be broadcast either directly to central community reception installations or to conventional broadcast stations, cable channels, ITFS, or low-powered translators from which they would be re-transmitted to homes, schools, and other clients.* A future possibility for the satellites will be a low-cost, national interconnection of computer banks, thus fostering the further development of existing electronic data-processing and transmission systems and opening up new opportunities for public access to informational and educational centers, medical services, libraries, and program centers.

The telecommunication centers can play a major role in the development of satellite interconnections and services. The centers might acquire and operate ground stations for satellite reception and, in some locales, up-links for feeding the satellite. The centers and their core public radio and television stations might also provide

---

*Although the status-of-the-art clearly projects development of the direct-to-home satellite, such a system may not be cost-effective in America, where the terrestrial system is so extensive and where immense "political" obstacles would stand in the way of its introduction.

logical sites for the storage of programs that can be accessed by the coupling of computers and satellites. Such a computer installation would be particularly appropriate in a telecommunication center located on a university or college campus.

Because the flexibility of satellite technology allows easy networking, another intriguing possibility would be the development of school "systems" that are educationally related in some way, but not geographically contiguous. For instance, an inner-city school system could be established electronically across the nation in order to provide special instruction for the children in these deprived locations. Similar programs could be instituted for rural education, for special language instruction, for professional training, and so on. In this way, distance need no longer be a barrier to the organization and application of our best educational and social resources. In addition, the satellites would permit service to special audiences which are too small to be economically viable in one community, but can be aggregated across the nation into a "market" of sufficient size.

I am also intrigued by the special power that the communication satellite seems to have as a catalyst for new uses of the technology. For example, the MPATI project, the first airborne instructional television experiment, persuaded school districts in seven states to agree on a common curriculum of televised courses. This experience encouraged use of the ATS-6 satellite in fostering the large-scale, multi-state institutional coordination that has taken place in the delivery of educational programs and health services in the Rocky Mountain and Appalachian regions and in Alaska. These programs led, in turn, to the WAMI project, in which medical training is jointly organized by the states of Washington, Alaska, Montana, and Idaho.

The special quality of the satellite technology is not merely that it facilitates cooperative undertakings of unprecedented scale and scope. The satellite also appears to have a potent psychological effect of placing people and things, jealousies and rivalries, terrestrial imperatives, and status prerogatives in a new and larger perspective. As Charles Wedemeyer observes, "It is one medium that need not be parochial; it sees the whole *community*, not only the *school*; it sees the *state*, not only the *community*; it sees the *region*, not only the *state*."[1] The satellite gives us perspectives that have never before been available, and it can help us induce the comprehensiveness and cooperativeness we need in the successful application of all the different modes of technology.

Three other technologies, which are variants of television and radio broadcasting, should be mentioned as important components of the telecommunication center. One is the Instructional Television Fixed Service (ITFS), which makes use of low-power television for multi-channel, point-to-point communication. ITFS is an effective system for delivery of instructional services over short distances, commonly within a single campus or school system; and it offers another opportunity for a telecommunication center to utilize a non-broadcast channel for specialized services.

Another important component of a telecommunication center is a flexible radio facility. FM multiplexing provides a means of adding side bands to the prime channel, thus affording additional avenues for serving special audiences. Two-way radio systems, such as that pioneered by the Albany Medical College for post-graduate study, afford an economical means for in-service professional training and for listener participation in public affairs forums. Both radio-vision (combining slides or static pictures with sound transmission) and slow-scan video transmission by FM are effective and economical means for enhancing the uses of instructional radio and/or extending and supplementing television services.

Other new technologies holding great promise are the several new audio-video devices — film and television cartridges, cassettes, and disc systems. These systems should be seen as valid *channels* for the flexible delivery of diversified, individualized instructional programs. The widespread availability of these devices, which can instantly record and play back visual and audio materials delivered by either broadcast or non-broadcast modes, will enormously enhance the flexibility and usability of fixed-schedule, real-time communication systems. Stations can rather easily enlarge the scope of their operations and range of services by applying the capacities and unique qualities of these new cartridge storage and playback systems to the extension of learning opportunities and a more economical and effective management of educational resources.

The public telecommunication centers should become major deposit libraries of video and audio materials in film, cassette, and disc form. Each library might be connected in turn with a national and a regional depository, so that it would have access to a larger body of material. The programs could be distributed electronically or by mail, or they might also be available for use on the premises of the center. The successful telecommunication center should also have playback equipment available for loan or lease to community agencies, and it could maintain viewing/learning centers in neighborhoods throughout a service area.

Problems in Implementation of
the Telecommunication-Center Plan

There are several problems present and predictable that will be inhibiting to the expansion of the telecommunication-center concept and the evolution of a truly comprehensive public service information/communication system for the nation:

Funding. Since lack of funding on a continuing basis has plagued public broadcasting from the start, it is reasonable to wonder how funds can be expected for the additional technologies and facilities of a system of telecommunication centers. In fact, many of the public broadcasting station people themselves contend that seeking monies for "futuristic" technologies is foolish and even damaging when there is clearly not enough money available to properly support the present single-channel broadcasting system. This contention was manifest in 1975 in connection with proposed federal legislation that would divert some of the public broadcasting funds to special demonstration projects of the new technologies.

While this opposition is understandable, it is also short-sighted and will eventually have an effect opposite to the intended one of protecting vested interests. The new communication aids give the stations an opportunity to build upon what they already have and, thereby, to achieve a system much more flexible, efficient, and responsive than the broadcast facility alone. True, expanded equipment and operations will require expanded support. But the opportunities for a multi-channel center to extend a vast new array of practical specialized services should bring in more than enough *quid* to compensate for the *quo*. Furthermore, the opportunities for economies of scale through these new devices and services will not be lost upon the telecommunication center's primary customers and founders — the legislators and the administrators and trustees of schools, hospitals, and social agencies. Taxpayers, too, will surely come to appreciate the efficiency and savings, as well as the new services, of the telecommunication center.

The federal government seems to be firmly embarked now upon a general policy of favoring and funding public communication facilities. That policy would strengthen the existing public broadcasting system while stressing the adaptation of existing facilities to additional uses and, most important, the extension of services for a more equitable coverage of the country by public channels of communication. Regarding coverage, it is generally agreed that 100 percent service of the population by public broadcasting is not realistic. A goal of 90 percent *is* realistic, however; and the government is eager to see that figure achieved.

Because incremental increases in coverage can only be achieved at high per-user cost, the government's approach is to phase down capital outlays for new broadcasting stations and to support alternative delivery facilities. This approach is considered the most economical means of fostering the growth and maturation of a complete public service communications capability.[2]

I am persuaded that this is an appropriate course for the government to follow, provided that there is a significant increase in funding for public broadcasting facilities, so that: (1) completion of the physical elements of the existing system will not be inhibited, and (2) the maintenance and up-grading of the present system will not be neglected. In addition, an increasingly large proportion of the federal grants should be readily available to the stations for acquisition of non-broadcast equipment. And, finally, there must be a substantial increase in all *operating* funds granted to telecommunication centers on a long-term matching basis. In this way, the multiple services of the new telecommunication centers will be limited only by their capacity of creativity, not by a debilitating lack of funds.

Two recent changes in federal legislation reflect the favorable attitude of the government toward the idea of telecommunication centers. One bill for long-range funding for the Corporation for Public Broadcasting was changed to permit stations to use their grants for "developing and using non-broadcast communications technologies for educational television or radio programming purposes." The bill also authorizes CPB to conduct related research, demonstrations, and training.

The other bill was at one time called the Educational Broadcasting Facilities Act, but has now been changed to the Educational Broadcasting Facilities and Telecommunications Demonstration Act. In addition to continuing support for broadcast facilities, its provisions include indirect support, through demonstration grants, of a wide range of telecommunications technologies. HEW has suggested that these technologies will provide, in some instances, a more efficient means of meeting national health, education and social service communications needs. The demonstration provisions in the facilities legislation also provide financial incentives for private industry to invest in special communications systems which will effectively employ modern technology in meeting both private and public-service needs. It is to be hoped that the federal government (and private foundations) will continue to play a vital role in providing risk capital for research and experimentation and for demonstrations of the applications and usefulness of the new communications technologies.

The development of communications hardware has always followed the market — and always will. Entrepreneurs are not about to lay out the enormous expenditures requisite for capitalization and development of these new devices until their feasibility is demonstrated and a consumer demand is evident. This is especially true now, in light of the bitter experiences of business in rushing into the publication/communications education industry to meet with such misadventures as the multi-million dollar stumble of CBS in the development of Electronic Video Recording (EVR).

HEW has recognized the importance of the federal role and has taken steps not only to complete nationwide coverage by the public communications system, but also to promote optimum utilization of the system's capacities and maximum return on the government's investment. In the latter regard, HEW has made a substantial grant to the Public Service Satellite Consortium (PSSC), an alliance of education, health-care, and other public organizations interested in the shared use of satellite services and facilities. HEW expects that PSSC will develop a coherent demand for multi-channel communication facilities to serve health, education, and social requirements, thereby demonstrating the market potential of such uses and encouraging commercial satellite developers to add the necessary capacity during the initial capitalization.

Complementing the help that federal and foundation stimulus can provide, the new telecommunication centers themselves must undertake continuous studies of audience interest patterns in order to determine critical levels of consumer potential for new devices. At the same time, they will have to stimulate consumer demand for these new devices. The alternative will be either failure of the telecommunication center concept of a commercial shaping of similar systems in ways that may adversely affect the interests of public telecommunications.

Regulation. It is ironic that while HEW and the Congress have followed a policy of fostering the development, first, of public broadcasting and, now, of public telecommunications, the regulatory agency for the industry, the Federal Communications Commission, has generally eschewed positive support or even active encouragement for the noncommercial part of the broadcasting industry. The FCC's policies can best be characterized as a kind of casual tolerance of educational communication systems, with a clear preference for commercial interests whenever they come into contention with those of the educators. The basic orientation of American broadcasting has always been, and will continue to be, commercial; and noncommercial broadcasting will continue to be considered supplemental or complementary to the commercial services.

The FCC's protectionist attitude toward commercial communication/entertainment interests has impeded the growth of the public telecommunications movement in many ways, most notably in the cable television industry. The FCC, in its zeal to protect the existing television broadcasting enterprise, has imposed a series of constraints on the infant cable industry that have slowed its development and limited its ability to compete in the marketplace. Coupled with rising costs and protracted disputes over changes in the copyright law, the vast uncertainty about the FCC attitudes and rulings has kept cable a perennially promising but unrealized enterprise for more than a decade.

This situation has profoundly affected not only cable (naturally, it must first succeed as a business before its potential for education and public service can be realized) but also the whole movement toward public communication centers. Capital-intensive as it is, cable requires too heavy an initial investment for extensive development by noncommercial interests. As a result, the opportunities for telecommunication centers to gain access to cable distribution channels (either free or by lease) is directly related to and limited by the expansion of the cable system by private enterprise.

Because of FCC regulations, public broadcasters are also foreclosed from direct ownership or participation in the cable enterprise. The FCC prohibits any multiple ownership of local television and cable systems in their own "markets." The NAEB has made repeated petitions seeking exemption from the cross-ownership constraint. The association points out that dual ownership by noncommercial licensees has been permitted for operation of one or more public radio and television stations without adverse impact upon the principles of diversification. Indeed, the result has been a far greater diversification in programming and positive advantages to the public interest. The NAEB argues, further, that ownership and operation of a cable system could be financially beneficial to an existing educational broadcasting station, affording the station a wider spectrum of broadband communication services, including two-way capability.

I can suggest no sound reason why local cable ownership should be prohibited for educational television licensees.* Indeed, there are two compelling reasons why this restriction should be removed. First, such cross-ownership would serve to advance the development of cable in the public service. Second, it would simultaneously advance the financial security and, thereby, the further development and extension of noncommercial stations. In this way, public broadcasting could enhance its capacity for achieving the diversity of voices, information sources, and programming that the FCC has announced as one of its primary long-range goals.

The potential social benefits of cable would be far more readily realized under the management of telecommunication centers, which have the resources, the competence, and the interest and dedication to develop distinctive and diverse programming and other services of substance and appeal. In addition, cable channels under the control and supervision of telecommunication centers could become a means for horizontal dialogue within our society, providing "channels for dissent" and fulfilling the desire for greater public participation in a system of true "communication" as opposed to

---

*It is understandable that the FCC would prefer a duopoly prohibition for commercial licensees. But anti-trust considerations — to promote diversity of ownership and competition and to eliminate the threat of undue economic advantage and concentration of media control — are hardly applicable to noncommercial licensees. The latter are not competing for advertising dollars; they seek multiple ownership solely to have more efficient and effective ways of serving the increasing diversity of community needs.

To achieve such a goal in an area of limited resources and frequencies, it is only sensible to coordinate planning and programming among public stations in a single community. Similarly, a combined ownership arrangement can minimize the costs of overhead, power, and maintenance, which means that waste and duplication can be decreased in the expenditures of public dollars. The multiple owner is also better equipped to serve minority audiences and specialized interests by avoiding the duplication of general programming that often occurs when stations in the same area compete for the same undifferentiated audience.

mere "information transmission.''*

Can anything be done to alter governmental policies that tend
to impede a greater and more rational use of communications technology in the furtherance of educational and social goals? Frankly,
I am not very sanguine about the ability of the educational broadcasting community to alter substantially the preferential and protectionist posture of the FCC toward commercial/entertainment
interests. Except in sporadic bursts, advocates of educational
interests have never been able to develop effective political strategies
to equal or counterbalance the communications/entertainment
lobbies in presenting their case to the Congress, the Executive, and
the FCC. Only when educational broadcasters have acted in concert
have they won their few important victories (reservation of channels
for ETV and FM radio, ITFS, etc.).

Perhaps if they can develop a consistent long-range policy for
technology in education and then organize the kind of united, grass-
roots power they should be able to command, they will make some
breakthroughs in the future. Their first goal should be to initiate
some important changes at the FCC. As an M.I.T. Communications
Policy Report has pointed out, governmental agencies have great
difficulty in adjusting to technological change, since they are constrained by internal bureaucratic forces as well as by the external
pressures of those determined to preserve the status quo.[3] The telecommunication-center concept would be considerably advanced,
however, if the FCC were persuaded to take three rather modest
steps:

1. Modification, clarification, and codification of FCC rules
   and policies affecting public telecommunications.
2. Revision of FCC rules to establish a separate section em-
   bracing all regulations relating to public telecommunications.
3. Creation of a separate Public Telecommunications Bureau
   at the FCC to replace the present Educational Broadcasting
   Branch.

The agencies which regulate communications and entertainment,

---

*Realistically, the high capitalization costs would probably preclude all but the largest
public television stations from establishing their own cable systems. They should not,
however, be foreclosed from the possibility of doing so; and, especially, they should not
be prohibited from participating in joint cable-ownership arrangements with commercial
or other public entities.

as Charles Wedemeyer has observed, have a responsibility to set policies and regulate in such a way that a concern for culture has at least as much priority as property and profit.[4] But the people in public telecommunications will need to rally a lot of their fellow citizens to share their concerns before the regulatory and legislative agencies recognize this solicitude and take appropriate action.

Copyright. Copyright regulations loom as another potential inhibition to the vigorous growth and fulfillment of public telecommunications. Attempts have been made for years to modify the 1909 federal copyright law, and it appears that 1976 may well bring the revision. As it is presently being discussed, the new copyright law will incorporate several changes that will have a severe impact upon educational and public-service communication systems. The doctrine of "fair use" permitted under existing law (though not expressly authorized) will be severely curtailed, so that public broadcasting will no longer be exempted from paying royalties to copyright holders of non-dramatic works. Only live instructional broadcasts and possibly closed-circuit instructional transmissions may continue to be exempted.

In addition to the prospect of royalty payments, the concept of telecommunication centers and of nationwide information systems is most threatened by possible provisions in the new law that would (1) prohibit the number of recordings that can be made; (2) limit the length of time that recordings could be retained before they must be destroyed; and (3) forbid not only copying for interlibrary purposes but also any *regular* copying on a large scale. The third provision, especially, would be a primary bar to the development of national computer-based information-transfer systems. It would, for example, prevent photocopying of most medical and scientific information for electronic transmission to another library or to universities, hospitals, and other receiving points.

It seems clear that whatever the specific provisions in the revised copyright law, education and other nonprofit entities will no longer have a free ride. There may be a few educational exemptions (for example, limited copying for teaching, scholarship, and research); but for the most part nonprofit institutions, including noncommercial stations and communications systems, will be obliged to begin compensating authors and composers for the use of their copyrighted materials. These reforms will most certainly have an adverse impact upon education and public telecommunications in terms of added costs and some diminution of the free flow of ideas and information. It is possible, however, that Congress will try to soften the blow somewhat by providing for a compulsory license that will relieve stations of the cumbersome, time-consuming, and expensive procedure of obtaining copyright clearances, work by work. Royalty payments would then be determined in accordance with prices fixed by a Copyright Royalty Tribunal.

The inertia of educators, bureaucrats and public broadcasters. It is not difficult to identify the source of major resistance to the spread of educational technology; for — lo! — the educators lead all the rest. Down through the ages men have feared innovations that seemed to threaten their jobs, and today's teachers and educational administrators are no exception. The history of educational radio and television and of audio-visual technology is continuously characterized by the insistent struggle of a few ardent media enthusiasts against the apathy and indifference — if not outright hostility — of the educational establishment.

This is not to say that considerable progress has not been made in the past two decades in gaining acceptance by teachers of the new technologies as valuable classroom aids. This more amenable attitude by teachers, professors, and administrators has been partly the result of a growing interest in open learning and non-traditional study. But equally important has been a changing strategy by the advocates of the technologies. Too often in the past, their thinking and their arguments were based upon "imagined possibilities rather than upon realizable probabilities." As a result, their "uncalibrated enthusiasm . . . initiated a cycle of high hopes, great activity, few perceived benefits, disenchantment, and finally, abandonment."[5]

The ineptitudes and the "blue-sky" predictions are now largely a thing of the past for the media advocates. Instead, they have learned to demonstrate, first, that the technologies can help a good teacher to be an even better teacher. Second, they have involved the teachers (and curriculum specialists, principals, national professional organizations, etc.) in the step-by-step planning, design, production, and presentation of the media-based programs.

The producers of instructional broadcasting materials have also come belatedly to realize the necessity of designing their products to meet the needs of the "consumer" and to continually test and validate product effectiveness. Early in the development of educational television, a mistaken effort was made to "sell" it to administrators and legislators primarily as a means of saving money. The broadcasters soon began to understand, however, that only when

The Future of Public Broadcasting

ETV was promoted as a method for achieving higher quality and greater availability of education did it begin to gain acceptance and support from the educational leadership.

Increasingly, educational administrators are seeing the application of technology as a strategy, rather than as gadgetry, and as a way to facilitate the efficient management and cooperation of people and resources. Even so, many of the old fears persist in the educational fraternity; and, of course, many people outside education are alarmed at the "future shock" that media development may bring to our society. The proper response is, first, sensitivity to these apprehensions and then the suggestion that, rather than stamp out these devices, concerned citizens and educators should help ensure that the new technologies are developed to their full potential in ways that guarantee their social usefulness. The innate suspicion of the professional educator or medical administrator toward the technical "practitioner" can only be overcome by a convincing demonstration of the latter's seriousness of purpose and dedication to common goals.

In discussing inertia, there is scarcely a need to mention the traditional foot-dragging of the bureaucracy at all levels — local, state, and federal. The resistance of the latter seems to rise automatically in response to any innovation, including public communication initiatives. It can be combatted only by the pressure of public opinion and by the legislative or administrative action which responds to that pressure. The growing membership of laymen on boards of directors and advisory councils for public communication entities, the rise of consumer action groups, the subscriber involvement in public station support, and the establishment of such organizations as the Friends of Public Broadcasting and the Advisory Council of National Organizations (to the CPB) — these are all ways of stimulating public participation and support.

Among the ranks of public communicators themselves, the inertia is generally more subtle and difficult to combat. Most station managers subscribe to the philosophy behind the concept of the telecommunication center. Very few, however, have actually set out to implement it in their own "shops." The typical station manager lives almost from day to day, barely keeping his station on the air. It is understandable, then, that the public broadcasters may find some difficulty in taking the long view.

The precarious and unpredictable nature of a public station's financial status is highly inhibiting to long-range planning, and an obsessive preoccupation with finding sufficient funds to maintain current services tends to preclude any managerial interest in an expanded operation requiring additional facilities and monies. In addition, some educational broadcasters apparently feel that the advent of new communications technologies will undermine the economic health of the conventional stations and even cause them to disappear. Therefore, the broadcasters are hesitant in fostering the growth of the telecommunication-center idea.

In my judgment, the real protectionist view should be quite the contrary: Public broadcasting managers should embrace these new channels as fully and quickly as possible in order to ensure an increase in the level and diversity of station services and thereby to build a wider, stronger base of support within the community. There is a growing tendency of school systems to require "on demand" services and to cancel contracts with stations because of the limitations of their one-channel systems. Stations cannot afford to lose this revenue (in the case of "community stations," the only non-federal tax base they have); nor can they risk the loss of political support which always accompanies public enterprises serving the needs of children. The one-channel public broadcasting system might well derive a lesson from the current moves of one-product industries to diversify.

If the public broadcasters need any further persuasion as to the benefits of the new channel capacities, they need only consider two important by-products of the new technologies:

(1) Precise and virtually instantaneous audience evaluation will be enabled by the new devices. This essential feedback process has always been at best imprecise and inefficient. The data are difficult and cumbersome and exorbitantly expensive to collect; the analysis of that data is generally suspect. Now computer and data-processing machinery is available for rapid analysis of audience data, and new low-cost telemetry techniques allow sample information to be rapidly fed to or from geographically diverse sources without the long delays of the past.

(2) Another management benefit to be derived from the new transmission/distribution systems is their capacity for easy tallying of the gross circulation of particular programs. For example, the new playback devices require consumers to select and lease or buy individual programs "over the counter." Pay-TV, when it becomes fully developed, will introduce a direct test of the marketplace in assessing the demand for particular programs and services. Two-

way service would have unlimited possibilities for audience feedback. Increasingly, all public program projects are being subjected to rigorous cost-effectiveness accounting procedures as a result of the desire for greater accountability and increased productivity in return for the investment of public dollars. The new enabling technologies are coming on the scene just as this fiscal policy is becoming not only desirable but a practical necessity.

The public broadcasting station represents a community's greatest capital investment in a physical plant and in high-quality equipment for communications. The typical station also provides a reservoir of professionally competent people with the experience and capacity to manage, operate, and maintain public telecommunications facilities. Consequently, station managers should not feel timid about a vigorous sales pitch to local, regional, and state agencies for the idea of building new community communications services around their stations.

Moreover, since money will inevitably be the major incentive for station managers to cast aside their fears and to begin looking forward in their planning, the advocates of public broadcasting and public telecommunication centers must join in a unified and relentless campaign for continued and increased support from the federal government. Of first priority is the proposed congressional action that will permit licensees to expand, improve, and operate their facilities for delivery of programming by means not limited solely to broadcasting.

Programming. It is hardly a flashing new insight to observe that the real problem for a public communications system is to have something worthwhile to communicate. Although technological innovations promise a vast increase in the number of channels, such proliferation will not be beneficial if it results in "multi-channel unanimity at the lowest level," or if the enlarged system becomes an improved means of spreading mediocrity. Public broadcasting will survive or fall, and the public communications system will grow or wither, depending on the quality of the programming and services that it carries.

This imperative mandates prime attention to creativity and diversity in program production. It also means finding and using better ways to define audiences and to determine what kinds of programming will meet the needs of those audiences. It means measuring the programming successes, not by numbers alone, but with appropriate evaluative criteria devised in terms of stated goals.

Finally, in the telecommunication-center concept particularly, all phases of the production process — assessment of needs, setting of goals, use of materials, and evaluation of results — must be accomplished in cooperation and collaboration with a wide range of other educational and social agencies in the community.

It is my opinion that because of their facilities, their pools of talent and technicians, their background as public and educational institutions, and their special concern for minority opinion and programming, the public broadcasting stations are the agents most likely to successfully implement the telecommunication-center idea. It is my further opinion that the public telecommunication center, with the public broadcasting station at its core, has the best chance of achieving the aim of the Carnegie Commission on Educational Television for "excellence in the services of diversity." Only the public telecommunication center would have the equipment, the personnel, the experience, the public support, and, above all, the multi-channel capacity to devise and deliver programs precisely according to specific audience needs and locations.

Leadership. There appears to be no individual or agency manifestly suited to leading the public telecommunications movement. In part at least, this is a consequence of the nature of the enterprise itself. The concept is characterized by an extraordinarily diverse and diffuse multi-purpose, multi-interest group of advocates. In addition, it necessitates an inherently cooperative and collaborative approach which is unsuited to individual proselytizing or special-interest promotion. In short, the telecommunication-center idea requires group initiative and action. Only to the extent that this can be achieved will the idea be successful.

Considerable collaborative effort in the advancement of telecommunicaitions is already under way at various levels and in a variety of configurations. In the federal government, there is an Interagency Telecommunications Committee which is keeping various departments informed and involved. At state and regional levels, there are a number of consortia actively engaged in the development and operation of telecommunication centers. Wisconsin and Virginia are good examples of the interactive use of existing and new technologies for the statewide expansion of educational and social services.

The University of Mid-America, initiated by the telecommunications center of the State University of Nebraska (SUN), is a four-state collaborative effort using telecommunications to support an open learning system in higher education. Miami-Dade has spear-headed the development of a successful experiment in the co-production of television courses by junior colleges. The Rocky Mountain Satellite Project was an eight-state cooperative experiment serving 60 rural school districts in that area with the ATS-6 satellite. The satellite was also used in training medical students in Washington, Alaska, Montana, and Idaho (WAMI) and for the Appalachia Educational Satellite Project, in which 22 colleges in that region cooperated in using a course in teacher education developed by the University of Kentucky and produced by the Kentucky state television center.

In the area of specialized professional computer-library access services, there are a number of on-going activities, such as EDUCOM and MEDLARS. The most recent cooperative enterprise in the field is the previously mentioned Public Service Satellite Consortium, which seeks to bring together a combination of groups interested in the sharing of communication satellite capacities for distribution of education, health, and other services. Its initial funding by HEW is another earnest of the government's intention to foster the telecommunications concept.

Though these and other current collaborative efforts are numerous and growing, the movement as a whole remains spotty, unintegrated, and uncoordinated. Given these conditions, the advocates and the pioneering organizers of telecommunication centers have an important role to play as prime catalytic agents. Public broadcasters and the telecommunication-center management should take the initiative in effectively explaining their efforts and their equipment to educators, librarians, public health officials, and others who are potential users of the multi-services made possible by the new multi-modes of communication. They should also seek a comprehensive responsibility for engaging with others in the cooperative planning and development of community, regional, and national facilities to serve the whole spectrum of social concerns.

A Commission on a National Public Information/Communications System

Unfortunately, it is going to be difficult to develop a consistent, long-range, cooperative national policy for communications technology in education. For one thing, every level of government traditionally separates responsibility for education from the authority for communications policy and regulation, copyright, etc. In addition, the private sector's enormous diversity of interests in communications, education, health, science, and other fields makes it difficult for any group in these fields to come to common agreements. Yet some sort of generally supportable schematic is a pressing requirement if we are to use the present and predictable communications technology in the service of our society.

This suggests, I submit, that the time has come for a high-level study, similar to that of the Carnegie Commission on ETV, which would produce recommendations for the design, implementation, and continuing assessment of a national public service information/communications system. As a preliminary step, the Office of Telecommunications Policy of the White House might convene a national conference that would document the need for such a commission, established with the help of HEW and a consortium of foundations. Whether the commission is initiated through a White House conference or Presidential study, or as a "Son-of-Carnegie," does not matter much. The important point is that this groundwork be so broadly supported, so boldly conceived, and so compellingly presented that it will energize the cooperative undertaking.

The commission's first responsibility should be to generate and coordinate a ten-year action plan that would delineate the fiscal, legislative, and political strategies necessary for the achievement of the national public service information/communications system. Such an outline would include measures for the maintenance and expansion of efforts already under way, as well as recommendations for the new initiatives that would be required.

A primary recommendation should be the establishment of a permanent commission that would serve as a central mechanism for the positive implementation of the study commission's strategies and for a continuing assessment of the system and the technologies in the light of changing societal needs.* In addition, the following strategies would, in my opinion, be an essential part of the program of the commission:

---

*Though I am as allergic as any to the establishment of another national agency, it is my opinion that none of the existing entities — CPB, NIE, PBS, NPR — can do the job asked for here. What is needed is a determined and single-minded new enterprise with no vested interests to protect.

The Future of Public Broadcasting

1. Complete the public radio and television broadcasting's physical system.
2. Establish a nationwide, low-cost satellite interconnection service for public broadcasting stations and other public service users. Eventually, a dedicated public service satellite should also be introduced with government help. Presumably, such a service would achieve economies of scale sufficient to make it rather quickly self-supporting.
3. Build a legislative program that (a) ensures higher-level, long-range funding on a matching basis for the operation of public telecommunication centers; (b) continues to provide matching funds for modernization of broadcast equipment but makes increasingly higher proportions of such funds available for nonbroadcast technology; and (c) incorporates provisions and grants for innovative equipment and for experimentation, demonstration, and research.
4. Organize a campaign to turn the FCC in the direction of the present favorable public telecommunications orientation of HEW, NASA, and OTP. The FCC must be persuaded not merely to lift restrictions but also to offer positive support and affirmative initiatives for the telecommunication-system concept. It should also create a new FCC Bureau of Public Telecommunications.
5. Lay out and coordinate a national applied-research program designed for the pursuit of *specific* data and guidelines that will be of use in planning and implementing operational telecommunication systems.
6. Promote the development of a multitude of administrative accords among public broadcasters, educational and social institutions, and units of government at all levels. These accords would set up consortia for the design, production, and delivery of educational program materials via new telecommunication centers.
7. Devise means for broad involvement of the public in the development, governance, and operation of the telecommunication centers. In addition, the commission should promote the development of mass clientele groups for the use of materials made possible by the new technologies and the new distribution centers.
8. Organize and carry out a sophisticated national public relations program that will introduce the general public

314

and governmental and civic leaders to the many benefits of the public telecommunications idea. The aim of the informational program should be not only to develop grass-roots support for the concept and to foster the favorable climate in which the system can evolve, but also to attract the many new interest groups which should be directly involved in the formation and operation of the system.

In 1963, when the first federal dollar was spent to assist in the construction of an educational television facility, it would have been difficult to predict exactly what the present system of educational and public broadcasting in the United States would become. So, it is difficult — and probably a futile exercise — to predict now what kind of public telecommunications arrangements we shall find in 1985. Nevertheless, it is vitally urgent now, as it was in 1963, to know the direction in which we should be moving.

The telecommunication-center concept is one proposal that deserves immediate and serious study. It promises a wholly new kind of community institution — a broadly based and truly "public" mechanism for enriching and streamlining education and job training, for stimulating an interchange of minority ideas and views, for show-casing developing talents, for debating public issues and involving the citizenry in a public forum for easing and increasing the flow of information, for improving medical services, and for shaping the sound social development of the community and of the society as a whole.

References

1. Charles A. Wedemeyer, "Satellite and Cable — No Highway in the Sky for Conventional Teaching and Learning", keynote address, Satellite/Cable Technology Conference, University of Wisconsin, June 1975.

2. These observations are based on (a) testimony delivered by HEW representatives in 1975 before the U. S. House of Representatives Subcommittee on Power and Communications and (b) informal memoranda prepared by the Department's Office of Telecommunications Policy.

3. "Research Program on Communication Policy," M.I.T., January 1974, p. 7.

4. See note 1.

5. Robert Wolp, "Educational Information System," unpublished outline, Pasadena, California, 1973.

Acknowledgement

    I want to acknowledge particularly my indebtedness to George L. Hall, who while a member of the NAEB staff (1970-73) initially outlined the telecommunications concept and whose several memoranda on this topic were invaluable in the writing of this essay. I also acknowledge with gratitude the assistance of George, and that of James Fellows, Frank Norwood, Holt Riddleberger, Robert Woods, and Harriet Lundgaard, in reading assorted drafts and making useful suggestions.

Conclusion:
Taking Stock and
Looking Ahead

Michael J. Nyhan

As originally conceived, this volume was intended to lay the foundation for a review and forecast of the policy choices facing public broadcasting in the next ten years, starting in 1976. The time frame was arbitrarily chosen, but as it turns out, the years 1975 and 1976 may well mark a major turning point for public broadcasting. Consider, for example, this statement from President Gerald R. Ford on January 1, 1976:

> I am pleased to sign H.R. 6461, the Public Broadcasting Financing Act of 1975. This legislation, while not perfect, represents a milestone in the history of public broadcasting. It will help assure that public broadcasting can concentrate on being the effective and innovative source of educational and cultural programming which the American people have come to expect.

Some would argue that this legislation is something less than the "milestone" suggested by the President. Indeed, the "milestone" may well have less to do with this marginally adequate piece of

Mr. Nyhan is assistant director of the Aspen Institute Program on Communications and Society.

legislation than with the fact that public broadcasting has survived, and that an American President, hand-picked by Richard Nixon, could reaffirm the importance of this communications system and affirmatively endorse its future. Public broadcasting had come a long way from the predicament it faced on June 30, 1972, when President Nixon vetoed a public broadcasting financing measure and left the future of the system much in doubt. Presidential aide Patrick Buchanan described that veto in blunt terms on the "Dick Cavett Show" in early 1973:

> So they sent down their $165,000,000 package voted 82 to 1 out of the Senate, thinking that Richard Nixon . . . wouldn't have the courage to veto something like that. And Mr. Nixon, I'm delighted to say, hit that ball about 450 feet down the right foul line right into the stands — and now you've got a different situation in public television . . .

That "different situation" brought public broadcasting perilously close to collapse. Not long after Mr. Buchanan's TV appearance, Thomas Curtis, a Nixon appointee and then chairman of the board of the Corporation for Public Broadcasting, abruptly resigned. Curtis left no doubt as to why he quit: "When it became clear that the White House was not respecting the integrity of the board, then I couldn't defend the integrity of the board the way I had." For several months thereafter, public broadcasting teetered on the brink, while desperately trying to devise a strategy for survival.

For some time to come, the system will have to contend with the trauma and repercussions of its premature politicization and the resultant internecine strife. Still, if one marks the episode of June 30, 1972, as the low point in public broadcasting's history, the chart since then points upward. By 1974, the system had settled most of its disputes (the "CPB/PBS Partnership Agreement"), reorganized itself (a new PBS), and come up with a program-selection mechanism (SPC) which began to meet the specifications for both decentralization and a more systematic operation and organization. By 1975, with the re-introduction of the federal long-range financing bill, there were signs that public broadcasting was over the hump, that the system was emerging from what may well have been its darkest hour with relatively few outward scars. The fact that it had emerged at all is no small feat.

Michael J. Nyhan

1975 as a Year of Transition

The financing bill signed by President Ford is a tangible step forward; but as several writers in this volume have indicated, it is not the panacea that many people in public broadcasting had been waiting for. The legislation provides a five-year *authorization*, not a five-year *appropriation*. Actual federal grants to the public broadcasting system will still be subject to frequent Congressional review. Also, as McKay points out, five years is hardly "long-range," and keeping that fact in mind will save public broadcasters the embarrassment of being caught unprepared in 1980. Nevertheless, for an institution whose fate in the past was so often tied to continuing resolutions from the Congress (in nearly half ot its first eight years of existence), this commitment by Congress and the Administration has to be viewed as a significant development which will give the system a certain degree of badly needed breathing space.

1975 was noteworthy for other reasons: Since 1962, under the Educational Broadcasting Facilities Act, federal money has been allocated to help build and upgrade the physical plants and the broadcast hardware of the nation's public radio and television stations. But concurrent with these developments — and particularly in recent years, when public broadcasting facilities have begun to overlap — a number of people have questioned the wisdom of further expansion of the broadcast system and, especially, of the broadcasting technology. The issues are two: one, whether public broadcasting should not be concentrating more of its energies on programming and on building greater public support; and two, whether broadcasting itself, as opposed to the newer technologies, is where the future of the system should or will be.

In 1975, the Facilities bill was changed in title to the Educational Broadcasting Facilities and Telecommunications Demonstration Act. This expanded law is still intended to aid in the "construction of noncommercial educational television or radio broadcasting facilities," but it will also "demonstrate the use of telecommunication technologies for the distribution and dissemination of health, education, and other public or social service information." Extensive tests and demonstrations are essential ingredients if non-broadcast technologies are to play an important part in the educational and social fabric of the nation in the years ahead. Thus, the change in the law's emphasis and the increased funding can represent an important turning point for public broadcasting. There is the promise that the public broadcasting system could be transformed over the next ten years into a network of public telecommunications centers serving a wide variety of community needs.

In another development in 1975, the Senate Communications Subcommittee for the first time killed a presidential nomination to the Board of Directors of the Corporation for Public Broadcasting. Joseph Coors, nominated by Nixon and renominated by Ford, was in effect rejected by the subcommittee because of the potential for conflict of interest. However one may feel about the nominee in this instance, those who care about public broadcasting should take encouragement from this heightened congressional awareness about appointees to the CPB board. The nominating procedures for the board may well need reform — this should be an agenda item for a second Carnegie Commission — but in the interim, Congress and the public should continue to scrutinize appointees and ensure that the directors of public broadcasting are high-caliber men and women who are sincerely dedicated to the success of the system.

Also in 1975, the Committee for Economic Development released its report and recommendations on U. S. communications policy, *Broadcasting and Cable Television: Policies for Diversity and Change*. The CED report included public broadcasting among its "five imperatives" for public policy and offered a series of recommendations for the future of the system:

> We believe that public broadcasting can provide greater quality, diversity, and choice in programming. Thus, it can serve the many specialized audiences that commercial broadcasting, with its mass appeal, is not geared to reach. Public television and public radio are in critical need of reliable long-range funding, but we consider recent government proposals for such funding inadequate. At the same time, we recognize that the success of any proposal for increased long-term funding *will depend on the establishment of realistic and firm goals for the future of the system*. Public television and radio must identify and address the needs of their audiences. Increased resources must be effectively managed. Moreover, public broadcasting must examine how it will fit into an era in which cable and other technologies could substantially widen program diversity and choice. [Emphasis added.]

On the programming side, 1975 was the year that public television attracted its biggest audience ever for a prime-time program. The National Geographic special, "The Incredible Machine," was actually more popular in some markets than any of the competing programs on the commercial stations. The significance of this accomplishment is threefold: (1) The program was produced by a prestigious organization, the National Geographic Society, which had moved its popular commercial television series to public television; (2) the sponsor and the underwriter combined efforts for a brilliant promotional campaign; and (3) millions of new viewers turned to public television channels.

In another development in programming in 1975, the Children's Television Workshop admitted that its elaborate health series, "Feeling Good," had failed to meet some of its goals. Rather than simply canceling the series or letting it run despite its faults, CTW made the laudable decision to take the program off the air, rethink and reevaluate the series, and then put an improved edition back on the air two months later. What is significant in this example is that public television and CTW had developed a program with specific goals, had gathered evidence that the series was not meeting those goals, and then had *acted* on that evidence. The example illustrates both the advantageous flexibility of public broadcasting and the benefits that can accrue for the system and for the public when careful planning, hard-nosed research, and thoughtful, innovative, courageous decision-making are elements in public broadcasting programming.

There were other significant developments in 1975. In that year, public broadcasting's Satellite Working Group — a task force representing PBS, CPB, the Ford Foundation, and National Public Radio — was completing its recommendations for satellite interconnection of the public broadcasting stations by 1978. Other potential nonprofit users of satellite communication were organizing themselves at the same time as the Public Service Satellite Consortium. The needs and goals of these two groups, while initially divergent, may ultimately merge through the development of a high-powered satellite system which will assist public broadcasting in serving remote locations not presently reached by ground transmissions.

If 1975 is to be judged a truly transitional year, then all of these advances — these loose pieces — need to be brought together into a coherent and intelligent plan for the future. In 1975, Jim

Lehrer of public television station WETA in Washington, D.C., said, "Public television is on the threshold of maturity." In early 1976, Lawrence Grossman, the newly appointed president of PBS, was more ebullient: ". . . we're on the threshold of . . . the Golden Age of public broadcasting." There are indeed a number of positive signs. Yet, one thing is clear: If public broadcasting is to cross that threshold, it will do so only through renewed vision, realistic and cooperative planning, and creative leadership.

The Challenge of Prognostication

Public broadcasting can finally state with some conviction that it has a future. The relevant question now is: What kind of a future will it be? The writers in this volume were asked to probe both the past and the next ten years and to give us their vision of public broadcasting's immediate future, as well as how that vision might be attained. The book proceeded from the conviction that too little attention has been given in public broadcasting to middle-range planning and policy, that the system has been allowed simply to drift into the future.

Pick out a few descriptive phrases about public broadcasting from the essays in this volume. The image that emerges is both surprising and alarming:

> . . . survival comes first . . .
> . . . severe developmental crisis of identity . . .
> . . . struggling infant institution . . .
> . . . under seige . . .
> . . . collision course . . .
> . . . bloody frontal assault . . .
> . . . endless slugfests . . .
> . . . crippling shackles . . .
> . . . establishing the ceasefire with CPB . . .
> . . . a threat to be contained . . .

This image portrays a broadcasting system tied in knots over its past, a past so twisted with time-consuming set-backs, with charges and counter-charges, with desperate, self-serving rationalizations that the people associated with the medium have had little time or energy for creative thinking and future planning. Most of them have been too busy maneuvering merely to stay in business.

Anyone who is part of an institution predominantly concerned with survival quite naturally becomes adept at devising short-range strategies. One also routinely adopts a rather skeptical attitude about "futuristic" scenarios. Inevitably in the early life of a new public institution, there is a flurry of forward thinking and goal-making, but as immediate problems seem to multiply and become more complicated, the long-range goals begin to appear ever more distant, and future planning becomes an exercise in frustration and futility. The people who work with immediate realities, coping as best they can, must necessarily gain ascendency in the bureaucracy.

An institution as vital and vulnerable as public broadcasting needs to have a cadre of people who can view the present objectively, keep sight of the immediate future in realistic terms, and then take the time to develop goals and strategies in middle-range blocks of five and ten years. This challenge would seem to be relatively reasonable and straightforward, but, in fact, it is not easily approached or accomplished. Perhaps one of the offshoots of our "future shock" age is a steadily declining band of willing and credible prophets. Social and technological change has become so pervasive and the variables so numerous that few dare venture their scenario for the future in any aspect of the society, let alone an area as complex and controversial as communications and, specifically, public broadcasting.

Consider Richard Moore's proposition: "Television is a function of the society as a whole; it changes as the society changes. Predicting the state of this nation, even over a five-year span, takes a kind of clairvoyance that no one has yet reliably demonstrated." In his essay on instructional television, Bernard Friedlander looks at the future and states: "I don't have the courage to make detailed predictions of exactly *how* ITV will become more important in the future than it has been in the past . . ." William Harley hopes that "The ineptitudes and the 'blue-sky' predictions are now largely a thing of the past . . ." What these writers and others tell us is that we've attempted to predict the future in communications before and have gotten burned. Now, if you don't mind, we'd just as soon not stick our necks out.

Who can blame them for their caution? If anything, the past decade has underscored the perils of wishful thinking about a radically different future, just around the corner, filled with all manner of communication marvels. Cable television in the late 1960s was

heralded as a "take-off" medium; six years later, it is still on the
runway. Public broadcasting was also launched in the late 1960s
with glowing phrases and grand dreams. In signing the Public Broadcasting Act in late 1967, President Johnson used the occasion to
propose an ambitious and exciting scheme: ". . . we must consider
new ways to build a network for knowledge — not just a broadcast
system, but one that employs every means of sending and of storing
information that the individual can use."

For a time, the excitement surrounding this new law and system
spurred many other far-reaching proposals. A few years later, as the
Nixon Administration began sniping at public broadcasting, the
balloon burst. It became quickly apparent how difficult it was
merely to build "just a broadcast system." The dreams had to be
postponed once again — things weren't going according to plan —
and the visionaries quietly retreated.

Looking Ahead

Rick Breitenfeld once described his vision of public broadcasting's future in the form of a news story:

> *Washington, December 1988* — Officials of PBS and CPB
> have agreed to meet during the next few months to iron
> out the apparent differences they've been having in de-
> ciding who is to do what in public telecommunications.

Breitenfeld's satirical gibe contains a serious warning: The past in
public broadcasting could be merely the prologue for an even shakier
and more aimless future.

One sign of institutional maturity is the ability of an organization to come to grips candidly with its own strengths and weaknesses, putting aside some of the myths, the rhetoric and public
relations hyperbole, that so often surround new social enterprises.
Public broadcasting, left to its present devices and delusions, could
drift back into the power struggles and organizational problems of
the past. If serious planning is to get off the ground, the system must
set aside the old images and rationalizations and develop new
goals and new, stronger steering mechanisms that will determine
the proper direction and set a steady forward course.

There is some evidence that public broadcasting has already

begun this task. Several authors in this volume have attempted to bare "myths" of public broadcasting, as they see them, and to propose alternative views and methods which might lead to a more effective system in the immediate future. Others have simply raised some hard — and often unpleasant — policy questions for which answers are not easily found. They have also examined some of the probable stumbling blocks along the way. Among the highlights of their conclusions are the following:

A new Carnegie Commission. One over-riding proposition emerges from this book to assure a thriving public broadcasting system for the 1980s: McKay, Rowland, and Harley explicitly suggest that the time is now propitious for a major comprehensive review of public broadcasting. Other writers hint at the need. Dr. Killian, who chaired the Carnegie Commission in the middle 1960s and later headed the CPB board, launched the idea of a new commission when he left the corporation in 1975. Clearly, those who have given deep thought to the evolution of public broadcasting and the changing American communications environment have ended up at the same point: The Carnegie Commission and its 1967 report helped public broadcasting conceptualize and plan its first decade. Public broadcasting now needs similar review and forward-planning in order to negotiate the next ten years.

Skeptics retort that public broadcasting is already over-burdened with committees and studies. As one public television veteran quipped: "Public broadcasting is a series of meetings interrupted by a few programs." The skepticism is understandable. The system has had and continues to have more than its fair share of identity crises. Hardly a year goes by without someone raising The Big Question: "What *is* public broadcasting?"

All this introspection may seem boring to an outsider — like a technology in search of a mission. But in the long run, it may well prove to have been a healthy regenerative mechanism — if the system will begin *now* to put aside its past problems and present squabbles and start thinking and acting in concert for a better future. It must be evident, for reasons articulated here and elsewhere, that the proposed Carnegie-type commission, carefully planned and carried out, makes sense as a first step in putting public broadcasting on the right track. The system came into being after a commission had set the stage. There's no reason why another commission cannot build on that precedent.

The public weal. One problem area that should be examined by the new commission is the role of the public in the operation and decision-making of the public broadcasting system. Several authors in this volume single out this issue as one of the most potentially explosive in the litany of public broadcasting's troubles. Certainly, if the experience of San Francisco station KQED in 1975 is any indication, there will be increasing pressure on the system and on the individual stations for greater public involvement in the affairs of public broadcasting.

A seemingly small matter, the cut-back of KQED's evening news program, "Newsroom," from one hour to one-half hour, sparked the formation of a citizens' group calling itself the "Committee to Save KQED." This group was not content simply to state its grievances with the station. Instead it attempted to gain voting power on the station's board of directors by obtaining a copy of the station's membership list and soliciting proxy votes from the station's 100,000 members for the December 1975 board election.

The committee reportedly received over 10,000 proxies before a San Francisco judge issued an injunction limiting the group's further activities. Nonetheless, the committee formulated a platform and fielded a slate of opposition candidates for the elections. None were elected, but the procedure is being challenged in the courts. The significant accomplishment here is that the committee managed to create a general public awareness of what was formerly a *pro forma* election. In the 1974 KQED board election, approximately 1,700 members of the station voted; in 1975 over 30,000 participated. Whatever one may think of the tactics and issues involved in this particular case, the message is clear: The "public" in public broadcasting can no longer be taken for granted simply as passive viewers/listeners/contributors.

The KQED experience may well occur elsewhere unless new mechanisms for public participation are developed and implemented. But this will be a two-edged sword. On the one hand, the fact that there are groups and segments of society taking public broadcasting much more seriously than in the past reflects an increasing public awareness of the value of the system. The "people's movement" in public broadcasting may be self-interested at times and scatter-shot in its approach; but, if it can be properly tapped and channeled by the leaders in public broadcasting, it could lead to a new and advantageous driving force for the system. Considering the lack of any widespread public support and involvement in the system in the past — a serious problem that McKay, Rowland and others mention

— this new interest should be neither discouraged nor dismissed.

On the other hand, with all types of conflicting requests and demands, the concept of public participation could be a formula for chaos. Thus far, the public broadcasting system has barely been able to function. It could be taxed to its limits by increased demands and programs for public participation. Stations cannot satisfy these demands merely by encouraging subscribers to vote in board elections or by sampling the opinions of the general public regarding programming (neither are very controversial propositions). For many vocal groups, public participation means setting quotas for minority employment, programming, and representation on governing boards. For others, it also means public access to programming decisions and even to program production and financing.

Many of these demands — perhaps all of them — are legitimate rights deserving recognition, but meeting them without harm to the efficiency and effectiveness of the system will be a very delicate task. When interest-group demands are shouted loud enough and long enough, and when political clout is well-exercised, the temptation at the receiving end is to give in rather than to contend with discrimination charges, law suits and tumultuous board meetings. The lesson learned by universities in the 1960s is relevant here: Somebody has to be able to say "No." Clearly, without strong and able leadership, public broadcasting could become everybody's mechanism for meeting his particular grievance and, in the process, ruining the effectiveness and integrity of the institution.

The problem won't go away — indeed, as public broadcasting gains increasing recognition, the demands and pressures could quickly escalate. It seems wise, then, that the system learn rather quickly to deal with this new force as positively and constructively as possible. Public broadcasting should begin now to design better mid-career training for its professionals in order to raise their consciousness concerning the social and cultural revolution around us and to help them to develop an appropriate aptitude and attitude for the future difficulties raised by the participation issue.

The problem of programming. Another vital problem area in public broadcasting is programming. At an Aspen Institute conference on public television, Thomas Moore of the CPB board stated: "What we end up with in the homes of this country is all that really matters. Structure, funding, everything else should lead to that one result." Robert Benjamin, chairman of the CPB board, stated it even more directly: "The priority today has to be programming; it's high time we got to it." When he became president of PBS in 1976, Lawrence Grossman stated: "My first three priorities are programming. Programming. And Programming!" Clearly, top-quality programming is the system's first order of business.

However, as a new growth period emerges for public broadcasting, the system and the stations (and the authors in this volume) confront a number of difficult questions: Where will this programming originate? Who will pay for it, and how? For whom will the programming be geared? For a wide audience, competitive with the commercial network offerings, or for "specialized," fragmented audiences that may (or may not) be neglected by American radio and television. Are the elaborate mechanisms now in existence sufficient for ensuring programming excellence?

Regarding the last question, several authors here would appear to be saying "No." Land argues for the advantages of independent production: "There is simply too much creative energy in this large, heterogeneous democracy for the stations to be able to foreclose others from the programming process." Katzman points to a vacuum in programming leadership: ". . . there are differences between a division of authority, a delegation of authority, and a dilution (or even avoidance) of authority." Public affairs programming, as several of the writers point out, can fall between the cracks unless some systematic plan is developed to guarantee its continued, vital role in the system. Morrisett and Friedlander underscore the need for some type of quality control, and Lyle summarizes the views of his colleagues when he says of some public television production: ". . . deep in our hearts we have known [it] to be not merely ineffective but downright bad."

Accountability. Like it or not, public broadcasting is going to be in the data collection and research business for years to come. In the past, it has been exempt from the FCC requirement that commercial broadcasters ascertain the needs and interest of their local community. In 1976, that exemption was lifted. In other areas as well, public broadcasters must expect to be carefully scrutinized by public legislative bodies. Public broadcasting's future, in short, may depend in part on its ability to devise the measurements and glean the facts that will demonstrate its accomplishments and its potential — not just in terms of how the dollars were spent but more importantly in terms of what services were rendered. In practical terms, this means a new, energetic and innovative commitment to research.

The instructional gap. Yet another perplexing issue for public broadcasting is its relationship with education. The noncommercial channels were originally set aside as an educational service; but in the efforts to build a "public" broadcasting system, the leadership has come to neglect the potential and the problems of educational or instructional broadcasting. There have been several efforts to bridge the ever-increasing gap, including the aborted CPB ALPS (Adult Learning Program Service) project, and a whole series of studies, such as the 1975 ACNO report, "Public Broadcasting and Education." But very little of a tangible nature has been accomplished.

This vital segment of the public broadcasting system can stand no more false starts or unproductive study projects. What it needs desperately are more breakthroughs on the order of the Children's Television Workshop. Unfortunately, neither the public broadcasting establishment nor the educational leadership has been eager to work together in formulating a mutually beneficial arrangement. There are some cooperative efforts at the state and local level, but the dramatic example of a partnership at the national level will be necessary to spur on this essential service.

Cooperative planning. Another area badly in need of new cooperative efforts is the problem of stations with overlapping signals. As Katzman and Wirt point out: ". . . the relatively poor communication between PTV stations with overlapping signals wastes a valuable resource for public broadcasting." The system prides itself on the independence of its stations; but the price for this independence has often meant a duplication of manpower and resources, as well as a tendency toward defensiveness, bureaucratic inertia, and parochialism. There are exceptions, but in most cases individual stations are so accustomed to fighting for survival that they are disposed neither to seize a larger turf nor to surrender territorial responsibilities which they cannot support or adequately fulfill.

The problem is not easily remedied. One possibility might be the creation of federal financing incentives, so that cooperative efforts among the stations would be encouraged and rewarded. As several writers in this volume have noted, public broadcasting can no longer afford to confront any of its problems as individual stations dealing with unrelated issues. As the system matures, and as we begin thinking in broader technological terms than traditional broadcasting, the guiding principle for the future of public broadcasting should be evident to all: Public broadcasting's continued development and expanded contribution to American society will be increasingly dependent upon its ability to view its problems as integrally related and to develop plans for action from that perspective.

Governmental policy-making bodies, too, must begin to alter short-sighted and negativist attitudes. As Branscomb argues, the FCC is a case in point. How much longer can we tolerate a less than affirmative endorsement of noncommercial communications by this major federal regulatory agency? William Harley offers three "modest steps" for changing the FCC position *vis-a-vis* public telecommunications. These and other proposals deserve public airing and serious consideration. If public broadcasting continues to be merely tolerated by the FCC, its future will no doubt be much like its past — filled with roadblocks and detours. Other federal agencies, such as HEW, the OTP, and even NASA, have adopted a relatively favorable position toward public, nonprofit uses of telecommunications. The FCC must follow their lead.

Perhaps 1975 was not the transition year posited here. Perhaps we are in store for more of the same for the next ten years. I would like to think not. The writers for this volume have given us a glimpse of the issues to be tackled and some possible solutions to consider. Not every problem is covered nor is every proposal of equal merit, but this can be a starting point. It *must* be a starting point. Media critic Ben Bagdikian addressed the public broadcasting community in late 1975 and put the challenge before them (and all of us):

> Our problem is to create in this generation the vision of what public broadcasting ought to be. People in this audience know the struggle of keeping public broadcasting merely alive. If it were not for you, there would be little hope. Someone needs to do more than that.
>
> . . . We need a new coalition of people to campaign for a permanent end to the shameful smothering of this great national resource. They will not be fighting only for money, for equipment, or support of hard-working employees. They will be fighting for something basic to freedom in a modern world. Democracy will not survive without an informed and thoughtful citizenry or without a rich and diverse reservoir of public ideas and activities. The American public has been denied the full growth of their radio and television toward those ends for 50 years. It is time to develop this most powerful communications instrument in the history of civilization, not for

the narrow goals of sales and profits, but for support of the beleaguered human spirit in our society.

A Selective Guide
to Sources on Public
Broadcasting

CHRISTOPHER H. STERLING

These pages present my own highly selective listing and discussion of useful sources on public, educational, and instructional radio and television mainly in the United States. The emphasis throughout is on relatively current material (much of it likely to be found in any good library), on public rather than educational/instructional aspects of broadcasting, and on books and reports rather than periodical articles. The sources are arranged into the following sections: (1) how public television developed; (2) overviews of public broadcasting and public policy; (3) financing of public broadcasting; (4) public television programming trends; (5) "Sesame Street" and other children's programs; (6) ETV/ITV services; (7) the public television audience; (8) public radio; (9) technological trends in public and educational communications; (10) public broadcasting regulation; (11) public broadcasting abroad; and (12) useful periodicals.

Dr. Sterling is associate professor of Communications at Temple University and is editor-publisher of *Mass Media Booknotes* and editor of the *Journal of Broadcasting*.

The Future of Public Broadcasting

1. *How Public Television Developed*

The first detailed analysis of educational television and what it might become was Charles A. Siepmann's *Television and Education in the United States* (Paris: UNESCO, 1952), in which the long-time media critic reviewed educational programming on commercial networks and stations, explored beginnings of university and school use of the medium, and concluded with his views of how the educational media would fit into a basically commercial system. Jennie Waugh Callahan's *Television in School, College, and Community* (New York: McGraw-Hill, 1953) covers similar ground and offers a good bibliography of other early studies. Both of these books, as well as the annual *Education on the Air* series (see section 8), describe early plans for public broadcasting prior to issuance of the FCC's *Sixth Report and Order* (1952), which reserved the first educational television channels. A full understanding of the beginnings of public television should also include background on public radio (see section 8), since many of the organizations and people were the same.

A review of the first few years after the educational allocation is found in the report *Four Years of Progress in Educational Television* (Washington: Joint Committee on Educational Television, 1956), while the best history of educational television to the early 1960s, before major government infusions of money, is found in John Walker Powell's *Channels of Learning: The Story of Educational Television* (Washington: Public Affairs Press, 1962). Details on how one organization operated and provided leadership during this critical period is in W. Wayne Alford's *NAEB History: 1954-1965* (Washington: NAEB, 1966). *Educational Television: The Next Ten Years* (Washington: Government Printing Office, 1965) offers a contemporary view of the system and its future in a collection of original essays on programming, community relations, instructional functions, financing, and resources and facilities. Intersting commentary on the rise of public television within the commercial system is found throughout Erik Barnouw's *Tube of Plenty: The Evolution of American Television* (New York: Oxford University Press, 1975).

To best understand the fundamental changes brought about at the close of the 1960s, one naturally begins with the Carnegie Commission on Educational Television's *Public Television: A Program for Action* (New York: Harper, 1967), which provides 12 recommendations for an improved system, detailed information on the status quo of educational television, and a series of appendices giving data on (a) legal aspects of the proposed Corporation for Public Television, (b) costs of a nationwide public television system, (c) technology and television, (d) relations with commercial TV, (e) the role of the FCC and public television, (f) financial and operating requirements of public TV, and (g) the mid-sixties audience for public television. Though now a decade old, this report remains the seminal document for the transformation in public television in the 1970s. To trace the background of the report, how it was received in various quarters, the role of the Johnson Administration, and the subsequent passage of the all-important congressional act of 1967, see John E. Burke's *The Public Broadcasting Act of 1967* (Washington: NAEB, 1972), which was reprinted from a series of three articles in *Educational Broadcasting Review*. Useful background on the state of public television in that epochal year is found in Allen E. Koenig and Ruane B. Hill's *The Farther Vision: Educational Television Today* (Madison: University of Wisconsin Press, 1967). This general overview included articles on the various types of educational TV stations, on NET and regional networks, on development of instructional television, on trends in programming and problems in financing, on the ETV management, and on the effects of the 1967 act and forthcoming technological changes.

2. Overviews of Public Broadcasting and Public Policy

An excellent starting place is Sydney W. Head's *Broadcasting in America: A Survey of Television and Radio* (Boston: Houghton-Mifflin, 1976, third edition), which is the best one-volume overview of broadcasting in general terms and includes several discussions of educational radio and public television. Les Brown's *Televi$ion: The Business Behind the Box* (New York: Harcourt, Brace Jovanovich, 1972) deals mainly with network broadcasting but includes a chapter on public television as it was in the early 1970s. Another useful chapter overview is found in Martin Mayer's *About Television* (New York: Harper & Row, 1972). Looking quite specifically at the economics and public-policy ramifications of public television is a detailed chapter in Roger G. Noll, Merton J. Peck, and John J. McGowan's *Economic Aspects of Television Regulation* (Washington: Brookings Institution, 1973).

Turning to works dealing specifically with public broadcasting, one of the most useful books is John Macy, Jr.'s *To Irrigate a Wasteland: The Struggle to Shape a Public Television System in the United States* (Berkeley: University of California Press, 1974). This book by the former president of CPB offers an impassioned discussion of the trials and limitations of public policy (especially financing and control) in public broadcasting and includes 40 pages of appendix matter: a glossary of organizational terms, a list of public television stations and locations, the full text of the 1967 act, and a series of statistical tables on the growth of public television as seen from several points of view (finance, population, program sources, etc.). A good analysis of the political football which Macy and others were dealing with in the early 1970s is found in Fred Powledge's *Public Television: A Question of Survival* (Washington: Public Affairs Press, 1972). In this work, a report of the ACLU, the author focuses on the problems of CPB versus the Nixon Administration.

A handy, relatively brief reference source is *The People's Business: A Review of Public Television* (Washington: Public Broadcasting Service, 1974), which provides an overview of the various public broadcasting organizations and their functions, a section on program sources and controversies, a discussion of public broadcasting's relationships with Congress and the Executive, an examination of public television funding, and speculation about the likely future of the system. The latter subject is the focus of George W. Tressel *et al.*, *The Future of Educational Telecommunication* (Lexington, Mass.: Lexington Books, [D. C. Heath], 1975). Half the book is devoted to the report's text (dealing with goals of educational broadcasting, analyzing recent Congressional action on financing, and discussing the current status of public broadcasting's distribution system, programming, funding, administration, and alternatives and recommendations for the future). The remainder is a series of appendices (minimum annual operating costs, financial statistics for public radio and TV licensees, new technologies, etc.).

There are a number of *annual* works of reference which are invaluable for those seeking relatively consistent textual and statistical-trend information. The single most useful title is *Status Report on Public Broadcasting* (Washington: CPB, 1975-date), the first issue of which provided data for 1973 on the growth of public radio and television; the role of foundations, HEW, and CPB; the finance and employment patterns of the system; broadcasting and program production for both public radio and television; national interconnection; and the public broadcasting audience — all of this in both text and dozens of tables and charts. Focusing more specifically and in greater detail on part of the picture is *Statistical Report on Public Television Licensees* (Washington: CPB, 1971-date), which has provided relatively consistent information for fiscal years since 1970. While data for 1970 and 1971 appeared in several booklets for each year, the data have been pulled together in a single volume since 1972 and include information on the number of licensees and stations, on finance and employment patterns, and on hours of broadcasting and production — with an average of 70 tables and charts per year. This series of reports also includes coverage of public radio (see section 8) and public television program trends (see section 4).

An annual guide/directory of value is the *NAEB Directory of Public Telecommunications* (Washington: NAEB, annual), which includes a statistical summary (taken from the series discussed just above), a list of NAEB members, and details on public radio and television stations, on state agencies and networks, on ITFS systems (see section 6), on colleges and universities offering educational broadcasting curricula, etc. A parallel source of value is *Broadcasting Yearbook* (Washington: Broadcasting Publications, 1935-date), which each spring publishes the standard industry directory to radio and television stations (including noncommercial operations and personnel) and the allied industry organizations. Another way to keep track of the cast of characters in the national public telecommunication organizations is to consult *Who Is Where* (Washington: NAEB, 1974), a frequently revised organizational and telephone directory of key personnel in several dozen private and government agencies.

To follow the activities of the most important organization in this field, see the annual reports of the Corporation for Public Broadcasting, which appear in January or February following the fiscal year covered. These reports provide useful text summations of program trends, organization, technological changes, grants to local stations, community relations, audience research, and financial data. (Another handy annual report is that for CTW — see section 5.) The concern of CPB and others over the status and needs of women is reflected in a recent data-packed analysis, Caroline Isber and Muriel Cantor's *Report of the Task Force on Women in Public Broadcasting* (Washington: CPB, 1975) which deals with the role of women in programming (and programming by and for women), the employment of women, and the role of women in public broadcasting management. The 60-page text is supplemented by several appendices and nearly 70 tables detailing program and employment trends. For further employment data, including that concerning minorities, see the statistical reports discussed in the paragraph above.

3. *Financing of Public Broadcasting*

The prime source for information on what public broadcasting actually receives and spends — and what it hopes to receive and spend — is found in the annual hearings before Congressional committees, most usually the House Interstate and Foreign Commerce Committee and the Senate Commerce Committee. As this book goes to press, the most recent of these are hearings before both committees on the *Public Broadcasting Financing Act of 1975* (94th Congress, 1st Session), and the resultant briefer reports from those committees to the full House and Senate. In addition, the House committee is apparently initiating an annual overview hearing on public broadcasting, held each March or April, in which both the past year and current controversies will be reviewed, with an emphasis on financing. There are also reports on public broadcasting financing going back to the late 1960s. A hearing of special value was on the *Role of Private Foundations in Public Broadcasting* (Senate Committee on Finance, September 1974, 94th Congress, 1st Session).

The Senate and House Appropriations Committees hold annual hearings, usually early in the spring, on federal monies appropriated for the Corporation for Public Broadcasting and related agencies (PBS, CTW, etc.). The discussions of public broadcasting usually appear (in both House and Senate committees) under the omnibus title *Department of Labor, Health, Education and Welfare, and Related Agencies*, and they generally provide 100-150 pages of testimony and tabular financial information. All of these hearings can be consulted in a nearby Federal Depository Library (usually a university or law school library), or they can be obtained either directly from the committee (addresses are in the *Aspen Handbook* — see section 12) or from your own Congressman or Senator.

There have been a number of valuable special reports on financial questions, most of which have come from the CPB. One such report was *Report of the Task Force on the Long-Range Financing of Public Broadcasting* (Washington: CPB, 1973), which was reprinted in the Senate Commerce Committee's hearings on the 1975 Financing Act. In addition, CPB often has a limited number of copies of specialized reports, sometimes researched by outside agencies, such as "A Study of Persons Who Pledge to PTV Stations," and "A Survey of Public Television Auctions." Naturally, further financial data can be found in the annual CPB statistical reports (see section 2), in the appendices to some of the books discussed in sections 2, and in the transcripts of the various Congressional hearings.

Reports from outside agencies on the funding problems are less common but no less useful. One of the most influential (and only the second such independent analysis since the 1967 Carnegie Commission Report) was Wilbur Schramm and Lyle Nelson's *The Financing of Public Television* (Palo Alto, Calif.: Aspen Institute Program on Communications and Society, 1972). Included in the text and tables are discussion of sources of support, support distribution, and assumptions and cost projections. An earlier analysis is found in two reports, *The State of Public Broadcasting* and Dick Natzer's *Long-Range Financing of Public Broadcasting* (New York: National Citizen's Committee for Broadcasting, 1968), which includes a good deal of station-by-station information as well as an overall picture. (For funding of children's programs with federal money, see section 5.)

4. *Public Television Programming Trends*

There are two types of current information available in this category: One is thematic, the other statistical in approach. The most recent of the thematic studies is Natan Katzman's *Program Decisions in Public Television* (Washington: CPB, 1976), which in just over 70 pages discusses the national system of public television, local public television programming (divided into the various types of stations by ownership and size), and school programming (again broken down by types of station ownership). Katzman's report is based on interviews and on information gathered in his statistical report, discussed in the next paragraph. His book is a valuable overview of a complicated and often controversial question. It also includes useful charts showing sources and funding of programming in recent years, and interesting reference materials, such as the map showing the different types of public television stations across the country in 1975. An earlier and more philosophical approach is found in Robert J. Blakely's *The People's Instrument: A Philosophy of Programming for Public Television* (Washington: Public Affairs Press, 1971). This volume deals with basic principles and concepts in its nine documented chapters and explores the limitations of commercial broadcasting content, the problem of quantity versus quality, station functions and goals, the making of audience constituencies, and varied types of programming priorities.

Of the statistical studies, the most recent is Natan Katzman's *Public Television Program Content: 1974* (Washington: CPB, 1975), which is based on a sample week of programming by PTV stations. Tables, charts, and text cover instructional television, children's programs (especially those from CTW — see section 5), general and news/public affairs programs, special or target-audience programs, local programming, and PBS and prime-time program content. A lengthy overview chapter examines programs by source, time of broadcast, distribution factors, etc. The first of what is to become an annual or biennial series, this volume is an invaluable reference. Earlier benchmarks for comparison are provided by *One Week of Public Television, April 1972* (Washington: CPB, 1973), and by similarly titled reports for 1970 and 1968 (published by the National Instructional Television Center, Bloomington, Ind.), and for 1966, 1964, 1962 and 1961 (published by Morse Communication Research Center, Brandeis University, Waltham, Mass.). All of these earlier reports (except for the 1974 analysis) used a specific sample week, usually in the spring of the year indicated.

5. *"Sesame Street" and Other Children's Programs*

There is quite a literature on the role and impact of the Children's Television Workshop and its most important single program: "Sesame Street." Richard M Polsky's *Getting to Sesame Street: Origins of the Children's Television Workshop* (New York: Praeger Special Studies, 1974) details the behind-the-scenes events of 1966-68 as CTW was just getting off the ground, and before any programs were broadcast. It is an invaluable study of management, of energy, and of innovation. Because CTW approached the commercial networks first, the study also serves as a useful comparison between commercial and educational television decision-making. Robert K. Yin's *The Workshop and the World: Toward an Assessment of the Children's Television Workshop* (Santa Monica, Calif.: Rand Corp., 1973) is a summary of the many studies of CTW's role as innovator and educator, as well as an outline of further research then needed to better understand what CTW was doing, had done, and might do in the future.

The "standard" book on the subject of CTW is probably Gerald S. Lesser's *Children and Television: Lessons From Sesame Street* (New York: Random House, 1974), but it is a view from the inside, as Lesser is deeply involved in CTW's operations. He covers the development of the system, planning and production of the series, the broadcasts themselves, and a review of audience research done on the series' impact, all supplemented by a detailed bibliography of further readings on CTW and related subjects. The *Annual Report* (New York: CTW, 1968-date) provides a year-by-year review of developments, funding, organization, and management. "Outside" analysis is found in The Network Project's *Down Sesame Street* (New York: Network Project Notebook No. 6, November 1973), which dissects the support operation, and impact of the CTW and its programs. A more detailed and less polemical outside analysis is found in Herman W. Land's *The Children's Television Workshop: How and Why it Works* (Jerricho, N.Y.: Nassau Board of Educational Services, 1972), a 200 page volume dealing with organization, applications of research in program construction, financial administration, audience promotion, and reaching the disadvantaged. A scholarly re-analysis of audience-research studies on "Sesame Street" is the focus of Thomas D. Cook et al., *"Sesame Street" Revisited* (New York: Russell Sage Foundation, 1975), which takes another look at the massive 1970 and 1971 audience studies done on the program. Cook and his colleagues find that all is not as well as some had assumed, that the program may not be having all the beneficial effects expected. (See section 7 for other studies of PTV/ITV audiences.)

Taking a broader view of children's television support is Keith Mielke, Rolland Johnson, and Barry Cole's *The Federal Role in Funding Children's Television Programming* (Bloomington, Ind.: Institute for Communication Research [copies available from NAEB in Washington], 1975). This study reviews the general factors in children's programming (soft-ware, hardware, distribution, alternative media, audience needs and desires, and types of federal funding used thus far); analyzes the current federal involvement in children's television (administration, selection of projects, methods of applying for funding, qualification requirements, lengths of time involved, and evaluation of results); examines policy issues;

and presents alternatives and recommendations (audience needs, copyright questions, other models for the federal role, and questions concerning production, distribution and evaluation). This unique study includes nearly 20 tables, a bibliography, and a glossary. (For related studies of funding see section 3.)

6. ETV/ITV Services

The literature is truly massive in this category, and the recommendations which follow are very selective, stressing only the most current and generally useful reference materials. For the background context of educational and instructional television, the best single source is Paul Saettler's *A History of Instructional Technology* (New York: McGraw-Hill, 1968), which offers extensive coverage of educational radio and television, the many organizations concerned with each, and the research on the effects of the system. Another detailed analysis with a strong British accent is George Bereday and Joseph Lauwery's *Communication Media and the School: The Yearbook of Education, 1960* (Tarrytown-on-Hudson, N.Y.: World Book Company, 1960), which is a 600-page study that includes some 50 original essays on the then-current status of the various educational media both here and abroad (see also section 11).

The most important single source of material in this field on a continuing basis, aside from the periodicals noted in section 12, is the ERIC Clearinghouse on Information Resources, Stanford Center for Research and Development in Teaching, School of Education, Stanford University, Stanford, California 94305. ERIC, the Educational Resources Information Center (funded by the National Institute of Education and founded in 1967), is a multi-center, computer-based storage and retrieval service dealing with all aspects of education, including the media and instructional technology. A general information brochure on ERIC and how it works is available on request. Those interested should also write for "Educational Media and Technology: Publications from ERIC at Stanford, 1967-1973," which covers nearly 60 documents covering the center's scope, and "Instructional Technology Subject Matter Descriptors: A Subset of the ERIC Thesaurus," which offers a sense of how to get computer access to the thousands of documents stored. (See also Brown — section 6 — for a discussion of ERIC and how it operates.)

Bibliographies devoted to this general topic are quite common, but the two most recent and useful appear to be John Ohliger and David Gueulette's *Media and Adult Learning: A Bibliography with Abstracts, Annotations, and Quotations* (New York: Garland Publishing, 1975), which exhaustively details some 1,650 studies under more than 50 subject headings, many of which deal with some aspect of educational radio-TV. Of great value is James W. Brown's *Educational Media Yearbook* (New York: Bowker, 1973-date), a continually updated annual which reviews organizations, new products, and research and development. With lengthy bibliographies of the previous year's books, periodicals, and video publications, this volume is becoming a standard reference source.

Noting just a few of the other titles in this category, we have first *Public Broadcasting and Education* (Washington: CPB, 1975), a detailed analysis by CPB's Advisory Council of National Organizations on the role of public stations in the educational/instructional process. The body of the report presents 11 major recommendations, while the rest of the book offers detailed task-force reports on public broadcasting's potential and actual role with various levels of instruction, from early childhood to adult education. A comparison of the views of professionals and professors is found in Wilbur Schramm, ed. *Quality in Instructional Television* (Honolulu: University Press of Hawaii, 1973), which focuses on the useful interrelationships of production and related research for better educational programs. Richard C. Burke, ed., *Instructional Television Bold New Venture* (Bloomington: Indiana University Press, 1971), provides eight original papers on most aspects of the subject, including ITV at various school levels, the TV teacher, administration of ITV, evaluation of results, etc. George N. Gordon's *Classroom Television: New Frontiers in ITV* (New York: Hastings House, 1970) takes a general view of ITV impact and a more specific approach to methods of ITV production, including equipment, personnel, preparation of instructional materials, cost figuring, etc. D. B. Carlson's *College Credit through TV: Old Idea, New Dimensions* (Lincoln, Neb.: Great Plains National Instructional Television Library, 1974) reviews the development of college-level ITV (including early commercial network ventures) and provides a lengthy analysis of current programs and administrative trends. Caleb Gattegno's *Towards a Visual Culture: Educating Through Television* (New York: Avon Books, 1969) garnered a great deal of attention as a seminal work which could guide our thinking in the proper ways to use television as a means of education. There is useful analysis of programming types and related audience (student) reactions. A helpful overview of research and thinking up to the mid-1960s is found in Judith Murphy and Ronald Gross, eds., *Learning by Television* (New York: The Fund for the Advancement of Education, 1966). The study looks at the whole process, from administration to impact, and projects the likely future of ITV in American education. A report doing a similar job on a broader front is James W. Armsey and Norman C. Dahl's *An Inquiry into the Uses of Instructional Technology* (New York: Ford Foundation, 1973), which discusses some past major applications of instructional television both here and abroad. (For ITV audience research, see section 7.)

7. *The Public Television Audience*

For years, the standard reference source was Wilbur Schramm, Jack Lyle, and Ithiel de Sola Pool's *The People Look at Educational Television* (Palo Alto, Calif.: Stanford University Press, 1963); but while its exhaustive research of educational stations in Boston, Pittsburgh, San Francisco, Denver, the Alabama network, Lincoln, Neb., and Columbus, Ohio, is useful historically (most of the data was gathered in 1960-61), it can provide only the most general guidance today. Badly needed is a full-scale replication of this study, using more stations and reflecting the great changes since the early 1960s. A partial step in that direction is Jack Lyle's *The People Look at Public Television: 1974* (Washington: CPB, 1975), which is based on the on-going research efforts of CPB, and shows in tables, charts, and text the audience use patterns existing for public TV today. There are sections on children's viewing of PTV, viewing variations by market, PTV viewing as a part of overall viewing, what kinds of people watch, etc. From time to time, copies of smaller CPB studies are available, such as "Public Television and the Urban Black Audience," "Public Television and the Mexican-American Audience in the Southwest," and various specific market analyses. Requests should be directed to the Office of Research, CPB, 1111 16th Street, N.W., Washington, D.C. 20036.

Specific studies of the effects of instructional television are best summed up in Godwin C. Chu and Wilbur Schramm's *Learning from Television: What the Research Says* (Washington: NAEB, 1968; with a revised and updated printing in 1974). The latter printing includes an 11-page essay with bibliography of studies done since 1967, while the remaining 116 pages are the key to a voluminous and often repetitive literature on just how effective all that ITV hardware and software really is. Another annotated bibliography approach to some of the same material is found in J. Christopher Reid and Donald W. MacLennan's *Research in Instructional Television and Film* (Washington: Government Printing Office, 1967), which covers and indexes more than 300 studies. (For more recent material and bibliographies, see the periodicals under section 12.)

Studies of children and television are common, but they tend to deal with the effects of entertainment television rather than with public/educational television viewing. Aside from the sources discussed under section 5, see Grant Noble's *Children in Front of the Small Screen* (Beverly Hills, Calif.: Sage Publications, 1975), and Robert M. Liebert, John M. Neale, and Emily S. Davidson's *The Early Window: Effects of Television on Children and Youth* (New York: Pergamon Press, 1973), both of which offer useful overviews of research findings and bibliographies of those studies. In addition, for the best bibliographical assessment of research into television's effects in general (on both children and adults), see George Comstock et al., *Television and Human Behavior* (Santa Monica, Calif.: Rand Corp., 1975), a three-volume set. The first volume lists some 2,300 studies, the second focuses on the contents of 450 "key studies," and the third looks at current research trends and future needs.

8. Public Radio

The history of educational (AM) radio is naturally a long one, and there are several places, aside from Saettler (see section 6) to get an outline of that development. A detailed history of the first 15 years of educational radio is in S. E. Frost's *Education's Own Stations: The History of Broadcast Licenses Issued to Educational Institutions* (Chicago: University of Chicago Press, 1937; reprinted by Arno Press in 1971), which provides the background of more than 175 stations, many of them short-term. The early organizational history of educational radio shows up in Saettler, in Harold E. Hill's *NAEB History: 1925 to 1954* (Washington: NAEB, 1954, 1965), and in Isabella M. Cooper's annotated and very useful *Bibliography on Educational Broadcasting* (Chicago: University of Chicago Press,

1942; reprinted by Arno Press in 1971). The latter covers all aspects of the subject and offers commentary on more than 1,700 sources. See also *Education on the Air* (Columbus: Ohio State University Press, 1930-1953), the summary of one of the longest-running annual conferences on educational broadcasting. This book is an interesting study of the wartime and post-war roles of both AM and FM educational radio.

For current data on the status of public radio, see first the *Statistical Report on CPB-Qualified Radio Stations* (Washington: CPB, 1973-date), which provides information for fiscal years (the first one in the series being 1971) and includes data on finance, employment, broadcasting and production, etc., in text, charts, and nearly 50 tables. A major drawback is that only a small minority of all educational/public radio stations are CPB-qualified, and therefore the image presented here is not as representative as that of comparable television material (see section 2). For what appears to be the first in a series of content-focused reports, see Natan Katzman's *One Week of Public Radio: December 9-15, 1973* (Washington: CPB, 1974), which is a content analysis, again restricted to those less than 150 CPB-qualified stations. An earlier analysis, Herman W. Land Associates' *The Hidden Medium: A Status Report on Educational Radio in the United States* (Washington: NAEB, 1967), remains one of the most useful overviews of public radio. It provides information on programming, the national radio network over the 1951-66 period, professional communication, nonbroadcast services, services to commercial stations, and possible new directions. There are many tables and case studies, making this a valuable benchmark of information.

For information on nonbroadcast applications of public radio, see *College Carrier Current: A Survey of 208 Campus-Limited Radio Stations* (New York: Broadcast Institute of North America, 1972), which discusses management, income and budget, programming and news, and other findings about these "wired wireless" operations. One aspect of the growing sub-carrier applications of public FM stations is covered in *Radio Information Services for the Print Handicapped* (Washington: NAEB, 1975), a loose-leaf manual dealing in a descriptive and how-to-do fashion with management and operations of services for the blind (talking books, local volunteer stations, etc.).

Finally, readers interested in the background of noncommercial, listener-supported radio should refer, first, to Lewis Hill's *Voluntary*

346

Listener-Sponsorship (Berkeley: Pacifica Foundation, 1958), which is the story as seen by Pacifica's founder. Eleanor McKinney, ed., *The Exacting Ear: The Story of Listener-Sponsored Radio, and an Anthology of Programs* (New York: Pantheon Books, 1966), analyzes the Pacifica Foundation's expansion from California to other areas and broader content. Steve Post's *Playing in the FM Band: A Personal Account of Free Radio* (New York: Viking Press, 1974) is a staff member's study of New York's WBAI operation.

9. Technological Trends in Public and Educational Communications

Most material on this topic is of a general nature and does not deal specifically with educational applications (but see section 6 for some of the latter). In addition, no production-oriented material is discussed here. Over the years, there have been a number of publications dealing with the need of educational or public stations for improved facilities. An important early volume is the NAEB's *The Needs of Education for Television Channel Allocations* (Washington: Government Printing Office, 1962), which was a plea for more reserved channels to supplement those given over by the FCC's *Sixth Report and Order* in 1962. The book includes detailed coverage maps and text on a state-by-state basis, and it describes then-existing plans for educational television expansion, much of which has occurred in the past 15 years. A more recent analysis is *A Report on the Minimum Equipment Needs and Costs to Upgrade the Facilities of the Public Television Stations in the United States and its Territories* (Washington: CPB Office of Engineering Research, 1975). This volume describes a survey on costs to PTV operations for new equipment, especially local station color capability. The long-term problem of equality between the two types of television services is explored in Philip A. Rubin's *A Quantitative Comparison of the Relative Performance of VHF and UHF Broadcast Stations* (Washington: CPB, 1974).

For a better understanding of television and how it works — as well as how it can be applied to education — see W. J. Kessler's clearly written *Fundamentals of Television Systems: A Technical Monograph for Non-Technical Personnel* (Washington: NAEB, 1968). A recent and extremely well-illustrated guide to all aspects of television and video systems, including recent technical developments, is found in Ken Marsh's *Independent Video: A Complete Guide to the Physics, Operation, and Application of the New Television* (San Francisco: Straight Arrow Books, 1974). Marsh's book is specifically aimed at nontechnical people. A standard reference with descriptive text and diagrams is Raymond Spottiswoode, ed., *The Focal Encyclopedia of Film and Television Techniques* (New York: Hastings House), which deals with equipment, technical history and development, and operational aspects of typical television-station facilities.

There are several useful readings on the potential of cable television for education. Richard Adler and Walter S. Baer's *Aspen Notebook: Cable and Continuing Education* (New York: Praeger Special Studies, 1973) presents a number of papers and excerpts from the discussion of an Aspen Program summer conference. Several of the papers deal with general aspects of the topic, while three focus on operating examples of what can be done. Polly Carpenter-Huffman et al., *Cable Television: Developing Community Services* (New York: Crane, Russak & Co., 1974), includes several sections on uses of cable television. Other useful sources include *Educational Uses of Cable Television* (Washington: Cable Television Information Center, 1974), *Cable Television and Education: A Report from the Field* (Washington: National Cable Television Association, 1973), and *Schools and Cable Television* (Washington: National Education Association, 1971).

For materials on the newer technologies, consult *Television Cartridge and Disc Systems: What Are They Good For?* (Washington: NAEB, 1971), or "The Videodisc: The Next Step in the Communications Evolution," *Journal of the SMPTE* 83:533-587 (July 1974). A more general discussion of where things may be going is found in James Martin's *Future Developments in Telecommunications* (Englewood Cliffs, N.J.: Prentice-Hall, 1971), and in George Gerbner, Larry P. Gross, and William H. Melody, eds., *Communications Technology and Social Policy: Understanding the New Cultural Revolution* (New York: Wiley-Interscience, 1973).

10. *Public Broadcasting Regulation*

The basic sources of rules and regulations of the Federal Communications Commission is the *Code of Federal Regulations, Title 47: Telecommunications* (Washington: Government Printing Office, annual), especially the third of the four volumes making up Title 47.

That volume contains "Parts 70-79," which cover all regulation of radio television broadcasting, as well as cable television. In several cases, it also includes special sections relating to public broadcasting stations (such as Part 73, Subpart C, which refers to educational FM stations). This volume is annually revised, thus containing all rule changes made in the previous year. For more of an overview, both of public broadcasting regulatory developments and of the broader context of FCC regulation, see the FCC's *Annual Report* (Washington: Government Printing Office, annual). Unfortunately, the report is lagging badly in publication, often appearing nearly two years after the closing date of the fiscal year. Both of these sources will be found in any law library, and they should also be available in any government depository or large university library.

Two more specific publications of value are Eugene N. Aleinikoff's "Copyright Considerations in Educational Broadcasting" (Stanford, Calif.: ERIC Clearinghouse, Stanford University, 1972), a 10-page analysis; and Bradley S. Greenberg et al., *An Ascertainment Handbook for Public Broadcasting Facilities* (Washington: CPB Office of Communication Research, 1975), a loose-leaf guide to the ascertainment of community needs by noncommercial stations.

11. *Public Broadcasting Abroad*

The literature on broadcasting abroad is growing at a rapid rate, and much of it deals with public services. A very useful single-volume reference is *World Communications: A 200-Country Survey of Press, Radio, Television, Film* (Paris: UNESCO [New York: Unipub], 1975), which offers details by continent and on a country-by-country basis. See also Ignacy Waniewicz's *Broadcasting for Adult Education: A Guidebook to World-wide Experience* (Paris: UNESCO [New York: Unipub], 1972), which is arranged topically rather than geographically; Henry Cassirer's *Television Teaching Today* (Paris: UNESCO, 1960), which offers dated but valuable developmental information; Wilbur Schramm et al., *The New Media: Memo to Educational Planners* and *New Educational Media in Action: Case Studies for Planners* (Paris: UNESCO, 1967), the latter of which is a three-volume analysis of present practices and future potential in industrial and developing nations; Bereday and Lauwerys (see section 6); and a number of the specific titles in UNESCO's periodical series, *Reports and Papers on Mass Communication*. The key to this topic is found in a variety of bibliographies of foreign and international media, which are described in the final section of the *Aspen Handbook on the Media* (see section 12).

For specific examples of public/educational broadcasting overseas, see the following: *Educational Television and Radio in Britain* (London: BBC, 1966); Burton Paulu, *Broadcasting on the European Continent* (Minneapolis: University of Minnesota Press, 1967) and *Radio and Television Broadcasting in Eastern Europe* (Minneapolis: University of Minnesota Press, 1974); Sydney W. Head, ed., *Broadcasting in Africa* (Philadelphia: Temple University Press, 1974); and Mitoji Nishimoto, *The Development of Educational Broadcasting in Japan* (Rutland, Vt.: Tuttle, 1969).

12. *Useful Periodicals*

There is constant research and publication in all aspects of public and educational broadcasting, and naturally most of what is current will appear in periodical rather than book form. The best quick guide to periodicals and organizations in broadcasting, including many of educational focus, is William L. Rivers and William T. Slater, eds., *Aspen Handbook on the Media: 1975-76 Edition* (Palo Alto, Calif.: Aspen Institute Program on Communications and Society, 1975). In addition, keep an eye on the following publications:

AV Communication Review (quarterly): research on all aspects of instructional technology.

Broadcasting (weekly): basic trade periodical of the industry, with regular reports on developments in public broadcasting.

CPB Report (weekly): newsletter of the Corporation for Public Broadcasting, with short articles and research reports on most aspects of public television and radio.

EBU Review (bimonthly): journal of the European Broadcasting Union, with useful coverage of public broadcasting in Europe and many former colonial areas.

Educational and Industrial Television (monthly): heavy emphasis on technology and equipment developments and operations.

Educational Broadcasting (10 times a year): combination trade/research journal, with frequent reviews of new developments.

JCET News (irregular): newsletter of Joint Council on Educational Telecommunications, which focuses on public broadcasting.

Journal of Broadcasting (quarterly): research journal, with continuous coverage of educational and public broadcasting material. The periodical is indexed annually, and a 15 year index appeared at the end of Volume 15 (1971).

Journal of College Radio (monthly): primarily concerned with the "wired wireless" stations, but covers some over-the-air broadcasting as well.

NAEB Letter (biweekly): newsletter of National Association of Educational Broadcasters, with a focus on that organization's operations and personnel.

PBS Newsletter (monthly): covers developments at the Public Broadcasting Service, as well as news items from public television stations around the country.

Public Telecommunications Review (bimonthly): the major journal of public broadcasting. PTR combines newsmagazine and research-journal formats. It replaces the earlier *Educational Broadcasting Review* (1967-1972) and the *NAEB Journal* (to 1967). An index for all three journals, covering a two decade period (to 1971), is available from NAEB.

TV Digest (weekly): one of the most respected sources of information on broadcasting and cable television, with constant coverage of public broadcasting.

The Future of Public Broadcasting

Topicator (monthly with annual cumulation): an indexing service, begun in 1965, for periodicals on broadcasting and advertising. It covers many of the titles listed here and includes citations for public broadcasting and related issues.

Glossary
of Terms
and Organizations

Advisory Council of National Organizations (ACNO) consists of 45 major professional, religious, public-interest and educational organizations in the United States. It counsels the CPB and works with both national and local organizations in public broadcasting. In 1974, the corporation commissioned ACNO to conduct a study and make recommendations on the role of the CPB in the relationship of public broadcasting and education. The ACNO report, *Public Broadcasting and Education*, was released in 1975.

Agency for Instructional Television (AIT) is a nonprofit American-Canadian organization created in 1973 to strengthen education through television and other technologies. AIT's predecessor organization was National Instructional Television (NIT). Located in Bloomington, Indiana, AIT's primary function is the development of joint program/projects involving state and provincial agencies. It also acquires, adapts, and distributes a wide variety of television, audio-visual, and related print materials for use in teaching and learning. AIT's major consortium projects have been "Ripples," "Images & Things," "Inside/Out," "Bread & Butterflies," and "Self Incorporated."

Appalachian Educational Laboratory (AEL) is one of the regional, nonprofit educational laboratories first funded under Title IV of

ESEA (1965) to develop, test, and adapt new concepts and technologies from the research stage to the point of practice. Located in Charleston, West Virginia, AEL's television activities have included materials for home-based preschool education, such as "Round the Bend."

Applications Technology Satellite "6" (ATS-6) was launched from Cape Canaveral by the National Aeronautics and Space Administration (NASA) in May 1974. The ATS-6 carries the largest antenna yet devised for space, and because of its size and other technical features, it is able to transmit powerful, highly directional signals to relatively small and inexpensive ground receivers. During its first year, the satellite was used for an extensive series of communications experiments, including health and educational television transmissions to the Rocky Mountain States, Alaska and Appalachia; air and ship navigation and traffic-control; transmissions to and from orbiting satellites; and other meteorological, scientific and engineering experiments. In the summer of 1975, the satellite was repositioned for use by the government of India in its Satellite Instructional Television Experiment (SITE).

Ascertainment is a procedure required by the FCC for all broadcast licensees (prior to 1976 noncommercial stations were exempted) "to ascertain the problems, needs and interests of the residents of . . . [the] community of license and [all] other areas . . . [the licensee] undertakes to serve. . ." The licensee must then determine "what broadcast matter . . . [the licensee] proposes to meet those problems, needs and interests, as evaluated." This procedure is required for all applicants for a new license and all licensees filing for renewal.

Association for Public Radio Stations (APRS) represents the interests of public radio stations before Congress, the executive branch, the regulatory agencies, and the CPB. APRS also endeavors to keep the general public informed about public radio.

Bicycling is an economical mail system in which videotaped materials are trans-shipped from one agency to another until they are returned to the distributor. A single program is usually available for multiple broadcasts at any one agency within a seven-day period. Prior to national interconnections of the public system, many instructional television materials were made available nationally through a bicycling system.

Bilingual Children's Television, Inc. (BC/TV) is a nonprofit organization formed to produce bilingual-bicultural educational television programs for Hispanic children. Located in Oakland, California, it is the producer of "Villa Alegre," under an ESAA award.

Cable television is any facility that receives and amplifies broadcast television signals and distributes them to individual subscribers. Some cable systems also provide additional services, including their own programming (local origination), public and educational access channels, pay television (special programming available for an additional fee), and so-called "automated" weather or news channels. Experiments in bi-directional, interactive services via cable are currently underway on a few systems.

Children's Television Workshop (CTW) is an independent nonprofit agency whose activities include the creation of children's public television programming and many associated educational products. CTW is the producing agency for "Sesame Street" and "The Electric Company."

Community Service Grant (CSG) is the primary means by which CPB passes federal money directly to the stations. Each qualified public television and radio station is entitled to apply for a grant, the size of which is established by a complicated formula reflecting the size of the station's market and its budget. CSG funds are "unrestricted," except that they cannot be used for construction or equipment.

Corporation for Public Broadcasting (CPB) is a private, nonprofit corporation established by federal law to promote the growth and development of noncommercial television and radio. The purposes of the corporation are to strengthen the ability of local noncommercial stations to provide services to their communities; to aid in the development of national interconnection services for the distribution of programs of noncommercial radio and television; to expand the national inventory of programs available for local station use, and to support the total public broadcasting system through talent development, through encouragement of innovative production and instructional techniques, and through audience research and public information efforts. CPB does not actually produce programs or operate networks; rather, it functions as a planner and developer for public broadcasting.

Eastern Educational Network (EEN) was founded in 1960 as a cooperative endeavor to share and exchange public and instructional programming. It is an interconnected network, most of whose members are in the northeast and middle Atlantic states.

Educational Development Center (EDC) in Newton, Massachusetts, is a publicly supported nonprofit corporation engaged in educational research and development. Numerous curriculum reforms can be credited to EDC's efforts, including "Man: A Course of Study" (MACOS) in social studies. Many of its projects have involved television and other audio-visual media. Most recently, it has been involved in an ESAA project, "The Infinity Factory."

Educom, the Inter-university Communications Council, was formed in 1964 to help colleges and universities make the most of computers and communications technology. It has established a 20-member Planning Council on Computing in Education and Research, which will conduct the research and development for a national educational computer network. This network will facilitate increased sharing of computer information and cut down on duplication of efforts.

Electronic Video Recording (EVR) was once heralded as the future video counterpart of the LP recording in sound, but in the early 1970s, the project was abandoned by CBS Laboratories because of the heavy investment and risk involved in mass production.

Emergency School Aid Act 1972 (ESAA) included a provision under which a certain proportion of funds were set aside for the development, production and distribution of television materials to be made available to commercial and noncommercial broadcast users. Its projects have emphasized programming for and by racial and ethnic minority groups. Among the series produced under ESAA funding are "Carrascolendas," "Villa Alegre," "Gettin' Over," and "Vegetable Soup."

Family Communications, Inc. (FCI) is the producing agency for

"Mister Rogers' Neighborhood" and associated "Mister Rogers" activities.

Foreign Language Elementary Study (FLES) was an instructional television project supported by the Modern Language Association in the late 1950s and early 1960s in an attempt to upgrade and expand foreign language instruction in elementary schools.

FM (Frequency Modulation) broadcasting is that part of the radio band from 88 to 108 MHz. FM has several advantages over the older amplitude modulation (AM) broadcasting, including higher fidelity characteristics and less static, fading and background overlapping of other stations' programs. Most of the noncommercial radio stations are in the FM band.

FM multiplexing is the simultaneous transmission of two or more signals on different portions of the channel to which an FM station is assigned. Examples of multiplexing are stereophonic broadcasting and "storecasting," a restricted service which provides background music to stores and offices.

Great Plains National Instructional Television Library (GPN) identifies and distributes, on a lease basis, videotaped instructional television courses to educational institutions and other agencies desiring such materials. The library, in addition to its extensive collection of videotapes, offers a large number of 16 mm and kinescope materials. GPN is located at the Telecommunications Center of the University of Nebraska in Lincoln.

Instructional Television Fixed Service (ITFS) was established by the FCC in 1963 as an aid to what was then called educational television. The FCC considers ITFS a "nonbroadcast" service, since it does not utilize standard VHF or UHF channels. Ordinary television receivers are used to view ITFS transmissions, but the signals must first pass through special antennas and converters.

Medical Library Analysis and Retrieval System (MEDLARS) is a library-automation project, developed by the National Library of Medicine, which uses computer and information-processing technology for publication, reproduction and reference-searching of medical literature.

Midwest Program for Airborne Television Instruction (MPATI), a nonprofit corporation in existence from 1959-71, transmitted instructional television courses from aircraft flying over a central location to schools within a 210-mile radius. The project was particularly notable for the cooperative arrangements it stimulated among educational systems in several states.

National Association of Educational Broadcasters (NAEB) is a professional association of individuals who use communications technology for educational and social purposes. Its members are drawn from public broadcasting, instructional communications, and related fields; its mission is to meet the professional needs and interests of members by providing tangible services, by functioning as a focus for member activities, and by articulating and defending standards of professional performance.

National Public Radio (NPR) is an interconnected network of public radio stations funded by the CPB. NPR distributes and produces programming for more than 153 members operating 176 stations in the U. S. and Puerto Rico. It is a "two-way" network, with extensive utilization of materials produced by both member stations and the network.

NET (National Educational Television) evolved in 1962 from the Michigan-based Educational Radio and Television Center. Initially a library facility, it moved to New York and developed into a basic source of national programming for public television as well as a manager of distribution for the system. In 1970, NET merged with the noncommercial station WNET in New York to form the Educational Broadcasting Corporation.

National Friends of Public Broadcasting acts as a resource for local volunteer groups working on behalf of public broadcasting stations within their home communities.

National Public Affairs Center for Television (NPACT), a division of the Greater Washington Educational Telecommunications Association (licensee of WETA-TV and FM), produces news and public affairs programming for public television stations. Supported by the CPB and the Ford Foundation, NPACT submits its productions to the Public Broadcasting Service for possible distribution over PBS's interconnection system.

Office of Telecommunications Policy (OTP) is the federal executive agency responsible for overall supervision of national communications matters. OTP is part of the executive office of the President and its director is appointed by the President with the advice and consent of the Senate. The OTP functions may generally be divided into four areas: (1) establishing the executive branch's policies and programs pertaining to communications matters and seeking to implement them through various means, including the proposal of legislation; (2) coordinating the planning and evaluation of the communications activities of the executive branch; (3) allocating and managing that portion of the radio spectrum (approximately one-half) used by the federal government; (4) developing and administering emergency mobilization plans for the nation's communications resources.

Public Broadcasting Service (PBS) is a private, nonprofit membership organization for the country's public television stations. Originally established by the CPB in 1969 to select, schedule, distribute and promote high quality national television programming, PBS reorganized in 1973 and added to those functions the tasks of representing public television licensees before the executive branch, Congress, CPB, and the public. A major part of the programming distributed by PBS is produced by the public television stations themselves and distributed through the Station Program Cooperative. PBS also seeks and obtains programming from a variety of local, regional and overseas sources.

Public Service Satellite Consortium (PSSC) is a nonprofit alliance of educational, health-care, and other public organizations interested in the shared use of communications satellites for social services. It was formed in February 1975 mainly by the organizations which participated in health and educational experiments on NASA's ATS-6 satellite. The PSSC's aims are to identify public users, to determine their needs, to utilize existing satellite services, and to design advanced services for the future.

Rocky Mountain Satellite Project was one of several experiments conducted with the ATS-6 satellite during the 1974-75 school year. The object was to test the feasibility of using communications satellites to deliver educational information to remotely located schools in the Rocky Mountain region. A series of programs on career education were beamed to 56 schools in the region. In addition, certain times were set aside for the transmission of filmed material which could be videotaped and stored for later use.

Station Acquisition Market (SAM) was inaugurated by PBS in 1975 and is designed to provide a collective procedure by which the stations can make group purchases from syndicators and other program sources at a lower per-station cost than the single-buyer purchase price. With PBS acting as their agent, the stations are offered a program, or package of programs, for purchase on a selective basis.

Station Independence Program (SIP) is a three-year public television project whose goal is to increase the number of families subscribing to public television stations from the 1974 total of 1 million to 1.5 million in 1975, 2.2 million in 1976, and 3 million in 1977. Such an increase would boost the subscriber revenues of public television from $20 million in 1974 to $60 million by 1977. The Station Independence Program is also attempting to promote public understanding and support of the system. The program is supported by a $1,045,000 grant from the Ford Foundation and by $150,000 in matching funds from participating stations.

Station Program Cooperative (SPC) allows the nation's public television stations the opportunity to select those programs they feel best meet their local needs. Cost of the program is shared equally among selecting stations, and only those programs with total financing are purchased. Stations make new program selections based on a written proposal in a catalog and on a segment of a program pilot seen on a PBS closed-circuit feed.

UHF (Ultra-High Frequencies) is the range of frequencies extending from 300-3,000 MHz and from television channels 14 through 83.

University of Mid-America (UMA) is a four-state, open-learning system that represents the first attempt in the United States to deliver higher education on a mass basis through a mix of television, radio, reading, and telephone and personal consultation. UMA evolved out of a statewide system developed by the University of

Nebraska and the Nebraska Educational Telecommunications Center. In 1974, it received major federal funding and expanded. A four-year degree program is offered, as well as noncredit courses for personal or professional enrichment.

VHF (Very-High Frequencies) is the range of frequencies extending from 30-300 MHz and from television channels 2 through 13.

WAMI is a consortium designed by the states of Washington, Alaska, Montana, and Idaho to test the feasibility of providing medical instruction to students via satellite.

Index

A

Advisory Committee of National Organizations (ACNO), 71, 89, 116, 256, 308, 329
"Advocates", 263
Agency for Instructional Television (AIT), 73, 79, 85, 95, 103
Albany Medical College, 299
"Alistair Cooke's America", 79, 269
"All Things Considered", 60, 194
Allen, Chuck, 289
American Broadcasting Company (ABC), 148, 176, 222, 228
Anderson Foundation, 258
"Animation Festival", 263
Appalachia Educational Satellite Project, 312
Applications Technology Sattelite-6 (ATS-6), 298, 312
Association of Public Radio Stations (APRS), 27, 60, 135, 151
Atlantic Richfield Company (ARCO), 14, 257
Ascent of Man, The, 227
Aspen Institute Program on Communications and Society, 5, 235, 238
"Assignment America", 263

B

Bagdikian, Ben, 330
"Beacon Hill", 222
Beebe, Jack, 142, 152
Benjamin, Robert, 327
Berkman, Dave, 95, 104
Bi-Lingual Children's Television (BC/TV), 80, 85, 276 ff.
"Bill Moyers' Journal", 259
"Black Journal", 263

ABOUT THE EDITORS

Douglass Cater

Mr. Cater is founder of the Aspen Institute Program on Communications and Society and executive editor of the Aspen Program's Series on Communications. He is also consulting professor in Political Science and Communication at Stanford University.

From 1964 to 1968 he served as special assistant to President Lyndon B. Johnson, concentrating particularly on education and health programs. During this time, he worked on the shaping and passage of the Public Broadcasting Act of 1967. Before his White House assignment, he was the Washington and national affairs editor for *The Reporter* magazine and an associate director of Wesleyan's Center for Advanced Studies.

Mr. Cater received a Guggenheim Fellowship and an Eisenhower Fellowship and is the recipient of the George Polk Memorial Award and the "Harry" award for his contribution to public broadcasting. His other books include *Power in Washington*, *The Fourth Branch of Government*, *Ethics in a Business Society* (with Marquis Childs), and *TV Violence and the Child* (with Stephen Strickland).

Michael J. Nyhan

Mr. Nyhan is assistant director of the Aspen Institute Program on Communications and Society and the Program's project editor for public broadcasting. He formerly served with the Agency for International Development in Vietnam and with the Peace Corps in Turkey. Mr. Nyhan is co-editor (with William L. Rivers) of the *Aspen Notebook on Government and the Media*. He received his B.A. in psychology from Gonzaga University and his M.A. in communications from Ohio University.